THERE WAS A CABARET AND THERE WAS A MASTER OF CEREMONIES...

. . . AND THERE WAS A CITY CALLED BERLIN IN A COUNTRY CALLED GERMANY. . . .

IT WAS THE END OF
THE WORLD . . .
AND I WAS DANCING
WITH SALLY BOWLES
AND WE WERE BOTH
FAST ASLEEP . . .

CABARET

THE ILLUSTRATED BOOK AND LYRICS

Book by Joe Masteroff   Music by John Kander   Lyrics by Fred Ebb

Production Photography by Joan Marcus   Backstage Photography by Rivka Katvan
Edited by Linda Sunshine   Designed by Timothy Shaner

Roundabout
Theatre
Company

NEWMARKET PRESS
NEW YORK

Credits and acknowledgments for permissions will be found on page 128.
Photographs and illustrations by Joan Marcus, Rivka Katvan and others
are identified on page 128 and copyrighted by the photographers and
artists credited.

99 00 01 02 10 9 8 7 6 5 4 3 2 1

Library of Congress Cataloguing-in-Publication Data

Masteroff, Joe; Kander, John; Ebb, Fred
    Cabaret: The Illustrated Book and Lyrics/Book by Joe Masteroff;
    Music by John Kander; Lyrics by Fred Ebb; production photography
    by Joan Marcus; backstage photography by Rivka Katvan; edited by
    Linda Sunshine; designed by Timothy Shaner. – 1st ed.

    ISBN 1-55704-383-3 hc.
    1. Cabaret: The Illustrated Book and Lyrics (Roundabout Theatre
    Company Production). I. Masteroff, Joe; Kander, John; Ebb, Fred.
    Cabaret: The Illustrated Book and Lyrics. 1999. III. Title. IV. Series.
    PN1999.M3653B73   1999
    791.43'72—dc20   99-22945
                                                CIP

Quantity Purchases
Companies, professional groups, clubs, and other organizations may
qualify for special terms when ordering quantities of this title. For
information, write: Special Sales Department, Newmarket Press,
18 East 48th Street, New York, New York 10017 or call (212) 832-3575
or fax (212) 832-3569.

Manufactured in the United States of America

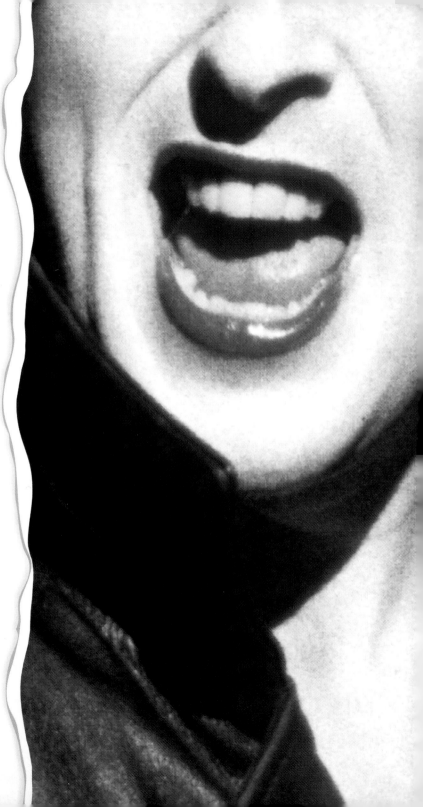

CABARET
CONTENTS

INTRODUCTION

This book is a celebration of the 1998 Broadway revival of *Cabaret*, one of those rare shows when the audience becomes part of the performance although, given the nature of this production, that's not always a comfortable place to be. An astonishing artistic expression of life at the brink of the millennium as seen through the prism of history, this revisionist production redefines the potential of live theater to mesmerize, transport, instruct, and profoundly influence an audience.

Included in this volume are the complete musical book and all the lyrics from the current revival, along with production and backstage photographs and archival material. The bones of this play date back sixty years. In 1929, Christopher Isherwood, an Englishman living in Germany, wrote, "I am a camera with its shutter open, quite passive, recording, not thinking." Among several other characters, he described a glamorous but eccentric English woman named Sally Bowles, "one of those individuals whom respectable society shuns in horror." Playwright John van Druten recognized Sally's potential for the stage and built a love story around her in his 1951 play, *I Am A Camera*. Julie Harris starred as Sally on Broadway and then reprised the role for the 1955 film which also featured Laurence Harvey as Cliff, Sally's asexual love interest.

A decade later director Hal Prince revolutionized the story by putting Sally in a cabaret and then making the cabaret a metaphor for Weimar Germany. With remarkable music and lyrics by John Kander and Fred Ebb and an

extraordinary book by Joe Masteroff, *Cabaret* featured a Master of
Ceremonies (the inimitable Joel Grey) who gave voice to this singing and
dancing commemoration of promiscuity, prostitution, abortion, anti-Semitism,
and the rise of Nazism. Starring Jill Haworth as Sally Bowles and Lotte
Lenya as Fräulein Schneider, here was the perfect musical for the Sixties.

In the 1972 film version, directed by Bob Fosse, Liza Minnelli played
Sally Bowles as an American torch singer, enriching the musical numbers but
confusing the plot. According to Joe Masteroff, "Sally was, originally, not a
very good singer. She was performing in the sort of seedy club where some of
the light bulbs were out. Sally singing well never made much sense." Audiences
didn't care, everything from Minnelli's haircut to Joel Grey's make-up became
pop icons of the Seventies.

Though a 1987 Hal Prince Broadway revival failed to find an
audience, perhaps overshadowed by the movie, British director Sam Mendes
was attracted to "the embryo of a dangerous show that was wrapped in a
conventional Broadway wrapping." In 1993, he re-imagined a *Cabaret*
performed in an actual nightclub. "When you walk in the front door, you walk
into their world. The rules are different," says Mendes. At the Donmar
Warehouse in London and later, co-directed by Rob Marshall on Broadway
(where the production was delayed almost two years before the Roundabout
found a suitable nightclub venue), the audience was seated at tables and served
food and alcohol by waitresses. Tattooed, bruised, and pierced, the chorus boys

and girls drag instruments onto the stage and double as the orchestra; they play out the story, quite literally, in our laps.

Mendes stripped his stage to the barest minimum; wooden chairs and an overhead fan replaced the automated train scenery Hal Prince used in his production. (In fact, no more than six chairs are allowed on stage at one time.) He refused to distribute *Playbills* when the audience arrives which, he felt, would only distract from the club atmosphere. (They're handed out at the end of the play.)

Mendes and Masteroff clarified the story by allowing all the characters—young, old, straight, gay, bisexual, and undecided—their sexuality. Though the play contains two juxtaposing love stories, Isherwood's landlady (the stoic German who endures) and her suitor (the Jew who refuses to accept the unthinkable) and Sally and Cliff, the focus always returns to Sally. She is English once again and only a marginal singer. Four moments were created where Sally is alone on stage emphasizing the difference between her public and private selves—the "Hello, darlings!" party girl and the drug addict. When Sally, the quintessential outsider who struggles to be inside, ultimately chooses to destroy her baby and herself ("a flash and burn," says Mendes), she becomes a much more tragic figure than in her previous incarnations.

Her descent, as well as everyone else's, is chronicled by the Emcee, brilliantly realized by Alan Cumming as an all-seeing theatrical dominance defining the production. Unlike the more subliminal character played by Joel

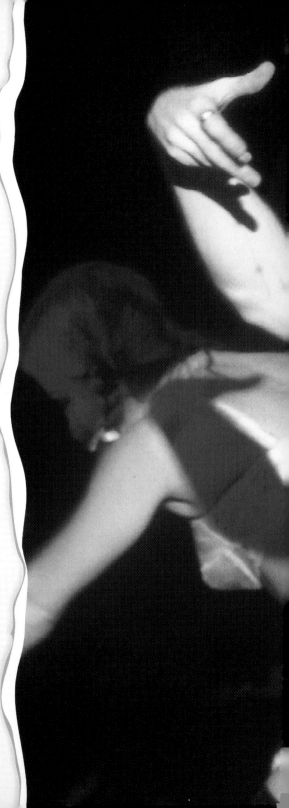

Grey, Cumming shape-shifts before our very eyes. He's a man, he's a woman, he's Hitler. He speaks all languages. He struts, he leers, he mocks, and he observes everything. At one point, he cajoles an audience member onstage for a dance, forever erasing any barrier between him and us.

We are in on the joke until his "If You Could See Her" duet with the lady gorilla that marks the turning point of the evening. Up until this number, the musical is filled with the life-force but when Cumming breathes the last line, "She doesn't look Jewish at all," the mood shifts from burlesque to grotesque. We don't know how to react. What have we been laughing at? This, according to Mendes, is when "the musical turns into a black-as-pitch play. The audience is a willing participant in the first part of the evening, but then the doors lock from the outside and they become prisoners." Suddenly, the music changes tempo, drained of energy. We are trapped in a place we never expected to be. This may explain why, at the end of the performance, the audience is shocked silent, often for several minutes, before they begin to applaud.

We leave the club in a daze. Not only have we been transported to Weimar Germany in the 1930s, we haven't strayed very far from home. Just when we thought no one could show us anything new about the rise of Nazism, along comes this *Cabaret* to remind us that art will always instruct in ways wondrous and enlightening, though sometimes terrifying.

–Linda Sunshine
December, 1998

ACT ONE

CABARET

ACT ONE   SCENE 1

(Darkness. Drum roll. Cymbal crash. Peep door opens. The EMCEE's eyes appear. The door opens and the EMCEE enters.)

EMCEE
(Sings)
WILLKOMMEN, BIENVENUE, WELCOME!
FREMDE, ÉTRANGER, STRANGER.
GLÜCKLICH ZU SEHEN, JE SUIS ENCHANTÉ,
HAPPY TO SEE YOU, BLEIBE, RESTE, STAY.

WILLKOMMEN, BIENVENUE, WELCOME.
IM CABARET, AU CABARET, TO CABARET.

(Spoken)
Meine Damen und Herren, Mesdames and Messieurs, Ladies and Gentlemen!
Guten Abend, bon soir, good evening!
Wie geht's. . . . Comment ca va?
Do you feel good? (I bet you do)
Ich bin euer conférencier, je suis votre compere . . . I am your host!

(Sings)
UND SAGEN -
WILLKOMMEN, BIENVENUE, WELCOME
IM CABARET, AU CABARET, TO CABARET!

(Spoken)
Leave your troubles outside . . .
So - life is disappointing? Forget it!
In here life is beautiful . . .
The girls are beautiful . . .
Even the orchestra is beautiful!

I told you the orchestra was beautiful . . .
And now, presenting the cabaret girls!
(crash) Rosie (ad lib), Lulu (ad lib),
Frenchie (ad lib), Texas (ad lib)
Fritzie (ad lib) and Helga (ad lib).

Rosie, Lulu, Frenchie, Texas, Fritzie . . .
Und Helga. Each and every one —
a virgin. You don't believe me?
Well, don't take my word for it.
Go ahead — try Helga!

(Spoken)
Outside it is winter. But in here it is so hot! Every night we have to battle with the girls to keep them from taking off all of their clothing. So don't go away.

19

Who knows? Tonight we may lose the battle!

ALL
WIR SAGEN –
WILLKOMMEN, BIENVENUE, WELCOME
IM CABARET, AU CABARET, TO CABARET!

EMCEE
(Spoken)
We are here to serve you!
And now presenting the cabaret boys!
Here they are …

Bobby (crash) …Victor (crash)
Or is it Victor (crash)… Bobby (crash)

There's really only one way to tell the difference … I'll show you later. Hans (crash) (ad lib), Hermann (crash) (ad lib)

And finally … Presenting the toast of Mayfair, Fräulein Sally Bowles!

EMCEE
BLEIBE, RESTE, STAY!

ALL
WILLKOMMEN, BIENVENUE, WELCOME (that's Victor)
IM CABARET, AU CABARET, WIR SAGEN
(Whisper)
WILLKOMMEN, BIENVENUE, WELCOME!
FREMDE, ÉTRANGER, STRANGER.
(Hello stranger)
GLÜCKLICH ZU SEHEN, JE SUIS ENCHANTÉ,
(Enchanté, madame)
HAPPY TO SEE YOU

EMCEE
BLEIBE, RESTE, STAY!

ALL
(Fellini)
WIR SAGEN –
WILLKOMMEN, BIENVENUE, WELCOME!
FREMDE, ÉTRANGER, STRANGER.
GLÜCKLICH ZU SEHEN, JE SUIS ENCHANTÉ, HAPPY TO SEE YOU

ALL
BLEIBE, RESTE, STAY!

"The angle on this production is that it's really true to the atmosphere of the John Van Druten play, *I Am a Camera*, and before that, of Christopher Isherwood's *Berlin Stories*, on which the play and musical are based. This *Cabaret* is real, rough, and raw--not sophisticated.

"The Kit Kat Klub is second-rate-- even third-rate. You'll see the runs in the stockings, the broken lightbulbs, the tackiness under the thin veneer of glitz...

"Although there's plenty of dancing, it's uncomfortable to watch...The choreography couldn't be too sophisticated or refined. I had to curb myself from doing something too slick and smart. I'd work on a piece and go back and distort it so that lines and angles are like a George Grosz or Otto Dix painting, where things are skewed or exaggerated. It's like choreographing everything twice. I'd say to myself, 'No, fray it purposefully with people on the wrong foot or out of step.' I always prepare much more than I need so that, if necessary, I can throw it away."

There were nineteen casting sessions before Marshall and co-director Sam Mendes (who directed the 1993 Donmar *Cabaret*) settled on the six Kit Kat Klub girls. "We had to turn down many who auditioned because they were too good," Marshall recalls. "Fabulous dancers who just couldn't let go of their technique. Each girl has to portray a distinct personality. In addition to singing, dancing, and acting, they also had to be able to play a musical instrument, because they make up the show's orchestra. And yet it's a wonderful show for me. At the beginning, it's very seductive. Then, half-way through, you kind of feel the doors lock and the chill of the encroaching Third Reich, and the Nazis taking over, along with the decadence of prewar Berlin."
                    --Rob Marshall quoted
                      in *Dance Magazine*
                        March 1998

WIR SAGEN –
WILLKOMMEN , BIENVENUE,
    WELCOME
IM CABARET, AU CABARET,
    TO CABARET

EMCEE
Thank you, thank you . . .
Bobby, Victor, Hans, Hermann,
Rosie, Lulu, Frenchie, Texas, Fritzie,
Helga, Sally and me!!
Welcome to the Kit Kat Klub!!

ACT ONE SCENE 2

A RAILWAY CARRIAGE

(CLIFF, then ERNST enter)

ERNST
Besetzt?

CLIFF
Nein.

ERNST
Sind die frei?

CLIFF
Ja . . . bitte.

*(ERNST places his suitcase
on the floor next to CLIFF's.
He puts his briefcase under an
empty seat next to CLIFF.)*

ERNST
American?

CLIFF
I might as well wear a sign: Yankee
Doodle.

ERNST
German. Berlin. Ernst Ludwig.

(THEY shake hands.)

CLIFF
Clifford Bradshaw. Harrisburg,
Pennsylvania. Are we slowing down
for the German border?

ERNST
Ja.

CLIFF
You've taken this trip before?

" In the original production, Cliff
was totally sexless. You
couldn't have a gay leading man
in those days. In the movie, he was
bisexual. In the 1987 revival, as we
traveled around the country, he was
sort of bisexual. When we got to New
York, we said, what the hell, let's
make him a homosexual."
                    --Joe Masteroff

21

ERNST

Many, many times. You are a tourist?

(ERNST sits.)

CLIFF

Not exactly. I'm a writer . . . and I give English lessons.

(ERNST looks out of the window)

Care for a cigarette? Herr Ludwig?

ERNST

Ja?

CLIFF

A cigarette?

ERNST

No, thank you.

(A GERMAN CUSTOMS OFFICER enters and turns to CLIFF)

OFFICER

Deutsche Grenzkontrolle. Ihren Pass, bitte.

(CLIFF passes him his passport)

Welcome to Germany, Mr. Bradshaw.

(He indicates CLIFF's bags)

Yours?

CLIFF

Yup.

(The OFFICER puts a customs mark on CLIFF's bag and typewriter without even looking in them. Then he turns to ERNST, who is deep in his newspaper)

OFFICER

Ihren Pass, bitte.

(ERNST hands over his passport)

Sie waren geschäftlich in Paris?

ERNST

Nein. Auf einer Urlaubsreise.

OFFICER

Bitte öffnen Sie Ihren Koffer.

(ERNST takes his suitcase from the floor, places it on a seat and opens it. The OFFICER goes through it.

While the OFFICER's back is turned, ERNST takes his briefcase from under the seat and puts it on the floor in front of CLIFF's bags. CLIFF is surprised but says nothing. The OFFICER marks ERNST's case.)

Haben Sie nur diesen Koffer?

ERNST
Ja. Das ist alles.

OFFICER
(To CLIFF)
I wish you will enjoy your stay in Germany. And a most Happy New Year.

(The OFFICER exits. As he exits, we hear him . . .)

Deutsche Grenzkontrolle . . .

(ERNST, very relieved, retrieves his briefcase)

CLIFF
What's in the bag?

ERNST
Baubles from Paris: perfume . . . silk stockings . . . But more than it is permitted. You understand?

CLIFF
I guess I've done a little smuggling myself.

ERNST
(Relaxing)
You are most understanding. I will thank you very much. You have been before to Berlin?

CLIFF
This is my first time . . .

ERNST
Then I will see to it that it will open its arms to you! We begin tonight — New Year's Eve — the Kit Kat Klub! This is hottest spot in the city. Telephones on every table. Girls call you — boys call you — you call them — instant connections.

CLIFF
Thanks — but I've still got to find a room . . .

ERNST
You have no room! But this is no problem!

(He takes out a card and writes on it)

I know the finest residence in all Berlin. Just tell Fräulein Schneider that Ernst Ludwig has spoken for you.

CLIFF
I can't afford the finest residence in all Berlin. I need something inexpensive.

ERNST
But this is inexpensive! Very inexpensive!

CLIFF
I don't care if it's awful — as long as it's cheap.

ERNST
But this is awful. You will love it!

(ERNST hands CLIFF the card.)

CLIFF
(reading card)
Fräulein Schneider.

ERNST

You see! You see! You have a new friend – Ernst Ludwig! You have a fine place to stay! And you are having perhaps even your first English pupil! So welcome to Berlin, my friend. Welcome to Berlin!

EMCEE

(Spoken)
Welcome to Berlin!
(Sings)
WILLKOMMEN, BIENVENUE, WELCOME.
FREMDE, ÉTRANGER, STRANGER.
GLÜCKLICH ZU SEHEN, JE SUIS ENCHANTÉ
HAPPY TO SEE YOU,
BLEIBE, RESTE, STAY!

ACT ONE SCENE 3

A ROOM IN FRÄULEIN SCHNEIDER'S APARTMENT

FRÄULEIN SCHNEIDER

So you see, Herr Bradshaw: all comforts! And with breakfast only one hundred marks.

CLIFF

It's very nice, Fräulein Schneider. But... you don't have anything cheaper?

FRÄULEIN SCHNEIDER

...but for a friend of Herr Ludwig...

CLIFF

I've very little money.

FRÄULEIN SCHNEIDER

But you will give English lessons. And you will have many pupils. And they will pay you... and then you will pay me. Ja?

CLIFF

Fifty marks. That's my absolute limit. If you've anything else... I don't care how small – how far from the bathroom...

FRÄULEIN SCHNEIDER

But for a Professor – this is more suitable.

CLIFF

I'm not a Professor. Think of me as a starving author. What do you have for a starving author?

FRÄULEIN SCHNEIDER
An author! A poet! You have the look!

CLIFF
A novelist.

FRÄULEIN SCHNEIDER
A novelist! And you will be most famous. It will be like years ago — when in all my rooms — persons of real quality ... this is your room! Here is for you to write. And look — your window! You can see the whole of the Nollendorfplatz! And there — that little house — the U-Bahn station. What you call the Metro. Ja? In ten minutes, you are anywhere in Berlin!

CLIFF
Subway ...

FRÄULEIN SCHNEIDER
Such a desirable window for a novelist!

CLIFF
I can still only afford fifty marks.

FRÄULEIN SCHNEIDER
This room is worth one hundred. More than one hundred.
(A pause)
Fifty?
(HE nods)
... Sit! You say fifty marks. I say one hundred marks, a —

(Spoken)
Difference of fifty marks —
Why should that stand in our way?
As long as the room's to let,
The fifty that I will get
Is fifty more than I had yesterday, ja?

(Spoken)
When you're as old as I —
Is anyone as old as I?
What diff'rence does it make?
An offer comes, you take.

(Sings)
FOR THE SUN WILL RISE AND THE MOON WILL SET
AND YOU LEARN HOW TO SETTLE FOR WHAT YOU GET.
IT WILL ALL GO ON IF WE'RE HERE OR NOT,
SO WHO CARES? SO WHAT?

SO WHO CARES? SO WHAT?

WHEN I WAS A GIRL, MY SUMMERS WERE SPENT BY THE SEA.
SO WHAT?
AND I HAD A MAID DOING ALL OF THE HOUSEWORK, NOT ME.
SO WHAT?
NOW I SCRUB UP THE FLOORS
AND I WASH DOWN THE WALLS
AND I EMPTY THE CHAMBER POT.
IF IT ENDED THAT WAY, THEN IT ENDED THAT WAY,
AND I SHRUG AND I SAY: SO WHAT?
FOR THE SUN WILL RISE AND THE MOON WILL SET
AND YOU LEARN HOW TO SETTLE FOR WHAT YOU GET.
IT WILL ALL GO ON IF WE'RE HERE OR NOT,
SO WHO CARES?
SO WHAT?
SO WHO CARES?
SO WHAT?

WHEN I HAD A MAN,
MY FIGURE WAS DUMPY AND FAT.
SO WHAT?
THROUGH ALL OF OUR YEARS
HE WAS SO DISAPPOINTED IN THAT.

SO WHAT?
NOW I HAVE WHAT HE MISSED
AND MY FIGURE IS TRIM,
BUT HE LIES IN A CHURCHYARD
PLOT.
IF IT WASN'T TO BE
THAT HE EVER WOULD SEE
THE UNCORSETTED ME,
SO WHAT?

FOR THE SUN WILL RISE AND THE
MOON WILL SET
AND YOU LEARN HOW TO SETTLE
FOR WHAT YOU GET.
IT WILL ALL GO ON IF WE'RE HERE
OR NOT,
SO WHO CARES?
SO WHAT?
SO WHO CARES?
SO WHAT?

SO ONCE I WAS RICH
AND NOW ALL MY FORTUNE IS
GONE,
SO WHAT?
AND LOVE DISAPPEARED
AND ONLY THE MEMORY LIVES ON,
SO WHAT?

IF I'VE LIVED THROUGH ALL THAT
(AND I'VE LIVED THROUGH ALL THAT)

FIFTY MARKS DOESN'T MEAN A
LOT.
IF I LIKE THAT YOU'RE HERE
(AND I LIKE THAT YOU'RE HERE)
HAPPY NEW YEAR, MY DEAR,
SO WHAT?
FOR THE SUN WILL RISE AND THE
MOON WILL SET
AND YOU LEARN HOW TO SETTLE
FOR WHAT YOU GET.
IT WILL ALL GO ON IF WE'RE HERE
OR NOT,
SO WHO CARES?
SO WHAT?
SO WHO CARES?
SO WHAT?

IT ALL GOES ON.
SO WHO CARES?
WHO CARES?
WHO CARES?
SO WHAT?!

**FRÄULEIN
SCHNEIDER**
The telephone is in the hall. I will fetch
towels . . .

(Knock on door)
(FRÄULEIN KOST enters)

FRÄULEIN KOST
Fräulein Schneider. There is no hot
water in the bathroom! The second
time this week!

**FRÄULEIN
SCHNEIDER**
If you will excuse me, Herr Bradshaw.

FRÄULEIN KOST
(seeing CLIFF)
Oh. . . you have finally rented this room.

**FRÄULEIN
SCHNEIDER**
This is Herr Clifford Bradshaw — the
world-famous American novelist.

CLIFF
How do you do?

FRÄULEIN KOST
Fräulein Kost. Across the hall . . . Please
feel free — at any time . . .

(A SAILOR runs in)

SAILOR
Fritzie — where are you?

FRÄULEIN KOST
My nephew. He is visiting me. From Hamburg.

FRÄULEIN SCHNEIDER
Come! We talk outside. We are disturbing Herr Bradshaw. And take your nephew with you – from Hamburg!

(FRÄULEIN KOST and the SAILOR exit)

Please accept my apologies, Herr Bradshaw. In the future I will keep her away.

CLIFF
Please don't.

FRÄULEIN SCHNEIDER
But are novelists interested in such persons?

CLIFF
Oh, yes.
(Knock at door)

FRÄULEIN SCHNEIDER
What is it now?

(SCHULTZ enters. He is carrying a bottle of schnapps.)

SCHULTZ
Fräulein Schneider – it is eleven o'clock.

FRÄULEIN SCHNEIDER
Ah, Herr Schultz! Eleven o'clock already? I have been showing Herr Bradshaw his room. Herr Bradshaw – Herr Schultz, who also lives here.

CLIFF
Pleased to meet you.

SCHULTZ
You are an American? I have a cousin in Buffalo. Felix Tannenbaum. It is possible you know him?

CLIFF
I hardly ever get to Buffalo.

FRÄULEIN SCHNEIDER
Herr Schultz is proprietor of the finest

fruit market on the Nollendorfplatz.

SCHULTZ
Italian oranges. Delicious.

FRÄULEIN
SCHNEIDER
I will dress now. Herr Schultz has been kind enough to invite me to join him in a glass of schnapps for the New Year.

SCHULTZ
And a little fruit.

FRÄULEIN
SCHNEIDER
And — after all — why not? Otherwise I am in bed with a hot-water bottle.

SCHULTZ
Perhaps Herr Bradshaw ...

CLIFF
No. Thank you.

SCHULTZ
Another time! I want to wish you much mazel in the New Year.

CLIFF
Mazel?

SCHULTZ
Yiddish. It means "luck!"

CLIFF
Thanks. The same to you.

SCHULTZ
I come to you, Fräulein, in ten minutes — with the schnapps!

FRÄULEIN
SCHNEIDER
And the fruit!

(SCHULTZ exits)

And now — please — anything you require — knock on my door. Anytime. Day or night. Also — welcome to Berlin!

(She exits)

KIT KAT KLUB
(Whispered)
Welcome to Berlin!

CLIFF
Welcome to Berlin — famous novelist. Open the Remington.

(CLIFF opens typewriter, TEXAS approaches him.)

TEXAS
Hello.

CLIFF
That's what you came here for . . .

TEXAS
Standing all alone like that you have happened to catch my eye.

(LULU and VICTOR appear)

Would you like to buy a girl a drink?

VICTOR
Would you like to buy a boy a drink?

CLIFF/EMCEE/ KIT KAT KLUB
Welcome to Berlin – famous novelist . . .

LULU
Ja? You would? Come on over!

(CLIFF slams the typewriter shut and exits into . . .)

ACT ONE SCENE 4

THE KIT KAT KLUB

EMCEE
Meine Damen und Herren – Mesdames et Messieurs – Ladies and Gentlemen – and now the Kit Kat Klub is proud to present a most talented young lady from England. Yes – England! She is so talented, so charming, so woo-who-who. Only yesterday I said to her, "I want you for my wife." And she said, "Your wife? What would she want with me?"

(A few members of the audience laugh)

Thank you! I give you – and don't forget to bring her back when you are finished with her – the toast of Mayfair – Fräulein Sally Bowles!!

(SALLY enters)

SALLY
(Sings)
MAMA THINKS I'M LIVING IN A
   CONVENT,
A SECLUDED LITTLE CONVENT
IN THE SOUTHERN PART OF FRANCE.

MAMA DOESN'T EVEN HAVE AN
   INKLING
THAT I'M WORKING IN A NIGHTCLUB
IN A PAIR OF LACY PANTS.

SO PLEASE, SIR,
IF YOU RUN INTO MY MAMA,
DON'T REVEAL MY INDISCRETION,
GIVE A WORKING GIRL A CHANCE.

(Girls enter)

HUSH UP, DON'T TELL MAMA,
SHUSH UP, DON'T TELL MAMA,
DON'T TELL MAMA, WHATEVER
   YOU DO.

IF YOU HAD A SECRET,
YOU BET I WOULD KEEP IT.
I WOULD NEVER TELL ON YOU.

I'M BREAKING EVERY PROMISE
   THAT I GAVE HER,
SO WON'T YOU KINDLY DO A GIRL
   A GREAT BIG FAVOR?
AND PLEASE, MY SWEET PATATER,
KEEP THIS FROM THE MATER,
THOUGH MY DANCE IS NOT
   AGAINST THE LAW.

YOU CAN TELL MY PAPA, THAT'S
   ALL RIGHT,

51

CAUSE HE COMES IN HERE EVERY
   NIGHT,
BUT DON'T TELL MAMA
WHAT YOU SAW!

ALL
MAMA THINKS I'M ON A TOUR OF
   EUROPE,
WITH A COUPLE OF MY SCHOOL
   CHUMS
AND A LADY CHAPERONE.
MAMA DOESN'T EVEN HAVE AN
   INKLING
THAT I LEFT THEM ALL IN ANTWERP
AND I'M TOURING ON MY OWN.

SO PLEASE, SIR,
IF YOU RUN INTO MY MAMA,
DON'T REVEAL MY INDISCRETION.

SALLY
JUST LEAVE WELL ENOUGH ALONE.
HUSH UP,

ALL
DON'T TELL MAMA.

SALLY
SHUSH UP,

ALL
DON'T TELL MAMA,

DON'T TELL MAMA
WHATEVER YOU DO.

SALLY
IF YOU HAD A SECRET
YOU BET I COULD KEEP IT.

ALL
I WOULD NEVER TELL ON YOU.
YOU WOULDN'T WANT TO GET ME
   IN A PICKLE,

SALLY
AND HAVE HER GO AND CUT ME
   OFF WITHOUT A NICKEL.

ALL
SO LET'S TRUST ONE ANOTHER,
KEEP THIS FROM MY MOTHER,
THOUGH I'M STILL AS PURE AS
   MOUNTAIN SNOW.

SALLY
YOU CAN TELL MY UNCLE
HERE AND NOW
CAUSE HE'S MY AGENT ANYHOW

ALL
BUT DON'T TELL MAMA WHAT
   YOU KNOW.

SALLY
YOU CAN TELL MY GRANDMA,
SUITS ME FINE;
JUST YESTERDAY SHE JOINED THE
   LINE,

ALL
BUT DON'T TELL MAMA WHAT
   YOU KNOW.

YOU CAN TELL MY BROTHER,
   THAT AIN'T GRIM
'CAUSE IF HE SQUEALS ON ME
   I'LL SQUEAL ON HIM,
BUT DON'T TELL MAMA, BITTE
DON'T TELL MAMA, PLEASE, SIR.
DON'T TELL MAMA WHAT YOU
   KNOW.

GIRLS
SSSH! SSSH!

SALLY
If you see my mummy, mum's
    the word!

EMCEE
Fräulein Sally Bowles! Thank you,
Sally! (Ad lib). Rosie, Lulu, Frenchie,
Texas, Fritzie, Helga! They're so hot!
Only half an hour 'til New Year's . . .
anything can happen . . .

ACT ONE   SCENE 5

SALLY
    (On the phone)
Table number three.

CLIFF
    (On the phone)
Hello.

SALLY
You're English!

CLIFF
Absolutely.

SALLY
Oh, you're American. But you speak
English beautifully, darling. I'm up here.

CLIFF
Oh, hello.

SALLY
Hello. Will you just keep talking, please?
You can't imagine how starved I've been.

CLIFF
Okay. Let's see: "Somewhere in this
favored land the sun is shining bright.
A band is playing somewhere and somewhere hearts are light. And somewhere
men are laughing and somewhere
children shout. But there is no joy in
Mudville, mighty Casey has struck out!"

SALLY
Oh, yes – don't stop, please.

CLIFF
I'm afraid that's all I know. My name is
Cliff Bradshaw.

SALLY
Where are you from?

CLIFF
Harrisburg, Pennsylvania. You never
heard of it.

SALLY
Did you like my number?

CLIFF
You bet!

SALLY
Are you alone?

CLIFF
Yes.

SALLY
Then let me buy you a drink.
    (MAX enters)
But not – right – at this moment.

    (SALLY exits. BOBBY, a waiter,
    calls CLIFF on the phone)

CLIFF
Hello.

BOBBY
Is that Cliff Bradshaw?

CLIFF
Who's this?

BOBBY
Bobby. We met in London. At the
Nightingale Bar.

CLIFF
Bobby. Oh, hello.

BOBBY
Hello. Listen — it's crazy tonight. But maybe you can come backstage. It's just through there.

CLIFF
Now?

BOBBY
Later — fifteen minutes. Alright?

CLIFF
Alright.

(CLIFF nods. BOBBY exits)

EMCEE
Meine Damen und Herren, Mesdames et Messieurs, Ladies and Gentlemen: It is almost midnight! Husbands — you have only ten seconds in which to lose your wives! Ten — nine — eight — seven — six — five — four — three — two — one — Happy New Year!

(To: The Dressing Room)

MAX
I can do anything I please. I own this Club.

SALLY
Part-owner!

MAX
And we all agree: It's a new year. Time for a new face.

SALLY
A new tart, you mean.

MAX
Is that so shocking, Fräulein Bowles?

SALLY
The only shocking thing is that nobody can see that I've been trying — against all odds — to give this seedy little dive a little . . . allure.

MAX
Allure? Our customers hate "allure." Every time we even mop the floor, they complain.

SALLY
But, darling, lots of people come here because of me.

MAX
No one will even notice you've gone!

(HE starts to exit)

SALLY
Max — I don't know about the laws here — but I'm sure it can't be legal to just . . . I mean — don't you have to give a girl a two-week notice? — Or at least a week . . .?

MAX
Why don't you organize a union? Go join all those Communists marching in the street!

(HE starts to exit)

SALLY
But Max! Max! Bastard!

(But HE is gone)
(SALLY snorts some coke)
(KNOCK at the door)

Come in!
                    (CLIFF enters)

CLIFF
I'm not sure I'm in the right place . . .

SALLY
(pulling herself together)
Oh, Chris!

CLIFF
Uh, Cliff.

SALLY
Ah, Cliff. Did you come for your drink?

CLIFF
Sorry?

SALLY
I promised to buy you a drink — and here you are! Is gin all right? Of course it is. It's all I've got.

CLIFF
Gin? I guess so. Why not?

SALLY
Will you pour?

(SHE continues to work on her make-up)

I only have a few minutes . . .

(CLIFF pours out two drinks)

Why did you say you were English?

CLIFF
I don't know, a whim. You ever had a whim?

SALLY
Constantly! I used to love pretending I was someone else—someone quite mysterious and fascinating. Until one day I grew up – and realized I was mysterious and fascinating. I'm Sally Bowles.

(Toasting)

Happy New Year, darling!

(She kisses him—he kisses her back)

Are you new in Berlin?

CLIFF
I've only been here three hours.

SALLY
Three hours! Welcome! How long are staying?

CLIFF
I'm working on a novel. I'll stay till it's finished.

SALLY
Oh, you're a novelist. How marvelous! You can write about what swine people are and have a huge success and make pots of money.

CLIFF
Let's talk about Sally Bowles. What part of England are you from? London? Stratford-on-Avon? Stonehenge?

SALLY
Oh, Cliff – you mustn't ever ask me questions. If I want to tell you anything, I will. Why did you come to Berlin to do your novel?

CLIFF
I'd already tried London and Paris.

SALLY
Just looking for a place to write?

CLIFF
Something to write about.

SALLY
Where are you staying?

CLIFF
On Nollendorfplatz.

SALLY
Nollendorfplatz! I'd love to live on Nollendorfplatz! It's so – racy! I just live upstairs here. It would be too divine to invite you up but Max is most terribly jealous . . .

CLIFF
Max? Your husband?

SALLY
Oh, no! He's just the man I'm sleeping with. This week. I say – am I shocking you, talking this way?

CLIFF
I say – are you trying to shock me?

SALLY
You're quite right, you know.

(SALLY's cue light flashes)

Ooh, there's my cue. Is there really a place called Mudville?

CLIFF
Absolutely. It's in New Jersey.

SALLY
Don't forget to leave your number – Toodle-pip!
(She exits quickly. CLIFF looks around)

(He goes to the dressing-table and looks in the mirror, starts to write his phone number on the mirror with her lipstick)

(BOBBY enters with VICTOR)

BOBBY
(To CLIFF)
That was never a good color for you. Cliff, this is Victor, he is sharing my apartment.

VICTOR
Hello.

CLIFF
(To VICTOR)
How do you do?

BOBBY
He's heard all about you.

VICTOR
All about you.

BOBBY
I can't stay. But will you ring me?

CLIFF
Of course.

BOBBY
You better had!

VICTOR
(At the door—urgently)
Bobby – come!

(VICTOR exits)

BOBBY
(To CLIFF)
Ja! Happy New Year!

(He goes to kiss him. CLIFF backs away)

Come on Cliff, this is Berlin. Relax. Loosen up. Be yourself.

(CLIFF and BOBBY have a real kiss)

(Cymbal crash. Lights snap up on SALLY)

SALLY

YOU HAVE TO UNDERSTAND THE
   WAY I AM, MEIN HERR.
A TIGER IS A TIGER NOT A LAMB,
   MEIN HERR.
YOU'LL NEVER TURN THE VINEGAR
   TO JAM, MEIN HERR.
SO I DO – WHAT I DO,
WHEN I'M THROUGH – THEN I'M
   THROUGH – AND I'M THROUGH –
TOODLE-OO!

BYE-BYE, MEIN LIEBER HERR,
FAREWELL, MEIN LIEBER HERR.
IT WAS A FINE AFFAIR, BUT NOW
   IT'S OVER.
AND THOUGH I USED TO CARE,
I NEED THE OPEN AIR.
YOU'RE BETTER OFF WITHOUT ME,
MEIN HERR.

DON'T DAB YOUR EYE, MEIN HERR,
OR WONDER WHY, MEIN HERR.
I'VE ALWAYS SAID THAT I WAS A
   ROVER.
YOU MUSTN'T KNIT YOUR BROW,
YOU SHOULD HAVE KNOWN BY
   NOW
YOU'D EVERY CAUSE TO DOUBT ME,
   MEIN HERR.

THE CONTINENT OF EUROPE IS SO

WIDE, MEIN HERR,
NOT ONLY UP AND DOWN, BUT
   SIDE TO SIDE, MEIN HERR.
I COULDN'T EVER CROSS IT IF I
   TRIED, MEIN HERR.
BUT I DO – WHAT I CAN –
   INCH BY INCH – STEP BY STEP –
MILE BY MILE – MAN BY MAN.

BYE-BYE, MEIN LIEBER HERR,
FAREWELL, MEIN LIEBER HERR.
IT WAS A FINE AFFAIR,
BUT NOW IT'S OVER.
AND THOUGH I USED TO CARE,

I NEED THE OPEN AIR,
YOU'RE BETTER OFF WITHOUT ME,
   MEIN HERR.

SALLY &
THE GIRLS
DON'T DAB YOUR EYE, MEIN HERR,

OR WONDER WHY, MEIN HERR.
I'VE ALWAYS SAID THAT I WAS
  A ROVER.
YOU MUSTN'T KNIT YOUR BROW
YOU SHOULD HAVE KNOWN BY NOW
YOU'D EVERY CAUSE TO DOUBT ME,
  MEIN HERR.
BYE-BYE, MEIN LIEBER HERR,
AUF WIEDERSEHEN, MEIN HERR.
ES WAR SEHR GUT, MEIN HERR
  UND VORBEI.
DU KENNST MICH WOHL, MEIN HERR,
ACH, LEBE WOHL, MEIN HERR.
DU SOLLST MICH NICHT MEHR
  SEHEN, MEIN HERR.

SALLY

BYE-BYE, MEIN LIEBER HERR . . .
BYE-BYE, MEIN LIEBER HERR,

GIRLS

AUF WIEDERSEHEN, MEIN HERR.
ES WAR SEHR GUT, MEIN HERR,
UND VORBEI. UND VORBEI.
DU KENNST MICH WOHL,
  MEIN HERR
DU KENNST MICH WOHL,
  MEIN HERR
ACH, LEBE WOHL, MEIN HERR
DU SOLLST MICH NICHT MEHR SEHEN
  AND BYE-BYE.

SALLY & THE GIRLS

BYE-BYE, MEIN LIEBER HERR,
FAREWELL, MEIN LIEBER HERR.
IT WAS A FINE AFFAIR,
BUT NOW IT'S OVER.
AND THOUGH I – USED TO CARE,
I NEED THE – OPEN AIR.

SALLY

YOU'RE BETTER OFF WITHOUT ME,
YOU'LL GET ON WITHOUT ME . . .

GIRLS

AUF WIEDERSEHEN, ES WAR
  SEHR GUT
DU KENNST MICH WOHL ACH,
  LEBE WOHL!

SALLY

MEIN HERR
BYE BYE, MEIN HERR,

GIRLS

AUF WIEDERSEHEN,
BYE BYE, MEIN HERR!

EMCEE

The final performance of
Sally Bowles!!
(ad lib)

Sally Bowles

As she dialled the number, I noticed that her finger-nails were painted emerald green, a colour unfortunately chosen, for it called attention to her hands, which were much stained by cigarette smoking and as dirty as a little girl's. She was dark enough to be Fritz's sister. Her face was long and thin, powdered dead white. She had very large brown eyes which should have been darker to match her hair and the pencil she used for her eyebrows. . .

A few days later he took me to hear Sally sing. . . .I was curious to see how Sally would behave. I had imagined her, for some reason, rather nervous, but she wasn't, in the least. She had a surprisingly deep husky voice. She sang badly, without any expression, her hands hanging down at her sides—yet her performance was, in its own way, effective because of her startling appearance and her air of not caring a curse what people thought of her.

–Christopher Isherwood
The Berlin Stories

ACT ONE   SCENE 6

CLIFF'S ROOM

ERNST
You know what is the trouble with English? It is not an exact language. Either one must memorize fifty thousand words either one cannot speak it correctly.

CLIFF
Either one must memorize—or one cannot speak . . .

ERNST
Aha! Either – or.

(ERNST makes a notation in his notebook – then closes it and looks at his watch)

The time is now finished.

CLIFF
I'm in no hurry.

ERNST
But the lesson is one hour. No? Another pupil is waiting.

CLIFF
What other pupil?

ERNST
No other pupil?
    (CLIFF shakes his head)
Then I make a suggestion: I have many friends. Most anxious for improving their English. I put them on to you. But for tonight, I will telephone a lady friend. She will bring a friend for you. Elsa. She is very loving of Americans – Gary Cooper in particular.

CLIFF
Not tonight, Ernst.

ERNST
But you have not seen this Elsa! Hot stuff – believe me! In one minute, I guarantee you are making a pass after her.

CLIFF
A pass at her.

ERNST
Aha!! A pass at her!

CLIFF
I've got a date tonight.

ERNST
A typewriter? But what can one do with a typewriter?

CLIFF
Not very much lately.

ERNST
Then come! Perhaps you and I only! We make a large whoopee!

CLIFF
    (shakes his head)
I've got a budget, Ernst – and it only allows for a very small whoopee – unfortunately.

ERNST
Then you will be my guest! I show you the real Berlin.

CLIFF
It's very tempting . . .

ERNST
    (moving close)
We will acquaint with one another.

CLIFF
As soon as I can afford it . . .

ERNST
It is difficult, you know – adjusting to the idea of a poor American. But I tell you a secret. There is no need for this poverty. Ja! If you are willing – I show you a most excellent way to supplement your income . . .

CLIFF
Doing what?

ERNST
Oh – by taking very brief trips – to Paris. A few days each time. Nothing more. But it will pay you well – extremely well.

(Knock)

CLIFF
Come in.

FRÄULEIN SCHNEIDER
Herr Bradshaw – there is a young lady to see you! A young lady in a fur coat!

CLIFF
A young lady?

FRÄULEIN SCHNEIDER
Fräulein Bowles . . .

CLIFF
Bowles?! Ask her to come in.

(FRÄULEIN SCHNEIDER exits)

ERNST
You are old friends . . . you and Fräulein Bowles? From London, perhaps . . . Ja?

CLIFF
From the Kit Kat Klub. Last night.

ERNST
Last night! You are some snappy operator!

(SALLY enters – wearing a fur coat – smoking a cigarette)

SALLY
Cliff, darling!

(She hands him her suitcase)

Ernst, dearest heart! Where were you last night?

ERNST
Ah – I have such a regret. But I have already explained to Herr Bradshaw – I was delayed on business. But I promise I will come to the Klub – very soon.

SALLY
Don't you dare! I don't want anyone going near that bloody Klub ever again!

(To CLIFF, still holding her suitcase)

Just put it anywhere. I'll unpack later.

FRÄULEIN SCHNEIDER
Unpack? – But Herr Bradshaw did not mention . . .

SALLY
Oh, I'll just be here temporarily.

FRÄULEIN SCHNEIDER
I am sorry, but this is not possible.

SALLY
(to CLIFF – sotto voce)

How much are you paying?

CLIFF
Fifty marks.

PREVIOUS SALLY BOWLES
Julie Harris (above) from the
1955 British film, *I Am a Camera*.
Liza Minnelli (below) from the
1972 American film, *Cabaret*.

SALLY
(to FRÄULEIN SCHNEIDER)
Sixty marks.

FRÄULEIN SCHNEIDER
(shaking her head)
It is not the money . . .

SALLY
Seventy?

FRÄULEIN SCHNEIDER
I cannot permit . . .

SALLY
Eighty—

FRÄULEIN SCHNEIDER
Eighty-five.

SALLY
(instantly shaking hands)
Done!

FRÄULEIN SCHNEIDER
And now — please make yourself cozy,
Frau Bradshaw.

(She exits)

ERNST
(to CLIFF)
Such a to-do! I will see you Friday for
the next lesson. But I am telling you
something: I think I am taking from you
the wrong kind of lessons!

(ERNST exits)

CLIFF
Sally — what the hell do you think
you're doing?

SALLY
Would you guess I was terrified?

CLIFF
Are you?

SALLY
(nods)
What if you'd thrown me out? Can
you imagine how that would feel — being
thrown out twice in one day?

CLIFF
You mean — Max?

4

SALLY

Dear Max. And you know whose fault it was, don't you? If you hadn't come to the Kit Kat Klub – and been so dreadfully attractive – and recited poetry – and forced your way into my dressing-room . . .

CLIFF

Sally – about your staying here . . .

SALLY

You know what I'd love, darling? A spot of gin.

CLIFF

Gin?

SALLY

You've got some? I mean – I think one must.

CLIFF

No, I don't have any gin.

SALLY

Oh, well – Prairie Oysters, then.

CLIFF

Prairie Oysters?

SALLY

I practically live on them. It's just raw

egg whooshed around in some Worcestershire Sauce. It's heaven for a hangover.

CLIFF
I haven't got a hangover.

(SALLY takes a container of eggs out of her large bag)

You carry eggs around with you?

SALLY
Of course! One never knows when one will have a desperate craving for an omelet – does one? Actually – I salvaged these from my previous digs.

(She takes a bottle of Worcestershire out of her coat pocket)

CLIFF
That's quite a coat.

SALLY
It should be. It cost me all I had. Little did I realize how soon I'd be unemployed.

CLIFF
I gather – your friend Max runs the Kit Kat Klub...?

SALLY
Oh, you're divinely intuitive! I do hope I'm not going to fall madly in love with

45

you. Are you in the movie business in any way?

(CLIFF shakes his head)

Then you're safe – more or less. Though I do believe a woman can't be a truly great actress till she's had several passion-ate affairs – and had her heart broken.

(She breaks the egg for the Prairie Oyster)

Damn. I should have let Ernst pay my cab fare. He's got all that money from Paris.

CLIFF
From Paris?

SALLY
He smuggles it in for some political party.

CLIFF
Ernst is in politics?

SALLY
Oh, it's all so terribly tedious. Hals and Beinbruch! It means neck and leg break. It's supposed to stop it happening. Though I doubt it does.

(She drinks)

Mmmmmm . . . It tastes like peppermint.

CLIFF
That's because it's my toothbrush mug.

SALLY
Well, it makes me feel terribly sensual.

CLIFF
Sally, you've got to understand . . .

(She picks up a book)

SALLY
Oh! This is your novel!
(squinting at it)
It's in German? "Mein Kampf"?

CLIFF
It's not my novel. I thought I should know something about German politics.

SALLY
Why? You're an American.

(She spots his typewriter)

Oh, a typewriter! How creative! You could be the next Dostoyevsky. Will you allow me to watch you work? Günther never would.

CLIFF
Who?

SALLY
Günther Werner, he does films. And guess who's going to be in his next one – "The Woman in Room 16"?

CLIFF
Are you The Woman?

SALLY
No, unfortunately. I play Penny, an English girl. It's a very good part . . . Günther wrote it specially for me.

CLIFF
What's it about?

SALLY
I haven't the foggiest. It's in German! Listen:
    (Reading with great bravura)
"Guten Tag. Ich heisse Penny und ich bin Engländerin."

CLIFF
Nobody's ever translated it for you?

SALLY
    (shakes her head)
Oh, but It's so much more fun not knowing. Oh, will you allow me to watch while you write? I promise to be incredibly quiet.

CLIFF
Look, I don't think I can work with someone else — on the premises.

SALLY
Then I'll go out — take long, invigorating walks ...

CLIFF
In the middle of the night? And there's another thing: I'm not a prude. At least ...

SALLY
Are you homosexual in any way? Bobby says you are.

CLIFF
Bobby?

SALLY
One of the boys at the Klub. He says he met you in London — at the Nightingale Bar ...

CLIFF
The Nightingale Bar?

SALLY
Is it possible?

CLIFF
I guess — anything's possible. I've been to lots of bars ...

SALLY
And did you and Bobby have an affair?

CLIFF
Did he say that?

SALLY
He implied it.

CLIFF
    (carefully)
I see ...

SALLY
Cliff — if you don't mind — I should like to withdraw the question. Because — really — it's none of my business.

    (Music begins)

I think people are people, I really do, Cliff. Don't you? I don't think they should have to explain anything. For example, if I paint my fingernails green and it happens I do paint them green, well, if someone should ask me why, I say: "I think it's pretty." So, if anyone

47

should ask about you and me one day, you have two alternatives: you can either say, "Oh, yes, it's true. We're living in delicious sin." Or you can simply tell the truth and say:

(Sings)
I MET THIS PERFECTLY MARVELOUS
  GIRL
IN THIS PERFECTLY WONDERFUL
  PLACE
AS I LIFTED A GLASS
TO THE START OF A MARVELOUS
  YEAR

BEFORE I KNEW IT SHE CALLED ON
  THE PHONE.
INVITING.
NEXT MOMENT I WAS NO LONGER
  ALONE,
BUT SAT RECITING
SOME PERFECTLY BEAUTIFUL VERSE,
IN MY CHARMING AMERICAN STYLE.
HOW I DAZZLED HER SENSES WAS
  TRULY NO LESS THAN A CRIME.
NOW I'VE THIS PERFECTLY
  MARVELOUS GIRL
IN THIS PERFECTLY BEAUTIFUL ROOM
AND WE'RE LIVING TOGETHER
AND HAVING A MARVELOUS TIME.

CLIFF
  (Spoken)
Sally, I'm afraid it wouldn't work.
You're much too distracting.

SALLY
Distracting? No, inspiring!
  (Sings)
SHE TELLS ME PERFECTLY
  MARVELOUS TALES
OF HER THRILLINGLY SCANDALOUS
  LIFE,
WHICH I'LL PROBABLY USE
AS A CHAPTER OR TWO
IN MY BOOK.

AND SINCE MY STAY IN BERLIN
  WAS TO FORCE CREATION,
WHAT LUCK TO FALL ON A
  FABULOUS SOURCE OF
  STIMULATION.
AND PERFECTLY MARVELOUS TOO
IS HER PERFECT AGREEMENT TO BE
JUST AS STILL AS A MOUSE
WHEN I'M GIVING MY NOVEL
  A WHIRL.

YES, I'VE A HIGHLY AGREEABLE LIFE
IN MY PERFECTLY BEAUTIFUL ROOM
WITH MY NEARLY INVISIBLE,
PERFECTLY MARVELOUS, GIRL.

CLIFF
Sally – I just can't afford . . . Do you have any money?

SALLY
A few marks . . . six.
(Triumphantly)

CLIFF
(very low)
Oh, God!

SALLY
Please, Cliff – just for a day or two? Please!

CLIFF
(Sings)
I MET THIS TRULY REMARKABLE
   GIRL
IN THIS REALLY INCREDIBLE TOWN,
AND SHE SKILLFULLY MANAGED
TO TALK HER WAY INTO MY ROOM.

SALLY
(Spoken)
Oh, Cliff!

CLIFF
(Sings)
I HAVE A TERRIBLE FEELING I'VE

SAID A DUMB THING.
BESIDES, I'VE ONLY GOT ONE
   NARROW BED.

SALLY
(sexily)
WE'LL THINK OF SOMETHING.

ACT ONE   SCENE 7

EMCEE
So you see, everybody in Berlin has a perfectly marvelous roommate. Some people have two people.

GIRL 1
(Sings)
BEEDLE DEE, DEEDLE DEE DEE!

GIRL 2
BEEDLE DEE, DEEDLE DEE DEE!

EMCEE
BEEDLE DEE, DEEDLE DEE DEE!
BEEDLE DEE, DEEDLE DEE DEE!

GIRLS
BEEDLE DEE, DEE DEE DEE,

EMCEE
TWO LADIES.

GIRLS
Beedle dee, dee dee dee,

EMCEE
Two ladies.

GIRLS
Beedle dee, dee dee dee,

EMCEE
And i'm the only man.
Ja!

GIRLS
Beedle dee, dee dee dee . . .

EMCEE
I like it.

GIRLS
Beedle dee, dee dee dee . . .

EMCEE
They like it.

GIRLS
Beedle dee, dee dee dee . . .

EMCEE
This two for one.
Beedle dee, dee dee dee . . .

GIRLS
Two ladies.

EMCEE
Beedle dee, dee dee dee . . .

GIRLS
Two ladies.

EMCEE
Beedle dee, dee dee dee,

GIRLS
And he's the only man.

EMCEE
Ja!

GIRLS
Beedle dee, dee dee dee . . .

GIRL 1
He likes it.

EMCEE
Beedle dee, dee dee dee . . .

GIRL 2
We like it.

EMCEE
Beedle dee, dee dee dee . . .

CABARET TIMELINE

1934 Christopher Isherwood publishes "Mr. Norris Changes Trains," a short novel about double agents, followed by four other novellas, including "Sally Bowles" in 1937. Hoping to write a novel "in the style of Balzac," Isherwood described the people he encountered while living in Berlin during the rise of the Nazis. His stories were eventually published in America as *The Berlin Stories*.

1952 *I Am a Camera*, the stage play by John van Druten based on Isherwood's "Sally Bowles" story, opens on Broadway starring Julie Harris as Sally. Isherwood met Harris in New York during rehearsals and wrote, "Miss Harris was more essentially Sally Bowles than the Sally of my book, and much more like Sally than the real girl who long ago gave me the idea for my character."

1966 *Cabaret*, the musical, directed by Hal Prince with music by John Kander, lyrics by Fred Ebb and a book by Joe Masteroff opens on November 20th and runs for nearly three years, for a total of 1,166 performances. The original cast included Joel Grey as the Master of Ceremonies, Bert Convy as Cliff, Lotte Lenya as Fräulein Schneider and Jill Haworth as Sally Bowles.

1955 *I Am a Camera*, the British movie, is adapted from the stage play and stars Julie Harris, Laurence Harvey as Cliff, and Shelley Winters as a Jewish girl who encounters anti-Semitism.

1972 *Cabaret*, the movie version of the stage musical, directed by Bob Fosse and starring Liza Minnelli as an American Sally Bowles, Joel Grey as the Master of Ceremonies and Michael York as Cliff opens in New York. Kander and Ebb wrote several new songs for the movie including "Mein Herr," "Money, Money," and "Maybe This Time."

1998 *Cabaret* is presented on Broadway by the Roundabout Theatre Company in a real nightclub setting after converting the former Henry Miller Theater into The Kit Kat Klub. Co-directed and choreographed by Rob Marshall, the musical stars Alan Cumming, Natasha Richardson, and Ron Rifkin and opens on March 19th. In November, the play moves to a new venue, the former Studio 54.

1987 *Cabaret* is revived on Broadway by Hal Prince. Joel Grey won acclaim reprising his role as the Emcee but the play was generally panned by the critics and closed after a brief run.

1993 *Cabaret* is staged by British director Sam Mendes at the Donmar Warehouse in London starring Alan Cumming and Jane Horrocks. The musical receives rave reviews and plays to sold-out audiences.

GIRLS
THIS TWO FOR ONE.

GIRL 2
I DO THE COOKING . . .

GIRL 1
AND I MAKE THE BED.

EMCEE
I GO OUT DAILY TO EARN OUR
    DAILY BREAD.
BUT WE'VE ONE THING IN
    COMMON,

GIRL 1
HE . . .

EMCEE
SHE . . .

GIRL 2
AND ME,

GIRL 1
THE KEY,

EMCEE
BEEDLE DEE DEE,

GIRL 2
THE KEY,

EMCEE
BEEDLE DEE DEE, THE KEY.

GIRLS
BEEDLE DEE, DEEDLE DEE, DEEDLE
DEE, DEE!

GIRLS
OOH! AHH!
OOH! AHH!

EMCEE
WE SWITCH PARTNERS DAILY
TO PLAY AS WE PLEASE.

GIRLS
TWOSIE BEATS ONESIE,
BUT NOTHING BEATS THREES.

EMCEE
I SLEEP IN THE MIDDLE,

GIRL 1
I'M LEFT,

GIRL 2
UND I'M RIGHT,

EMCEE
BUT THERE'S ROOM ON THE
    BOTTOM
IF YOU DROP IN SOME NIGHT.

GIRLS
BEEDLE DEE, DEE DEE DEE . . .

EMCEE
TWO LADIES.
BEEDLE DEE, DEE DEE DEE . . .

GIRLS
TWO LADIES.
BEEDLE DEE, DEE DEE DEE,
AND HE'S THE ONLY MAN.

ALL
JA!
BEEDLE DEE, DEE DEE DEE . . .

EMCEE
I LIKE IT,

GIRLS
BEEDLE DEE, DEE DEE DEE . . .

EMCEE
THEY LIKE IT!

GIRLS
BEEDLE DEE, DEE DEE DEE . . .

ALL
THIS TWO FOR ONE.

BEEDLE DEE, DEEDLE DEE, DEEDLE
DEE, DEEDLE DEE, DEE!

EMCEE
Thank you! Bobby, LuLu and Me!!
(ad lib)

ACT ONE SCENE 8

THE LIVING ROOM OF FRÄULEIN SCHNEIDER'S APARTMENT

*(FRÄULEIN KOST is entering
with a SAILOR. Suddenly
FRÄULEIN SCHNEIDER
enters from her room)*

FRÄULEIN SCHNEIDER
That sailor! Out of my house!

FRÄULEIN KOST
This sailor – dear lady – is my brother!

FRÄULEIN SCHNEIDER

Out! Out!! Out!!!
(SAILOR exits)

FRÄULEIN KOST

Wait! Wait! How dare you! You think it is easy — finding a sailor? This was only my second one since New Year's. And what is it now? April!

FRÄULEIN SCHNEIDER

Your second?

FRÄULEIN KOST

Ja.

FRÄULEIN SCHNEIDER

Your second?

FRÄULEIN KOST

Ja.

FRÄULEIN SCHNEIDER

You think I do not know what goes on here? Sailors — all the time: in — out — in — out! God only knows what the neighbors think I am running here — a battleship? Fräulein Kost, I give you fair warning! One sailor more — I call the police!

FRÄULEIN KOST

And if I cannot pay the rent?

FRÄULEIN SCHNEIDER

The rent is due each Friday — as always.

FRÄULEIN KOST

No sailors. No rent. I move.

FRÄULEIN SCHNEIDER

Move?

FRÄULEIN KOST

Move!!

FRÄULEIN SCHNEIDER

And what am I supposed to do with your room? Out of the blue — she tells me "I move!" Is that gratitude for you? Only last week I gave you another new mattress!

FRÄULEIN KOST

All right! All right!! So I will leave the end of the week — since you insist.

FRÄULEIN SCHNEIDER

I insist? You insist!

FRÄULEIN KOST

So what about the sailors?

FRÄULEIN SCHNEIDER

The sailors? Fräulein Kost — if you wish to continue living here, you must not let me catch you bringing in any more sailors! You understand?

FRÄULEIN KOST

Very good. So it is the same as always.

(She goes into her room and closes the door.)

FRÄULEIN SCHNEIDER

No, it is not the same as always!

(She knocks on FRÄULEIN KOST's door)

Fräulein Kost. Do you hear me? I have put my foot down.

(She knocks again)

Fräulein Kost! Fräulein Kost!!

(SCHULTZ enters from his room carrying a paper bag)

SCHULTZ

Fräulein Schneider! Good evening!

FRÄULEIN SCHNEIDER

Oh, Herr Schultz! Such a surprise!

SCHULTZ

You are occupied?

FRÄULEIN SCHNEIDER

No. No. Free as a bird. Please forgive my appearance.

SCHULTZ

But it is most becoming.

FRÄULEIN SCHNEIDER

Thank you.

SCHULTZ

I have brought you a little something from the shop.

FRÄULEIN SCHNEIDER

Another little something?

(SCHULTZ hands her the bag)

SCHULTZ

With my compliments.

FRÄULEIN SCHNEIDER

So heavy! But what can it be? Pears? Last Wednesday you brought me pears. And such pears! Apples, possibly? Friday was apples.

SCHULTZ

Ja, Ja. Friday was apples.

FRÄULEIN SCHNEIDER

So I cannot guess . . .

SCHULTZ

Then open!

FRÄULEIN SCHNEIDER

Herr Schultz. Can I believe what I see?
But this is – too much to accept. So rare
– so costly – so luxurious . . .

(Sings)

IF YOU BROUGHT ME DIAMONDS
IF YOU BROUGHT ME PEARLS
IF YOU BROUGHT ME ROSES
LIKE SOME OTHER GENTS MIGHT
    BRING TO OTHER GIRLS,
IT COULDN'T PLEASE ME MORE
THAN THE GIFT I SEE:
A PINEAPPLE FOR ME.

SCHULTZ

IF IN YOUR EMOTION
YOU BEGAN TO SWAY
WENT TO GET SOME AIR
OR GRABBED A CHAIR
TO KEEP FROM FAINTING DEAD
    AWAY,
IT COULDN'T PLEASE ME MORE
THAN TO SEE YOU CLING
TO THE PINEAPPLE
I BRING.

BOTH

AH . . .

FRÄULEIN SCHNEIDER

I CAN HEAR HAWAIIAN BREEZES
    BLOW.

BOTH

AH . . .

SCHULTZ

IT'S FROM CALIFORNIA.

FRÄULEIN SCHNEIDER

EVEN SO.
HOW AM I TO THANK YOU?

SCHULTZ

KINDLY LET IT PASS.

FRÄULEIN SCHNEIDER

WOULD YOU LIKE A SLICE?

SCHULTZ

THAT MIGHT BE NICE,
BUT FRANKLY,
IT WOULD GIVE ME GAS.

FRÄULEIN SCHNEIDER

THEN WE SHALL LEAVE IT HERE
NOT TO EAT,
BUT SEE:

BOTH
A PINEAPPLE . . .

**FRÄULEIN
SCHNEIDER**
FOR ME.

SCHULTZ
FROM ME.

ALL
AH . . .

(They dance)

**FRÄULEIN
SCHNEIDER**
But you must not bring me any more
pineapples. Do you hear? It is not proper.
It is a gift a young man would present to
his lady-love. It makes me blush.

SCHULTZ
But there is no one — no one in all of
Berlin who is more deserving. If I could,
I would fill your entire room with
pineapples!

BOTH
(Sing)
A PINEAPPLE . . .

FRÄULEIN SCHNEIDER
FOR YOU,

FRÄULEIN SCHNEIDER
FROM YOU.

ALL
AH ...
AH ...

(The music continues)

FRÄULEIN SCHNEIDER
(Spoken)
I think I will lie down for a few minutes. My head is spinning!

SCHULTZ
Fräulein Schneider, Good evening.

FRÄULEIN SCHNEIDER
Good evening, Herr Schultz.

(FRÄULEIN SCHNEIDER opens her bedroom door — then turns to SCHULTZ)

I am — overwhelmed!

(She goes in and closes the door. The music ends. SCHULTZ is all a-tingle. He makes a decision. He is about to knock on FRÄULEIN SCHNEIDER's door when suddenly FRÄULEIN KOST opens her door and comes out — obviously on her way out to find some business. She wonders why SCHULTZ is so far from his own door. But her natural flirtatious instincts take over.)

FRÄULEIN KOST
Good evening, Herr Schultz.

SCHULTZ
Good evening, Fräulein Kost. I am looking for — I think I dropped — a small coin — a groschen ... it rolled this way.

FRÄULEIN KOST
You're looking for a groschen?
(Meaningfully)
I'm looking for two marks.

(SCHULTZ gets her meaning. He shakes his head negatively. FRÄULEIN KOST exits. SCHULTZ goes again to FRÄULEIN SCHNEIDER's

door. He knocks. Immediately the door swings open. He swiftly enters. The door closes.)*

ACT ONE SCENE 9

(The EMCEE enters with a small wind-up gramophone. It is a boy's voice, singing beautifully ...)

THE SUN ON THE MEADOW IS SUMMERY WARM,
THE STAG IN THE FOREST RUNS FREE.
BUT GATHER TOGETHER TO GREET THE STORM,
TOMORROW BELONGS TO ME.

THE BRANCH OF THE LINDEN IS LEAFY AND GREEN,
THE RHINE GIVES ITS GOLD TO THE SEA.
BUT SOMEWHERE A GLORY AWAITS UNSEEN,
TOMORROW BELONGS
(The EMCEE takes off the needle)

EMCEE
... TO ME
(Cymbal crash)

ACT ONE   SCENE 10

(It is rather dark in CLIFF's room, SALLY is sitting alone – drinking. A bottle of gin is nearby. CLIFF enters, opening a letter)

CLIFF

I got the letter ... all seven pages. Are you alright? ... Sally?

SALLY
(nods)
I'm just not speaking today.

CLIFF
(Affably)
Okay.
(Looking at the letter)
My mother says: "Tell Sally to lay off the gin."

SALLY

She does not!

CLIFF

And here's the check!!

(He pulls out a check)

SALLY

Hurray!!! Fifty dollars? How much is that in real money?

CLIFF

More than enough to pay the rent ...

SALLY
(hopefully)
And dinner at the Adlon? With a bottle of champagne? Oh, Cliff!
(He looks at her as if she's off her rocker)
A glass of champagne?

CLIFF
Alright.
(SALLY kisses him)
Why so gloomy?

SALLY
(evading the question)
Because we never have dinner at the Adlon any more.

CLIFF
We never did.
(Reading the letter)
"I'm so excited you've finished your novel, Clifford darling, too." What a liar I am.

SALLY

Poor Cliff. It's my fault – If I weren't always dragging you off to party after party ...

CLIFF

But I love those parties. I like this whole town. It's so tawdry and terrible and everyone's having such a great time. Like a bunch of kids playing in their room – getting wilder and wilder – and knowing any minute their parents are going to come home.

SALLY

Maybe you should write about your childhood.

CLIFF

That was my first novel.

SALLY

There must be something else to write about ...
(SALLY beams a smile)

CLIFF

Sally Bowles?

SALLY

Of course! I told you I'd inspire you.

"Les amours du Sally." But make me ravishing and sublimely seductive – so no man can resist me. Not even a rather strange, handsome young American, who allows me to share his room – and his bed – and falls desperately in love with me . . .
  (He turns his head away from her)
Don't worry! It's only fiction!

CLIFF
  (nods)
Now all I've got to do is write it.

SALLY
I wish I were less distracting.

CLIFF
It's true. Nobody could work with you around. Not Hemingway – not Tolstoy – not even Proust . . .
  (She starts packing her suitcase)
Oh, no – Sally – I didn't mean . . .

SALLY
But it's time, Cliff. I've never stayed with anyone so long. One must keep mobile, musn't one?

CLIFF
What's the matter? Got a better offer?

SALLY
Dozens. I'm sure you've offers, too.

CLIFF
Oh, dozens
  (A game)
A couple
  (SALLY gives him a look)
Not one.

SALLY
Not even Bobby? He phoned today, by the way.

  (She picks up her suitcase ands starts to exit)

CLIFF
  (Suddenly)
Don't go.

SALLY
What?

CLIFF
Please, don't go.

SALLY
Are you serious?

CLIFF
The hell with Bobby. Maybe – I like you here. I need you. I need . . . The truth is, Sally – when you're out all night – I can't sleep. Our little bed suddenly seems so empty. I've never felt this way before about – anyone – anyone at all.

SALLY
You truly mean this?

CLIFF
More than I've ever meant anything.

SALLY
Oh, darling . . .

CLIFF
You want to tell me what's wrong?

SALLY
Nothing. Not a thing.
  (She sits)
I'm pregnant.

CLIFF
Are you sure?
  (SALLY nods)
Well – what are we going to do?

SALLY
What am I going to do? The usual thing, I suppose.

CLIFF
You've done it before?

SALLY
Thousands of times.

CLIFF
Don't you think you ought to check with the father?

SALLY
Why?

CLIFF
Well – to help pay for the doctor – for one thing.

SALLY
I do so hate it, Cliff. That awful doctor.

CLIFF
Then maybe . . .

SALLY
And – anyway – who is the father?
(laughing)
Could be anyone!

CLIFF
(dawning realization)
Could be me. Sally, it could be me.

SALLY
(considering it a possibility for an instant)
True.

CLIFF
And Sally – if it's mine . . .

SALLY
We'll never know – will we?

CLIFF
We could.

SALLY
Oh, yes! Nine months of being sick every morning. And then – the happy day! And whom does it resemble? Max! A horrid little German infant – with a moustache – ordering us about.

CLIFF
I'm willing to take that chance.

SALLY
Or – perhaps – an Oriental. I seem to recall a rather taciturn Malaysian . . .

It's the audience that blends into the scenery in *Cabaret*: Mendes spent more than two years looking for a place in New York to duplicate the cabaret setting he devised for his London production in 1993, eventually doing a makeover on the former site of Xenon, a once hot disco. A lover of movie musicals like *Mary Poppins* since childhood, Mendes was drawn to *Cabaret* when he read the original Broadway script and discovered how much had been left out of the movie--including an entire subplot about Cliff's landlady (originally played by Lotte Lenya, here by Mary Louise Wilson). Mendes made further revisions in the book with writer Joe Masteroff and then cast actors who mostly had little or no musical experience. "I don't want a produced sound," Mendes says. "The singing voices come out of their speaking voices." Even the orchestra members, who also play roles in the show, were cast for their acting and singing ability--and only then for their prowess with an instrument. And though the Nazi shadow looms large in the production, Mendes resists trotting out swastikas for an easy reaction. "It's become a cliche--," he says. "You can't act the beginning of Nazism with a knowledge of the ending. The point is to show how seductive it was, to draw the audience in."

--Richard Zoglin
Time
March 30, 1998

CLIFF

Sally — will you do me a favor and shut up! Can we just be serious for a minute?

SALLY

(suppressing hysteria)

I doubt it, Cliff.

CLIFF

This could be the best thing that ever happened to us . . .

SALLY

I doubt it, Cliff.

CLIFF

We're drifting — We have no focus to our lives. A baby would make all the difference. I know it would to me. I'd get a job. I'd have to. I'd stay home nights, write the novel — wash the diapers — the whole bit! Listen, Sally — will you do one thing for me — please? At least — think about it — before you see the doctor . . . ?

SALLY

(sings)

MAYBE THIS TIME, I'LL BE LUCKY
MAYBE THIS TIME, HE'LL STAY
MAYBE THIS TIME

FOR THE FIRST TIME
LOVE WON'T HURRY AWAY

HE WILL HOLD ME FAST
I'LL BE HOME AT LAST
NOT A LOSER ANYMORE
LIKE THE LAST TIME
AND THE TIME BEFORE

EVERYBODY LOVES A WINNER
SO NOBODY LOVED ME:
'LADY PEACEFUL,' 'LADY HAPPY,'
THAT'S WHAT I LONG TO BE
ALL THE ODDS ARE IN MY FAVOR
SOMETHING'S BOUND TO BEGIN
IT'S GOT TO HAPPEN, HAPPEN
    SOMETIME
MAYBE THIS TIME I'LL WIN

EVERYBODY LOVES A WINNER
SO NOBODY LOVED ME:
'LADY PEACEFUL,' 'LADY HAPPY,'
THAT'S WHAT I LONG TO BE
ALL THE ODDS ARE IN MY FAVOR
SOMETHING'S BOUND TO BEGIN
IT'S GOT TO HAPPEN, HAPPEN
    SOMETIME
MAYBE THIS TIME. . .
MAYBE THIS TIME I'LL WIN.

(ERNST knocks and enters)

65

ERNST

Clifford – Sally –

SALLY

Ernst.

ERNST

I do not wish to intrude.

SALLY

Would you like a drink, darling?

ERNST

Only if you'll join me.

SALLY

(making a bee-line for the bottle)

Well, just this once.

CLIFF

(to ERNST)

What's on your mind, Ernst?

ERNST

You remember – I mentioned the possibility of an occasional business trip to Paris. If you are interested, I think in the next few days. Thank you. And I promise you are giving help to a very good cause.

CLIFF

Well, whatever it is, don't tell me. I don't want to know.

ERNST

As you wish.

CLIFF

How about going tomorrow?

ERNST

Tomorrow? But, we are all going to the party . . .

CLIFF

I think I'll skip it.

ERNST

But why, Clifford?

CLIFF

Let's just say: I'm turning over a new leaf.

SALLY

Turning over a new tree.

ERNST

And you, Sally . . . ? You are turning over as well?

SALLY

Who knows? I mean – Cliff and I may just turn out to be the two most utterly boring people you ever met!

CLIFF

So, what would I have to do?

ERNST

It is so very simple: You go to an address I will give you – you pick up a small briefcase – you bring it back to Berlin. And I pay you seventy-five marks!

SALLY

Seventy-five marks!

ERNST

Yes, and that is only the beginning.

(to CLIFF)

So, you will go to Paris?

CLIFF

Absolutely. Anything for a buck. Prosit!

ERNST

(toasting)

Prosit!

SALLY

Prosit!

EMCEE

So, you see? There's more than one way to make money . . .

MONEY MAKES THE WORLD GO
    AROUND
THE WORLD GO AROUND
THE WORLD GO AROUND
MONEY MAKES THE WORLD GO
    AROUND
IT MAKES THE WORLD GO 'ROUND

A MARK, A YEN, A BUCK, OR A
    POUND
A BUCK OR A POUND
A BUCK OR A POUND
IS ALL THAT MAKES THE WORLD
    GO AROUND,
THAT CLINKING CLANKING SOUND
CAN MAKE THE WORLD GO ROUND.

GIRLS

MONEY MONEY MONEY MONEY
    MONEY MONEY
MONEY MONEY MONEY MONEY
    MONEY MONEY
MONEY MONEY MONEY MONEY
    MONEY MONEY
MONEY MONEY

EMCEE

GIRLS

IF YOU HAPPEN
TO BE RICH, . . . OOOOH
AND YOU FEEL LIKE A
NIGHT'S ENTERTAINMENT,
. . . MONEY
YOU CAN PARTY FOR
A GAY ESCAPADE.
MONEY MONEY MONEY
MONEY MONEY MONEY
MONEY MONEY

IF YOU HAPPEN
TO BE RICH, . . . OOOOH
AND ALONE,
AND YOU NEED A
COMPANION . . . MONEY
YOU CAN RING TING-A-LING
FOR THE MAID.

IF YOU HAPPEN
TO BE RICH . . . OOOOH
AND YOU FIND YOU ARE LEFT
BY YOUR LOVER, . . . MONEY
THOUGH YOU MOAN
AND YOU GROAN QUITE A LOT
MONEY MONEY MONEY
MONEY MONEY MONEY
MONEY MONEY
YOU CAN TAKE IT
ON THE CHIN, . . . OOOOH
CALL A CAB, AND BEGIN . . . MONEY

TO RECOVER,
ON YOUR FOURTEEN
CARAT YACHT.

EMCEE

MONEY MAKES THE WORLD GO
AROUND,
THE WORLD GO AROUND,
THE WORLD GO AROUND,
MONEY MAKES THE WORLD GO
AROUND,
OF THAT WE CAN BE SURE.
(- - - -) ON BEING POOR.

ALL

MONEY MONEY MONEY MONEY
MONEY MONEY
MONEY MONEY MONEY MONEY
MONEY MONEY
MONEY MONEY MONEY MONEY
MONEY MONEY MONEY MONEY
MONEY MONEY MONEY MONEY

ALL

MONEY MONEY MONEY - MONEY
MONEY MONEY
MONEY MONEY MONEY - MONEY
MONEY MONEY
MONEY MONEY MONEY MONEY

MONEY MONEY MONEY MONEY
MONEY MONEY MONEY MONEY

EMCEE & GIRLS
(in Canon)

IF YOU HAVEN'T ANY COAL IN THE
STOVE
AND YOU FREEZE IN THE WINTER
AND YOU CURSE TO THE WIND AT
YOUR FATE
WHEN YOU HAVEN'T ANY SHOES
ON YOUR FEET
AND YOUR COAT'S THIN AS PAPER
AND YOU LOOK THIRTY POUNDS
UNDERWEIGHT.
WHEN YOU GO TO GET A WORD
OF ADVICE
FROM THE FAT LITTLE PASTOR
HE WILL TELL YOU TO LOVE
EVERMORE.
BUT WHEN HUNGER COMES A RAP,
RAT-A-TAT, RAT-A-TAT AT THE
WINDOW
(RAT-A-TAT, RAT-A-TAT, RAT-A-TAT)

GIRLS

AT THE WINDOW . . .

EMCEE

WHO'S THERE?

69

GIRLS
HUNGER!

EMCEE
OOH, HUNGER!

ALL
SEE HOW LOVE FLIES OUT THE
DOOR ... FOR

EMCEE	GIRLS
MONEY MAKES	
THE WORLD ...	...GO AROUND
THE WORLD ...	...GO AROUND
THE WORLD ...	...GO AROUND
MONEY MAKES THE - - -	
GO AROUND	...GO AROUND
THAT CLINKING CLANKING	
SOUND OF	
MONEY MONEY MONEY MONEY	
MONEY MONEY MONEY MONEY	

EMCEE	GIRLS
GET A LITTLE,	
GET A LITTLE,	MONEY MONEY
	MONEY MONEY ...
MONEY MONEY MONEY MONEY	
	MONEY MONEY
	MONEY MONEY ...
A MARK, A YEN, A BUCK	

OR A POUND	GET A LITTLE
	GET A LITTLE
THAT CLINKING CLANKING	
CLUNKING SOUND	GET A LITTLE
	GET A LITTLE
IS ALL THAT MAKES	
THE WORLD GO ROUND	

MONEY MONEY MONEY MONEY...
MONEY MONEY MONEY MONEY...
MONEY MONEY MONEY MONEY...
MONEY MONEY MONEY MONEY...
IT MAKES THE WORLD GO ROUND!

ACT ONE   SCENE 11

(FRÄULEIN KOST is smuggling SAILORS out of her room. She is halfway across the floor with one of them when FRÄULEIN SCHNEIDER enters)

FRÄULEIN KOST
All right! There is no need to say it. I know it by heart already. So – no lectures, please–about sailors. They are just lonesome, patriotic German boys. I have a duty.

(SCHULTZ comes out of FRÄULEIN SCHNEIDER's room and takes in the scene. It is clear he has been inside with FRÄULEIN SCHNEIDER. The atmosphere crackles. Now, glorying in the moment, and for FRÄULEIN SCHNEIDER's benefit, FRÄULEIN KOST hugs and kisses the third SAILOR at great length)

FRÄULEIN KOST
Goodnight, Rudy – you must be sure to come back again soon. At any time.

(Looking at FRÄULEIN SCHNEIDER)

Bring your friends. Go home.

(The SAILOR exits. FRÄULEIN KOST waltzes up to FRÄULEIN SCHNEIDER)

Ah – good evening, Fräulein Schneider. A busy evening – no? I see we are – after all – sisters under the skin.

SCHULTZ
Fräulein Kost!

FRÄULEIN KOST
Yes?

SCHULTZ

This fine lady is not your sister! This fine lady has just honored me by consenting to give me her hand in marriage!

FRÄULEIN KOST

(Really amazed)

Marriage?

SCHULTZ

Yes, we marry in – three weeks.

FRÄULEIN KOST

Three weeks!

SCHULTZ

So a little respect for the future Frau Schultz – if you please!

FRÄULEIN KOST

Ja! Ja! Frau Schultz?

(Fräulein Kost – chastened – exits into her room)

FRÄULEIN SCHNEIDER

Thank you – Herr Schultz. You were – supreme.

SCHULTZ

But what else could I do?

FRÄULEIN SCHNEIDER

Such a magnificent lie to preserve my reputation.

SCHULTZ

But why did I say three weeks? Why not three months? Three years? This way she will find out the truth so quickly ... Unless ...

FRÄULEIN SCHNEIDER

Unless?

SCHULTZ

Unless what?

FRÄULEIN SCHNEIDER

You said: "unless."

SCHULTZ

But it is foolish! I mean – after all – who would have me? An elderly widower – balding – with heartburn – and a little fruit ...

FRÄULEIN SCHNEIDER

Am I such a bargain then? An unbeautiful spinster with some rooms to let – poorly furnished.

SCHULTZ

I work fourteen hours a day.

FRÄULEIN SCHNEIDER

I do my own scrubbing.

SCHULTZ

My right leg bothers me.

FRÄULEIN SCHNEIDER

I have such palpitations.

SCHULTZ

I'm not a well man.

FRÄULEIN SCHNEIDER

Am I a well woman?

SCHULTZ

What are we talking about? We're alive! And what good is it – alone? So if you would even consider – marriage ...?

(A long pause)

FRÄULEIN SCHNEIDER

I will consider it.

SCHULTZ

But take your time, by all means.
No hurry.

FRÄULEIN SCHNEIDER

We should discuss it. We must not marry merely to humiliate Fräulein Kost.

SCHULTZ

I assure you, Fräulein Schneider.
This is not the case.

FRÄULEIN SCHNEIDER

But let us be honest. Had she not seen us — you would not have proposed today.

SCHULTZ

Then tomorrow.

FRÄULEIN SCHNEIDER

You mean this?

SCHULTZ

(nods)
I had it in my mind.

FRÄULEIN SCHNEIDER

It is all so impulsive.

SCHULTZ

(shakes his head)
You hesitate because you have never been married. It frightens you.
But believe me, it can work wonders . . .

(Sings)
HOW THE WORLD CAN CHANGE,
IT CAN CHANGE LIKE THAT —
DUE TO ONE LITTLE WORD:
"MARRIED."

SEE A PALACE RISE
FROM A TWO ROOM FLAT
DUE TO ONE LITTLE WORD:
"MARRIED."
AND THE OLD DESPAIR
THAT WAS OFTEN THERE
SUDDENLY CEASES TO BE
FOR YOU WAKE ONE DAY,
LOOK AROUND AND SAY:
SOMEBODY WONDERFUL
MARRIED ME.

CHANTEUSE

O WIE WUNDERBAR,
NICHTS IST SO WIE-ES-WAR,

The only thing that the new "Cabaret" has in common with the movie version is green nail polish--worn then by Liza Minnelli, and now, onstage at Henry Miller's Theatre (renamed the Kit Kat Klub, in honor of the show), by Natasha Richardson . . . Everything about this production is more raw and immediate, including the audience's proximity to the actors: in this intimate night-club setting, seated at round tables for four and sipping drinks (you can, if you like, buy a bottle of Roederer Cristal for three hundred dollars), you're uneasily aware of having bought into the evening's entertainment--of being more than a spectator at the passing parade.

And it is a parade you can't tear your eyes away from: the figures onstage are garish, ghoulish, and aggressively arresting, beginning with the astonishing Alan Cumming in the part of the Emcee (the Joel Grey role). Cumming, a Scottish actor well known in England and here making his Broadway debut, comes on wearing a long black leather coat and boots, his lips colored blood red, and he stares at you with big eyes out of a long, pointy pale face; the look in his eyes--eyes highlighted with blue eye shadow, and the edges of the lids ringed with red-- tells you he knows that you're both dreading and dying to know what's under that coat. And you know that he's going to show you. There is a bow tie, as befits a master of ceremonies, but it's attached to a parachute harness, which wraps around his body in a way that deliberately emphasizes his crotch. His nipples have been rouged and glittered, and he appears to have bruises on his torso. Cumming is a spectacle of mixed messages, and he forces you to ask yourself what you think you're seeing, and what it might mean.

--Nancy Franklin
The New Yorker
April 6, 1998

DURCH EIN WINZIGES WORT:
"HEIRAT."

AUF DEM ERDGESCHOSS
DURCHEN EIN MÄRCHEN SCHLOSS
MIT EINEM WINZIGEN WORT:
"HEIRAT."

UND DAS GRAU IN GRAU
WIRD AUF EIN MAL BLAU,
WIE NOCH KEIN BLAU JEMALS WAR.
UND DANN STEHT MAN DA
SAGT BESELIGT `JA`
HEUT WIRD MEIN TRAUM NICHT
SO GRAU IN GRAU.

(Spoken)
O wie wunderbar,
Nichts ist so wie-es-war,
Durch ein winziges wort:
"Heirat"

Auf dem Erdgeschoss
Durch ein Märchenschloss
Mit einem winzigen Wort:
"Heirat."

SCHULTZ

CHANTEUSE

AND THE OLD DESPAIR
        UND DAS GRAU IN GRAU
THAT WAS OFTEN THERE
        WIRD AUF EIN MAL BLAU
SUDDENLY CEASES TO BE
        WIE NOCH KEIN BLAU
        JEMALS WAR

SCHULTZ & SCHNEIDER

FOR YOU WAKE ONE DAY,
LOOK AROUND AND SAY:

SCHULTZ

"SOMEBODY WONDERFUL

FRÄULEIN SCHNEIDER

"SOMEBODY WONDERFUL

BOTH

MARRIED ME."

ACT ONE   SCENE 12

THE FRUIT SHOP

(SALLY is carrying a large gift-wrapped package. CLIFF enters, carrying a briefcase.)

SALLY

Darling, at last – you're here – just in time!
(They kiss.)
Was Paris divine?

CLIFF

I don't know. I didn't see much of it.

SALLY

Why . . . Was there any trouble?

CLIFF

(the briefcase)
No. But I'll be glad to get rid of this.
It's so good to see you.

(CLIFF goes to her and starts to hug her.)

SALLY

Spare the child!

CLIFF

Oh, my God! I always forget . . .

SALLY
(dramatically)
Well – of course you do! You're not mortally ill every morning.

CLIFF
Neither are you.

SALLY
Well – there's still time – Come! I can't wait to give them their present!

SCHULTZ
Herr Clifford – you are back!

CLIFF
Herr Schultz.

SALLY
Fräulein Schneider, Herr Schultz, this is for you—but be careful!

FRÄULEIN SCHNEIDER
Ah – Herr Schultz – look! Crystal!

SALLY
Cut-crystal. It's for fruit.

FRÄULEIN SCHNEIDER
Beautiful.

SCHULTZ
I promise to keep it filled. As long as we live, this bowl will not be empty.
(FRÄULEIN KOST enters with a SAILOR)

FRÄULEIN KOST
Fräulein Schneider – I am welcome?

FRÄULEIN SCHNEIDER
Fräulein Kost – forgive me. It is my fault – I did not invite you. But only because I know you work in the evening.

FRÄULEIN KOST
Tonight I am free.

FRÄULEIN SCHNEIDER
I should live so long.

FRÄULEIN KOST
Rudy. Come! It's Fräulein Schneider's party. Why don't you dance with her?

SAILOR
(to FRÄULEIN SCHNEIDER)
Oh. It will be my pleasure, Fräulein.

FRÄULEIN SCHNEIDER
But I cannot ... and you are so young ... It is out of the question ... unthinkable ... Absolutely unthinkable ... Absolutely.

(During this, the SAILOR dances with FRÄULEIN SCHNEIDER)

(ERNST enters. He comes up to CLIFF and SALLY)

ERNST
Clifford – Sally . . .

SALLY
Ernst!

ERNST
You have the briefcase?

CLIFF
Baubles from Paris – Perfume – Silk stockings . . . ?

(ERNST takes the briefcase. He hands CLIFF the envelope, SALLY grabs it)

SALLY
Seventy-five marks! It's a gift from heaven!

ERNST
And now – I must find Fräulein Schneider. If you will excuse me . . . ?

SALLY
(to CLIFF)
Dance with me.

CLIFF
Do I have to?

SALLY
Yes!

(They join the dancers upstage, FRÄULEIN SCHNEIDER approaches ERNST)

ERNST
Ah, Fräulein Schneider. I wish you much happiness.

FRÄULEIN SCHNEIDER
Thank you, Herr Ludwig.

ERNST
I am sorry to be late, but there was a meeting. An important meeting.

FRÄULEIN SCHNEIDER
One does what one must.

ERNST
And now – I should like to meet the groom-to-be.

FRÄULEIN SCHNEIDER
Herr Schultz. But where can he be?

He's been having a glass of schnapps with everybody. But you will forgive if he is a little – "who-who" – you understand?
(SCHULTZ comes up)

SCHULTZ
(to ERNST)
Good evening. Good evening. You will have a drink with me?
(to FRÄULEIN SCHNEIDER – whispering)
Who is this?

FRÄULEIN SCHNEIDER
Herr Ludwig. An old friend.
(to ERNST)
Herr Ludwig – Herr Schultz.

SCHULTZ
And you are most welcome, Herr Ludwig. You will join me in a schnapps.

Then you must eat — there is so much food. And so many pretty girls. I will introduce you to them — except I do not know their names, so you will introduce yourself? — You will dance — Would you like another schnapps?

(ERNST is laughing and enjoying SCHULTZ's happiness)

FRÄULEIN SCHNEIDER
You did not give him the first one yet.

SCHULTZ
No?

FRÄULEIN SCHNEIDER
Here, let me do it.

(FRÄULEIN SCHNEIDER takes the bottle and pours a drink for ERNST)

ERNST
Thank you.

SCHULTZ
Nothing for me?

FRÄULEIN SCHNEIDER
You have had enough.

SCHULTZ
You hear? You hear? Not even married yet — and already she is in charge. And it is — pleasant. At last, someone who cares if I am foolish.

ERNST
Many, many happy years to an outstanding couple.

SCHULTZ
Beautiful dancing!

(FRÄULEIN KOST approaches ERNST)

FRÄULEIN KOST
Herr Ludwig — remember me? Fräulein Kost? You must dance with me! Come!

ERNST
A pleasure, Fräulein.
(To CLIFF)
Clifford, bitte — will you watch the briefcase? And my coat?

(He takes off his coat, revealing a Nazi armband. CLIFF grabs him and stares)

I am sorry, since you did not wish to know my politics.

CLIFF
Is this the good cause?

ERNST
Our party will be the builders of the new Germany.

CLIFF
Yes. I've been reading your leader's book . . .

ERNST
But enough politics. What does it matter? We are friends — close friends. Buddies!
(ERNST returns to dance with FRÄULEIN KOST)
With your permission? . . . A delightful party. Herr Schultz is a most generous host. Ja?

FRÄULEIN KOST
He should be. He could afford ten times as much. They have all the money — the Jews.

ERNST
Herr Schultz?
(FRÄULEIN KOST nods)
I think — I have changed my mind. If you will excuse me, Fräulein . . .

(ERNST *goes to* FRÄULEIN SCHNEIDER)

Fräulein Schneider – I must speak to you. You and I are old acquaintances. I have sent you many new lodgers. So let me urge you – think what you are doing. This marriage is not advisable. I cannot put it too strongly. For your own welfare . . .

FRÄULEIN SCHNEIDER

What about Herr Schultz's welfare?

ERNST

He is not a German.

FRÄULEIN SCHNEIDER

He was born here.

ERNST

He is not a German. Good night.
    (He goes to CLIFF *for his briefcase and coat)*
Sorry, Clifford. Good night.
    (FRÄULEIN KOST sees them)

FRÄULEIN KOST

Herr Ludwig – wait! You are not leaving so early?

ERNST

I do not find this party amusing.

FRÄULEIN KOST

Oh – but it is just beginning. Come, we will make it amusing – you and I – ja? Ladies and gentlemen –Wait – ! Herr Ludwig – this is for you:

(*Sings*)

THE SUN ON THE MEADOW IS SUMMERY WARM.
THE STAG IN THE FOREST RUNS FREE.
BUT GATHER TOGETHER TO GREET THE STORM,
TOMORROW BELONGS TO ME.

THE BRANCH OF THE LINDEN IS LEAFY AND GREEN,
THE RHINE GIVES ITS GOLD TO THE SEA.
BUT SOMEWHERE A GLORY AWAITS UNSEEN.
TOMORROW BELONGS TO ME.
(*Spoken*)
Herr Ludwig! Sing with me!

BOTH

THE BABE IN HIS CRADLE IS CLOSING HIS EYES.
THE BLOSSOM EMBRACES THE BEE.
BUT SOON, SAYS A WHISPER: "ARISE, ARISE,
TOMORROW BELONGS TO ME"

FRÄULEIN KOST
(*Spoken*)
Everyone!

(*All begin to sing except FRÄULEIN SCHNEIDER, SCHULTZ, CLIFF and SALLY, who stand watching*)

ALL

OH FATHERLAND, FATHERLAND,
SHOW US THE SIGN
YOUR CHILDREN HAVE WAITED TO SEE.
THE MORNING WILL COME WHEN THE WORLD IS MINE.
TOMORROW BELONGS TO ME!

OH FATHERLAND, FATHERLAND,
SHOW US THE SIGN
YOUR CHILDREN HAVE WAITED TO SEE.
THE MORNING WILL COME WHEN THE WORLD IS MINE.
TOMORROW BELONGS TO ME!

Every night at *Cabaret*'s Kit
Kat Club, Alan Cumming as
the Emcee brings a pair of
audience members on stage to
share a dance. Early in his
career, Cumming was a stand-up
comedian, so he feels at ease
ad-libbing these encounters--but
there have been a few notable
incidents. One night, for
instance, Mikhail Baryshnikov
was his dance partner. "I try
not to take celebrities, but
Tasha (Richardson) told me
he was out there and said,
'Wouldn't that be a laugh?'
The other day, I took Walter
Cronkite up by accident. I
know who he is, but I didn't
recognize him. I'd been refused
that night, so I was walking
back to the stage pretending to
be all upset because this man
wouldn't come with me. I grabbed
an older man from the back and
said, 'Okay you'll do!' The
audience went mad clapping. I
said 'What's your name?' and
he said, 'Walter Cronkite.'"
Another night, Cumming plucked
New York Times book critic
Michiko Kakutani from the crowd.
That bit of blind casting turned
out well: The Pulitzer Prize-
winning writer was so taken
with *Cabaret* that she wrote a
valentine to Cumming and the
show in the April 26 Sunday
Times Magazine.

"I always go for the butchest
men," Cumming explains, "because
(the dance segment is) about
humiliation in a way. The
cabaret exists to unsettle the
audience, and that's why some
people refuse to go up. That's
quite embarrassing, of course,
but they're more embarrassed
than I am. And I get to say
things like, 'You know you
want to.'"

--Kathy Henderson
InTheater
May 15, 1998

ACT TWO

The supporting cast--notably Denis O'Hare, Fred Rose, and Michele Pawk--delivers staunchly, and Mendes's idea of making the chorines double as members of the band is terrific, including the final touch when they appear wearing identical Louise Brooksian Lulu wigs. Such double duty is quite an accomplishment: Whether they lend a whiff of George Grosz to the orchestra or twist themselves into Marshall's burlesque choreography, these young ladies rate unstinting kudos.

--John Simon
New York
March 30, 1998

ENTR'ACTE:

(The EMCEE, now dressed as a girl, and the Women's Ensemble assemble on stage for a kick line.)

(The kick line progresses and builds. The EMCEE reveals himself. Then suddenly, at a given point, it becomes a row of goose-stepping, "Heil Hitlers.")

(The line marches off stage, leaving the EMCEE to introduce the next scene . . .)

85

ACT TWO SCENE 2

THE FRUIT SHOP

SCHULTZ
Fräulein Schneider—good morning.

FRÄULEIN SCHNEIDER
Good morning, Herr Schultz.

SCHULTZ
New apples. Fresh off the tree. Delicious—Please....

FRÄULEIN SCHNEIDER
Perhaps later.

SCHULTZ
About the party last evening...I do not remember it too well. Was I that inebriated? Can you ever forgive me?

FRÄULEIN SCHNEIDER
For what? A few glasses of schnapps?

SCHULTZ
I promise you — no more drinking. On our wedding day, you will be proud of me.

FRÄULEIN SCHNEIDER
I am already proud of you. But — as far as the wedding is concerned . . .

SCHULTZ
Yes?

FRÄULEIN SCHNEIDER
There is a problem. A new problem.

SCHULTZ
A new problem?

FRÄULEIN SCHNEIDER
New to me — because I had not thought about it. But at the party last night my eyes were opened.

SCHULTZ
And . . . ?

FRÄULEIN SCHNEIDER
I saw that one can no longer dismiss the Nazis. They are my friends and neighbors. And how many others are there?

SCHULTZ
(impatiently)
Of course — many. And many are Communists — and Socialists — and Social Democrats. So what is it? You wish to wait till the next election — and then decide?

FRÄULEIN SCHNEIDER
But if the Nazis come to power . . .

SCHULTZ
You will be married to a Jew. But also a German. A German as much as anyone.

FRÄULEIN SCHNEIDER
I need a license to rent my rooms. If they take it away . . .

SCHULTZ
They will take nothing away. And Fräulein Schneider — it is not always a good thing to settle for the lowest apple on the tree — the one easiest to reach. Climb up — a little way. It is worth it! Up there the apples are so much more delicious!

FRÄULEIN SCHNEIDER

But if I fall...?

SCHULTZ

I will catch you, I promise. I feel such tenderness for you. It is difficult to express. Are we too old for words like love?

FRÄULEIN SCHNEIDER

Far too old. I am no Juliet. You are no Romeo. We must be sensible.

SCHULTZ

And live alone? How many meals have you eaten alone? A thousand? Five thousand?

FRÄULEIN SCHNEIDER

Twenty thousand.

SCHULTZ

Then be sensible. Governments come — governments go. How much longer can we wait?
(FRÄULEIN SCHNEIDER says nothing)
Let me peel you an orange...

(SCHULTZ starts peeling an orange - rather clumsily)

FRÄULEIN SCHNEIDER

I will do it.
(Underscoring from "MARRIED" begins)

SCHULTZ
(Sings)
AND THE OLD DESPAIR THAT
  WAS OFTEN THERE
SUDDENLY CEASES TO BE.
FOR YOU WAKE ONE DAY,
LOOK AROUND AND SAY:
"SOMEBODY WONDERFUL
  MARRIED —

(EMCEE drops a brick between them)

(The fruit shop window shatters loudly)

(Spoken)
It is nothing! Children on their way to school. Mischievous children! Nothing more! I assure you! School children. Young — full of mischief. You understand?

FRÄULEIN SCHNEIDER

I understand.

ACT TWO   SCENE 3

(The EMCEE and a Gorilla enter)

EMCEE

I KNOW WHAT YOU'RE THINKING:
YOU WONDER WHY I CHOSE HER
OUT OF ALL THE LADIES IN THE
   WORLD.
THAT'S JUST A FIRST IMPRESSION,
WHAT GOOD'S A FIRST
   IMPRESSION?
IF YOU KNEW HER LIKE I DO
IT WOULD CHANGE YOUR POINT
   OF VIEW.

IF YOU COULD SEE HER THROUGH
   MY EYES,
YOU WOULDN'T WONDER AT ALL.
IF YOU COULD SEE HER THROUGH
   MY EYES
I GUARANTEE YOU WOULD FALL
   (LIKE I DID)
WHEN WE'RE IN PUBLIC TOGETHER
I HEAR SOCIETY MOAN.
BUT IF THEY COULD SEE HER
   THROUGH MY EYES
MAYBE THEY'D LEAVE US ALONE

HOW CAN I SPEAK OF HER
   VIRTUES?

I DON'T KNOW WHERE TO BEGIN
SHE'S CLEVER, SHE'S SMART, SHE
   READS MUSIC
SHE DOESN'T SMOKE OR DRINK GIN
   (LIKE I DO)
YET, WHEN WE'RE WALKING
   TOGETHER
THEY SNEER IF I'M HOLDING
   HER HAND,
BUT IF THEY COULD SEE HER
   THROUGH MY EYES
MAYBE THEY'D ALL UNDERSTAND.

(dance break)

EMCEE

WHY DON'T THEY LEAVE US
   ALONE?

(Spoken)

Meine Damen und Herren, Mesdames
et Messieurs, Ladies and Gentlemen – Is
it a crime to fall in love? Can we ever
tell where the heart truly leads us? All
we are asking is ein bisschen Verständnis
– A little understanding –Why can't
the world "leben and leben lassen" –
"Live and let live?"

I UNDERSTAND YOUR OBJECTION,
I GRANT YOU THE PROBLEM'S

NOT SMALL.
BUT IF YOU COULD SEE HER
   THROUGH MY EYES . . .
SHE WOULDN'T LOOK JEWISH
   AT ALL.

ACT TWO   SCENE 4

CLIFF'S ROOM

*(SALLY is dressed to go out as
CLIFF enters from the street.)*

SALLY

Cliff – did you get a job?

CLIFF

I'll try again tomorrow.

SALLY

But there's no need! I've got the most
marvelous news! Guess who was
summoned to the Kit Kat Klub today?!
(She bows)
Ta da! It turns out they want me back –
desperately!

CLIFF

(darkly)
Why?

SALLY

Why? Because they've finally realized how valuable I am! Bobby and Victor tell me it's been deadly since I left. So – I start tonight! Isn't that heaven!

CLIFF

Heaven.

SALLY

Think of the money, Cliff. We need it so badly.

CLIFF

Not that badly.

SALLY

I don't understand you. Really I don't. First you tell me you're not going to Paris for Ernst any more – even though it does seem the very easiest way in the world to make money . . .

CLIFF

Or the hardest. You know, Sally, someday I've got to sit you down and read you a newspaper. You'll be amazed at what's going on.

SALLY

You mean – politics? But what has that to do with us?

CLIFF

You're right. Nothing has anything to do with us. Sally – don't you understand – if you're not against all this – you're for it. Or you might as well be.

(Knock at the door)

SALLY

Come in.

(FRÄULEIN SCHNEIDER enters. She carries the box containing the fruit bowl)

Fräulein Schneider . . .

FRÄULEIN SCHNEIDER

I intrude?

SALLY

No. No. Come in.
(She notices the package)
Is that the fruit bowl? Is something wrong with it?

FRÄULEIN SCHNEIDER

(shaking her head)
I cannot keep it.

SALLY

But why?

FRÄULEIN SCHNEIDER

An engagement present. But there is no engagement.

SALLY

What do you mean?

FRÄULEIN SCHNEIDER

We have – reconsidered – Herr Schultz and I.

CLIFF

Fräulein Schneider, you can't give up that way!

FRÄULEIN SCHNEIDER

Oh, yes I can! That is easy to say! Easy for you. Fight!
(Music starts)
And – if you fail – what does it matter? You pack your belongings. You move to Paris. And if you do not like Paris – where? It is easy for you. But if you were me . . .

(Sings)
WITH TIME RUSHING BY,
WHAT WOULD YOU DO?
WITH THE CLOCK RUNNING DOWN,
WHAT WOULD YOU DO?
THE YOUNG ALWAYS HAVE
  THE CURE,
BEING BRAVE, BEING SURE
AND FREE.
BUT IMAGINE IF YOU WERE ME,

ALONE LIKE ME,
AND THIS IS THE ONLY WORLD
  I KNOW.
SOME ROOMS TO LET,
THE SUM OF A LIFETIME, EVEN SO,
I'LL TAKE YOUR ADVICE.
WHAT WOULD YOU DO?
WOULD YOU PAY THE PRICE?
WHAT WOULD YOU DO?

SUPPOSE SIMPLY KEEPING STILL
MEANS YOU MANAGE UNTIL
  THE END?
WHAT WOULD YOU DO?
MY BRAVE, YOUNG FRIEND?

GROWN OLD LIKE ME,
WITH NEITHER THE WILL NOR
  WISH TO RUN.
GROWN TIRED LIKE ME,
WHO HURRIES FOR BED WHEN
  DAY IS DONE.
GROWN WISE LIKE ME,
WHO ISN'T AT WAR WITH ANYONE,
NOT ANYONE!

WITH A STORM IN THE WIND,
  WHAT WOULD YOU DO?
SUPPOSE YOU'RE ONE FRIGHTENED
  VOICE
BEING TOLD
WHAT THE CHOICE
MUST BE,
GO ON, TELL ME,
I WILL LISTEN.
WHAT WOULD YOU DO IF YOU
  WERE ME?

CLIFF
(Spoken)
Fräulein Schneider . . . If you marry Herr Schultz – whatever problems come up – you'll still have each other.

FRÄULEIN SCHNEIDER
All my life I have managed for myself – and it is too old a habit to change. I have battled alone, and I have survived. There was a war – and I survived. There was a revolution – and I survived. There was an inflation – billions of marks for one loaf of bread – but I survived! And if the Nazis come – I will survive. And if the Communists come – I will still be here – renting these rooms! For, in the end, what other choice have I? This – is my world!

(Softly)
I regret very much returning the fruit bowl. It is truly magnificent. I regret – everything.

(FRÄULEIN SCHNEIDER exits)

SALLY
Oh, Cliff – should I speak to her?

CLIFF
What would you say?

SALLY
Oh – that it will all work itself out. Remember how she was about my staying here?
(imitating FRÄULEIN SCHNEIDER)
"It is not possible! And I cannot consider . . ."

89

CLIFF
Shut up, Sally.

SALLY
What?

CLIFF
It's not funny.

SALLY
Well, it seems nothing amuses you anymore. It was such fun today with Bobby and Victor. They laugh at everything. Especially the thought of you and me in a cottage at the end of a lane. They found that hysterical.
(She gets her coat)
They're waiting for me this very minute – to rehearse my numbers. So I really must go.
(CLIFF dusts off his typewriter)

CLIFF
The fact is – you're going a lot further than the Klub.

SALLY
I am?

CLIFF
We're going home. My home.

(SALLY looks at him blankly)
Pennsylvania.

SALLY
You're joking!

CLIFF
(indicating the typewriter)
I'm going to sell this. The money should get us as far as Paris. And I'll cable home for steamship fare.

SALLY
What are you talking about?

CLIFF
We've got to leave Berlin – as soon as possible. Tomorrow!

SALLY
But we love it here!

CLIFF
Sally, wake up! The party's over! It was lots of fun – but now it's over. So how could we live here? How could we raise a family?

SALLY
But is America the answer? Running away to America?

CLIFF

We're not running away. We're going home.

SALLY

Oh, certainly — that's fine for you. But what about me? My career?

CLIFF

You've got a new career.

SALLY

(Goes to CLIFF)
But I can work at the Klub for several months at least. And then — in November — Oh, Cliff, I want the world for our baby — all the most elegant, expensive things . . .

CLIFF

We'll talk about it tomorrow—on the train.

(CLIFF closes the typewriter and goes to get his coat)

SALLY

Cliff — wait! We can't just — uproot our lives — that quickly!

CLIFF

Oh, no? You give me one hour! Sit down!!
(He pushes her down.)
And don't move! Or, better yet — start packing! There's plenty to do.
(He goes towards the door, carrying his typewriter)
Call the Klub. Tell them goodbye.

(He exits. SALLY sits alone. She thinks.)

(The EMCEE appears and sings)

EMCEE

I DON'T CARE MUCH,
GO OR STAY,
I DON'T CARE VERY MUCH
EITHER WAY.

(SALLY exits)

HEARTS GROW HARD ON A
    WINDY STREET.
LIPS GROW COLD WITH THE RENT
    TO MEET.
SO IF YOU KISS ME,
IF WE TOUCH,
WARNING'S FAIR,
I DON'T CARE
VERY MUCH.

I DON'T CARE MUCH,
GO OR STAY,
I DON'T CARE VERY MUCH
EITHER WAY.

WORDS SOUND FALSE WHEN
    YOUR COAT'S TOO THIN.
FEET DON'T WALTZ WHEN THE
    ROOF CAVES IN.
SO IF YOU KISS ME,
IF WE TOUCH,
WARNING'S FAIR,
I DON'T CARE VERY MUCH.

ACT TWO   SCENE 5

THE KIT KAT KLUB

("I Don't Care Much" continues through the early part of the scene. SALLY aapproches MAX. CLIFF enters and goes to them.)

CLIFF

What the hell are you doing here?

SALLY

I beg your pardon?

CLIFF
Get your things. I'm taking you home.

SALLY
Pennsylvania, you mean? To live on your mummy's charity?

CLIFF
I'll get a job.

SALLY
The stock market.

CLIFF
I'll find something.

SALLY
Maybe. But this is sure.

CLIFF
This? What the hell is this? You keep talking about this as if it really existed. When are you going to admit, Sally – the only way you got this job – any job – is by sleeping with someone!

SALLY
Will you shut up, Cliff?

CLIFF
All this talk about your "career." My god – for once in your life – face the truth about yourself!!

SALLY
(Shouting back)
Maybe I will. But now don't you think it's your turn??!

(She runs off)

CLIFF
(Starts to follow her. Calls)
Sally . . .

(He is stopped by MAX, then ERNST appears.)

ERNST
Clifford – will you join me for a drink?

CLIFF
Not now, Ernst.

ERNST
I have been trying to reach you at Fräulein Schneider's. I have another urgent errand for you.

CLIFF
Sorry.

ERNST
This time I pay – one hundred-fifty marks.

CLIFF
The answer is no.

ERNST
But what is wrong, Clifford? You are angry with me?

CLIFF
I am?

ERNST
It is because of politics? If you were a German – you would understand these things.

CLIFF
Goodbye, Ernst.
(ERNST goes towards CLIFF)

ERNST
Wait! It is very important – this errand! I pay two hundred marks.

CLIFF
Go to hell.

ERNST

But this is most upsetting. I am your close friend, Clifford. So fond of you. I have sent you many new students.

CLIFF

Oh, sure. Your Nazi friends, to polish up their English! What an idiot I've been!

ERNST

I know you need the money. So there must be something else . . . It is because of that Jew at the party.

(CLIFF hits ERNST. As he does this, MAX and BODYGUARDS come to ERNST's help. ERNST leaves them to finish CLIFF off. A drum break accompanies this. The EMCEE appears as lights dim)

EMCEE

Thank you. And now meine Damen und Herren – Mesdames and Messieurs – Ladies and Gentlemen – once again the Kit Kat Klub is so happy to welcome back – an old friend. I give you, the toast of Mayfair – Fräulein Sally Bowles.
(SALLY appears. Something is not right.)

SALLY

(Sings)

WHAT GOOD IS SITTING ALONE IN
   YOUR ROOM?
COME HEAR THE MUSIC PLAY.
LIFE IS A CABARET, OLD CHUM,
COME TO THE CABARET.

PUT DOWN THE KNITTING, THE
   BOOK AND THE BROOM.
TIME FOR A HOLIDAY.
LIFE IS A CABARET, OLD CHUM,
COME TO THE CABARET.
COME TASTE THE WINE,
COME HEAR THE BAND.
COME BLOW A HORN,
START CELEBRATING;
RIGHT THIS WAY,
YOUR TABLE'S WAITING.

NO USE PERMITTING SOME
   PROPHET OF DOOM
TO WIPE EVERY SMILE AWAY.
LIFE IS A CABARET, OLD CHUM,
COME TO THE CABARET!

I USED TO HAVE A GIRLFRIEND
   KNOWN AS ELSIE,
WITH WHOM I SHARED FOUR
   SORDID ROOMS IN CHELSEA.
SHE WASN'T WHAT YOU'D CALL A

BLUSHING FLOWER.
AS A MATTER OF FACT SHE RENTED
   BY THE HOUR.

THE DAY SHE DIED THE NEIGHBORS
   CAME TO SNICKER:
"WELL, THAT'S WHAT COMES OF
   TOO MUCH PILLS AND LIQUOR."
BUT WHEN I SAW HER LAID OUT
   LIKE A QUEEN,
SHE WAS THE HAPPIEST CORPSE
   I'D EVER SEEN.

I THINK OF ELSIE TO THIS VERY DAY.
I REMEMBER HOW SHE'D TURN
   TO ME AND SAY:

"WHAT GOOD IS SITTING ALONE IN
   YOUR ROOM?
COME HEAR THE MUSIC PLAY.
LIFE IS A CABARET, OLD CHUM,
COME TO THE CABARET.

PUT DOWN THE KNITTING, THE
   BOOK AND THE BROOM.
TIME FOR A HOLIDAY.
LIFE IS A CABARET, OLD CHUM,
COME TO THE CABARET."

AND AS FOR ME, AS FOR ME,
I MADE MY MIND UP, BACK

94

IN CHELSEA,
WHEN I GO I'M GOING LIKE ELSIE.

(Sally begins to break down)

START BY ADMITTING,
FROM CRADLE TO TOMB
ISN'T THAT LONG A STAY.
LIFE IS A CABARET, OLD CHUM,
ONLY A CABARET, OLD CHUM,
AND I LOVE A CABARET.

ACT TWO   SCENE 6

CLIFF'S ROOM

(It is late morning. CLIFF is busily packing. His face is bruised. A knock at the door)

CLIFF
(Opens door)
Herr Schultz!

(SCHULTZ enters. He has a suitcase in one hand and a paper bag in the other)

SCHULTZ

Excuse me – but I have come to say goodbye.
(He sees CLIFF's face)
Your face –?

CLIFF

It's nothing. A little accident. Where are you going?

SCHULTZ

I've taken a room on the other side of Nollendorfplatz. I think it will be easier for her.
(He notes all the packing)
You are leaving also? You and Fräulein Bowles?

CLIFF

We are going home. To America.

SCHULTZ

America! I have sometimes thought of going there –

CLIFF

Why don't you? The way things look here –

SCHULTZ

But it will pass – I promise you!

CLIFF

I hope you're right.

SCHULTZ

I know I am right! Because I understand the Germans . . . After all – what am I? A German.

(The door opens and SALLY enters. She looks ill and exhausted. She wears a rather thin dress and is carrying her bag.)

Ah – Fräulein Sally! I have come to say goodbye . . . all good fortune.

SALLY

Herr Schultz.

SCHULTZ

And I have brought a little farewell gift.
(He gives SALLY the paper bag)
Italian oranges. Delicious.
(SALLY hugs him)

CLIFF

Goodbye, Herr Schultz. I wish you mazel.

SCHULTZ

Mazel. That is what we all need.

Sally Bowles has just stepped into the spotlight, which is, you would imagine, her very favorite place to be. Yet this avidly ambitious chanteuse recoils when the glare hits her, flinching and raising a hand to shade her face. Wearing the barest of little black dresses and her eyes shimmering with fever, she looks raw, brutalized and helplessly exposed. And now she's going to sing us a song, an anthem to hedonism, about how life is a cabaret, old chum. She might as well be inviting you to hell.... For pleasurable listening, you would of course do better with Liza Minnelli, who starred in the movie version. But it is to Ms. Richardson's infinite credit that you don't leave the theater humming the tune to "Cabaret," but brooding on the glimpses it has provided of one woman's desperation.
—Ben Brantley
The New York Times
March 20, 1998

(SCHULTZ exits, closing door behind him)

CLIFF

I've been packing for you. You won't be able to find a thing. We go today to Paris, remember?

SALLY

With that face?

96

CLIFF

I was in a little fight last night. Didn't you hear about it? You should see the other three guys. Not a mark on them. It's about time to leave for the station.

SALLY

The thing is, Cliff . . .

CLIFF

Don't say it. Whatever it is. Let's just forget the last twelve hours. Forget what I said at the Klub. Forget you've gotten even with me staying out all night.
(He takes her hand)
You're so cold.

SALLY

You know what I'd love? A spot of gin.

CLIFF

First thing in the morning? How about a Prairie Oyster?

SALLY

No, gin!

(She pours herself a drink)

CLIFF

That can't be good for expectant mothers. Where's your coat? Your fur coat? Did you leave it at the Klub?

SALLY

I left it at the doctor's office.

CLIFF

Were you sick last night? Is that why you didn't come home?

SALLY
(Drinking)
Oh, darling – you're such an innocent. Really! My one regret is I honestly believe you'd have been a wonderful father. And, I think someday, perhaps you will be. Oh yes, and I've another regret: That greedy doctor! I'm going to miss my fur coat.
(CLIFF slaps her)
Isn't it funny – it always ends this way? Even when I do finally love someone quite terribly – for the first time. But it's still not – quite – enough. I'd spoil it, Cliff. I'd run away with the first exciting thing that came along . . . or you would.

CLIFF

But that's not true. I'd never have run away from you–for any reason–not if there was a baby...

SALLY

To hold us together, you mean? Oh, Cliff–what a terrible burden for an infant–don't you think?
(CLIFF starts getting his things together – preparing to leave)

CLIFF

It's time for the train. Sally – I could go tomorrow – the next day –
(She shakes her head)
This is your ticket to Paris.
(With deep feeling)
– if for any reason–you decide to use it . . . You can reach me at the American Express Office. I'll be there till Friday...

SALLY

But – the truth is, Cliff: I've always rather hated Paris.

CLIFF

Oh, Sally.
(He starts to exit)

SALLY

Oh, Cliff!
(CLIFF turns in the doorway)
Dedicate your book to me.

(CLIFF exits. The lights fade)

ACT TWO   SCENE 7

*(Before the lights come
up – we hear –)*

LOUDSPEAKER
VOICE

Letzte Ansage! Berlin–Paris Express
Abfahrt vier Uhr Bahnsteig siebzehn.
Alle einsteigen, bitte! Letzte Ansage!

*(Lights up on a railroad compartment.
CLIFF and a CUSTOMS
OFFICER are discovered in it.)*

EMCEE/
OFFICIAL

Deutsche Grenzkontrolle. Ihren Pass, bitte.
*(CLIFF hands it to him, he hands it
back to CLIFF)*
I hope you have enjoyed your stay in
Germany, Mr. Bradshaw. And you
will return again soon.

CLIFF

It's not very likely.

OFFICIAL

You did not find our country
beautiful?

98

CLIFF
(tonelessly)
Yes. I found it … beautiful.

OFFICIAL
A good journey, sir.

(CLIFF makes a few notes in his notebook. Then reads.)

CLIFF
There was a Cabaret and there was a Master-of-Ceremonies and there was a city called Berlin in a country called Germany. It was the end of the world…

(We begin to hear the music of "WILLKOMMEN")

and I was dancing with Sally Bowles and we were both fast asleep …

(Sings)
WILLKOMMEN, BIENVENUE, WELCOME.

(The EMCEE appears)

FREMDE, ÉTRANGER, STRANGER.

BOTH
GLÜCKLICH ZU SEHEN, JE SUIS ENCHANTÉ. HAPPY TO SEE YOU. BLEIBE, RESTE, STAY …..

(They look up to see SCHNEIDER, SCHULTZ, KOST, ERNST and SALLY)

EMCEE
(Spoken)
Meine Damen und Herren – Mesdames et Messieurs – Ladies and Gentlemen. Where are your troubles now? Forgotten? I told you so. We have no troubles here. Here life is beautiful – the girls are beautiful … Even the orchestra is beautiful.

(The bandstand is now empty as the music continues)

(SCHNEIDER, SCHULTZ, KOST, and ERNST come down the stairs and form a line US and slowly move DS.)

(As they turn and walk US, the door wall, and brick wall behind the band, fly out to reveal the COMPANY.)

(The set disappears. We are in a white space)

EMCEE
AUF WIEDERSEHEN! Ä BIENTÔT.

(The EMCEE slowly takes off his coat. He is wearing the clothes of a concentration camp prisoner.)

(Drum roll. Cymbal crash. Blackout)

END

BA

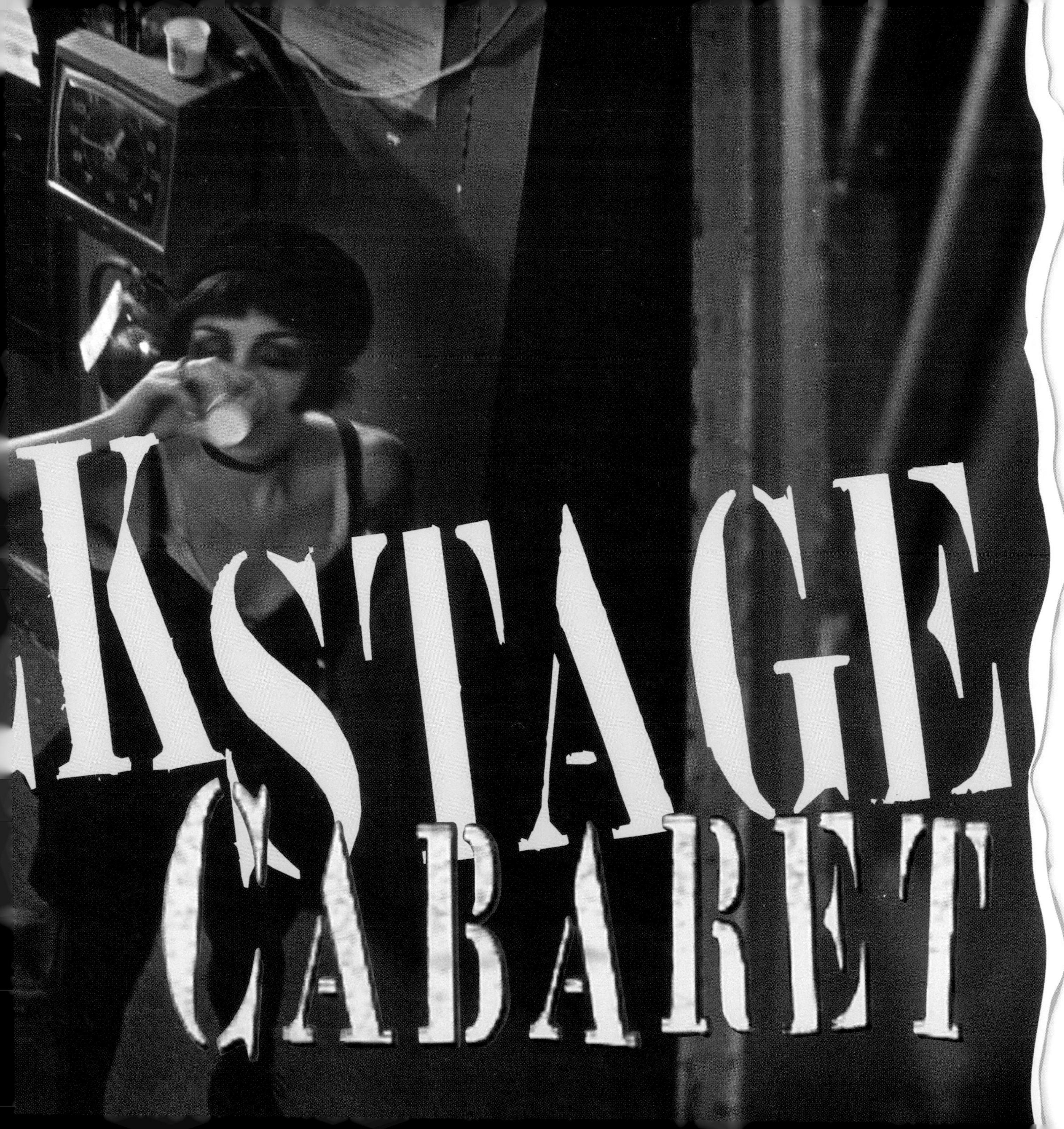

KSTAGE CABARET

From the diary of Alan Cumming, written for a magazine in Scotland.

DECEMBER 29, 1997 Oh God, what a scary day. The read-through of *Cabaret*! As usual on these occasions I wanted to vomit several times, but tried to remember that everyone else felt the same. It's just so horrible having to say your lines in front of strangers. I know that sounds weird considering acting is all about saying lines in front of strangers, but on first days you just feel so JUDGED. Not only the cast but the designers, sound engineers, press people, casting people, producers, marketing, etc., and probably the man from the bagel shop down the street are all there waiting to see how good you are. And what if you are having a bad day? Hence the potential vomiting.

I even had a cigarette. (Very difficult in the States these days—I eventually squat on the step of a fire exit with Natasha Richardson who's playing Sally Bowles, and who luckily smokes like a chimney.) But this only increased the vom factor. Ah well, at least I didn't have to sing. We just read our lyrics today (very embarrassing considering 'Two Ladies' mostly consists of 'beedlee beedlee dee') and tomorrow is the big vocal day.

Try to calm down at dinner with friends. Tell them I can't believe I've agreed to this. I am trapped in a musical on Broadway. Me. Something's rotten in the state of Denmark.

JANUARY 3, 1998 All my friends have gone home. I am alone in New York. However, the fact that the choreography of my role consists of lots of touching the genitals of my fellow cast members (and a few twirls) I am getting to know people here very quickly.

JANUARY 9 I have a day off. Just as well, as my legs are aching. I am now a Broadway hoofer. There's so much more dancing than in London. Every time I hear the words "new dance break," I am crushed.

JANUARY 10 I can't remember anything about the London production. Even when I'm shown photos I can't place that weird-looking person as me. In one way this is good, because I don't feel I'm recreating my role, instead I'm starting afresh and it feels very different and new. But in another way, I feel I must have really bad short memory loss or a terrible brain-wasting disease. I ask Sam Mendes, the director, if he feels the same. He can't remember. Ha ha.

JANUARY 17 *Spiceworld* is coming to the States. Columbia has a screening to which the *Cabaret* cast is invited. I suddenly go from being eccentric Scottish boy to Mr. Cool, friend of the stars. The Spiceys are going to conquer the world, I know it. They are in New York plugging the film so I go out with them tonight. We have a laugh and do a spot of clubbing—except when Mel B and I go for a dance we have to be accompanied by a bodyguard. The girls are really excited about me doing *Cabaret*. They're going to come and see it in June when they come to New York on tour.

JANUARY 28 Our first full run-through. It goes pretty well and I so enjoy seeing the bits of the show I'm not in, especially the Sally/Cliff story. The book has been extensively rewritten and seems a lot less clunky than before. Cliff's bisexuality is much more focused on. Also, the Fräulein Schneider/Herr Schultz scenes are incredibly moving and much wittier than I remember. I'm in awe of the ensemble—they play at least one instrument, dance, sing and act, and because New York is much more a musical theatre city than any other I've worked in, they're all shit hot. I managed to get through without forgetting too much. I've made up lots of new lines, which I know I won't be able to progress with until I do them with an audience. But I feel very relieved that I can actually sing after all. Stopping drinking has certainly worked.

FEBRUARY 8 Hysteria and lots of cast bonding. We are in the middle of a two-week tech period, and seem only to have done about two lighting cues. Also, the theatre, formerly a dodgy club, is still in a bit of a state and none of us can believe it will be transformed into the Kit Kat Klub in time.

FEBRUARY 13 We are right—first preview cancelled due to the balcony having no seats. Start drinking again.

FEBRUARY 18 Just the scariest day. The show goes on as seats have materialised, and it goes down a storm. The sort of 'get them laughing, pull the rug from under them, then make them embarrassed and question why they were laughing in the first place' element is much stronger here. No idea why. But I feel the show is really powerful in that the audience is really shocked by the outcome, and how they had in some way contributed to it, too. Whoopi Goldberg is standing outside the shower when I come out from washing off my druggie body make-up. Drip on her a bit. She's very nice.

FEBRUARY 19 Lauren Bacall came tonight and told me I was a sensation and a killer. I suddenly don't give a toss about the *New York Times*. Betty Bacall likes me, so there.

FEBRUARY 28 So many superstars are coming to previews that I am embarrassed to list them here in case you think I am a shallow, mindless, name-dropper. But Meryl Streep came to my dressing room tonight and said she's always admired my work. I forget that I've done films that have been quite big in the States, and wonder at how she'd

caught *Take the High Road* or *The High Life*! Have to have a lie down when she goes.

MARCH 7 Two-show day, and I'm starting to feel really exhausted. We're in rehearsal and changing bits every day as well as performing at night. Also, there's loads of press to do and American journalists can be pretty exhausting. Actually all journalists are exhausting, American ones just ask more questions with Joel Grey in them. I have never talked so much about someone I don't know.

MARCH 12 We open a week from today. All the fun of the last month of previews drained out of my memory bank as I wrote that. Help! At least we have more free time now, so I must try to sleep during some of it. New York is a great seductress for night people like myself.

MARCH 16 My last day off before we open. I talk to no one, as I'm trying to rest my voice. Suddenly, because the press are coming, I feel I should look after it. However, as I'm playing the MC of a second-rate, drug-fuelled, glorified sex club, a wee bit of a croak now and then shouldn't matter.

MARCH 18 Can't write anymore. We open tomorrow. I hate myself for having agreed to do this job and putting myself through this stress, though I know by tomorrow night at 10pm I'll feel fab because I'll have felt the fear and done it anyway. Funny old world.

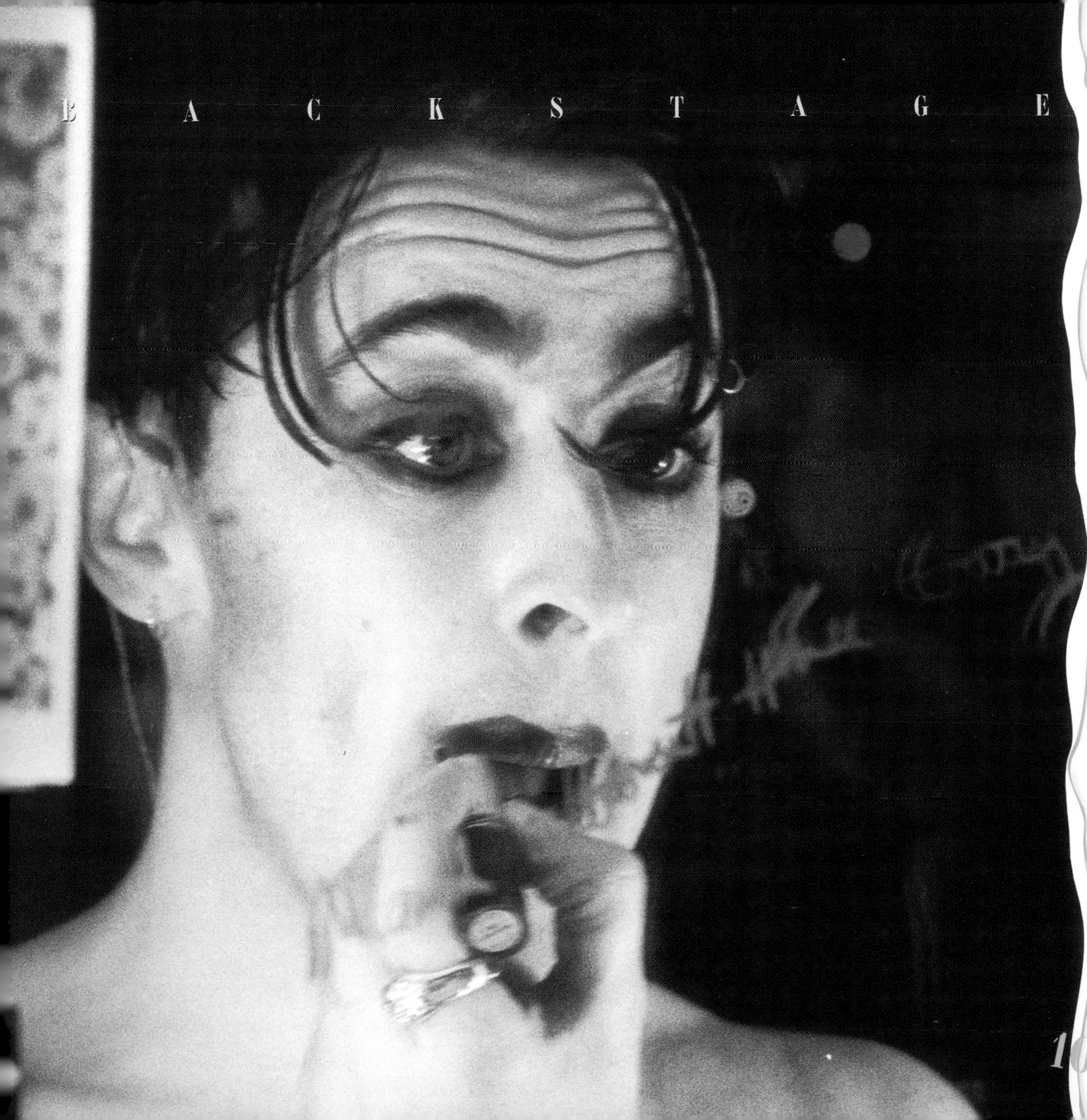

Natasha Richardson keeps a photograph of actress Judi Dench taped to her dressing room mirror for inspiration. Thirty years ago, Dench played Sally Bowles in a London production of the play, a part she won out over Vanessa Redgrave, Richardson's mother. Also on the mirror is an opening night note from Mike Nichols, imploring Richardson not to break "one of those gorgeous legs."

In an interview with *Playbill*, Richardson described Sally Bowles as "an eccentric, and vulnerable and strange and extraordinary. She's like a lot of girls around today—people who want the life but don't really understand about putting in the work. I love what Christopher Isherwood said about her: 'She was loveable in a way that no human could ever quite be, since, being a creature of art, she had been created out of pure love.' I think that's true. She can be so spoiled and myopic and selfish, but you can't help adoring her."

Backstage, on a small balcony outside their dressing rooms, Richardson and Alan Cumming, still in costume, clown around for photographer Rivka Katvan.

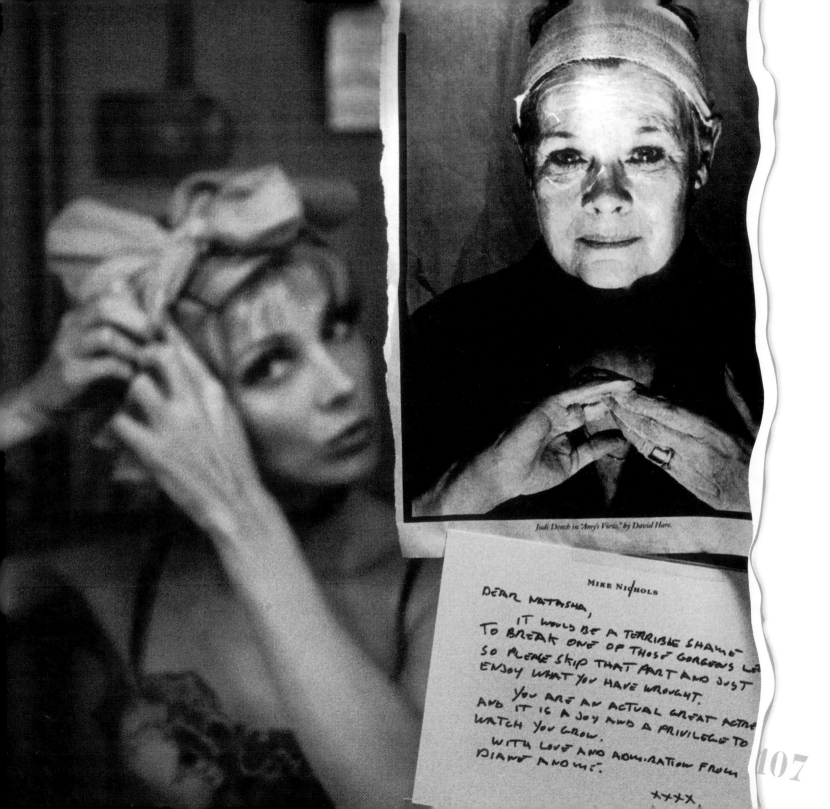

Judi Dench in "Amy's View," by David Hare.

MIKE NICHOLS

Dear Natasha,
    It would be a terrible shame
to break one of those gorgeous legs
so please skip that part and just
enjoy what you have wrought.
    You are an actual great actress
and it is a joy and a privilege to
watch you grow.
    With love and admiration from
Diane and me.

xxx.

107

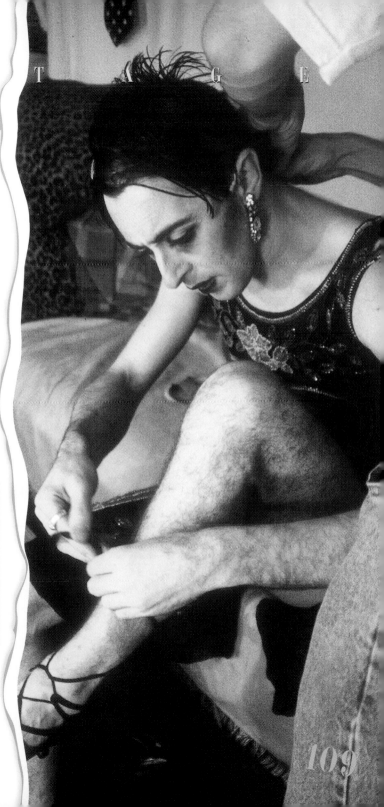

"The emcee in this production is the overseer of the whole show and not just the club. The atmosphere of the evening is very much of his making. He's down and dirty. He's come up from he streets and he brings the streets with him. My take is that he's a drug addict. You can see the track marks on his body from the drugs. And as the play progresses, with the rise of fascism, the emcee gets more and more debauched."

—Alan Cumming
Playbill

Left: Leenya Rideout and Joyce Chittick.

109

Left: Ron Rifkin, Michele Pawk, Denis O'Hare.
Above: Musical Director, Patrick Vaccariello.
Right: Mary Louise Wilson.
Below: John Benjamin Hickey.

111

The Kit Kat Klub boys and girls. *Clockwise from top:* Michael O'Donnell, Michele Pawk, Christina Pawl. *Left (top to bottom):* Vance Avery, Michael O'Donnel Erin Hill, Linda Romoff, Joyce Chittick.

Below: Brill constructed this 1/4 inch scale model of the theatre at the Kit Kat Club. The crooked picture frame is reminiscent of the 1966 Hal Prince production where a hanging mirror reflected the audience, making them part of the production. Brill says this was purely coincidental.

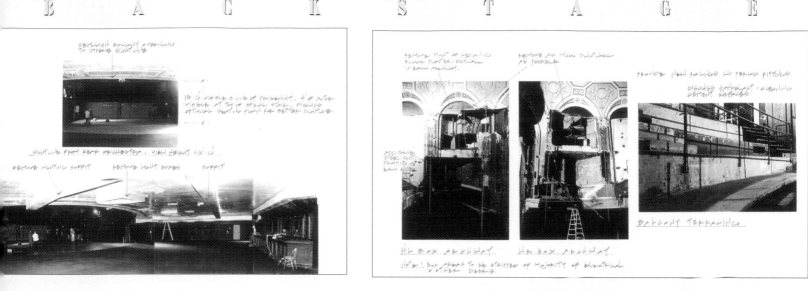

Above: Set and club designer, Robert Brill, photographed Studio 54 and then laid out his plans for converting the disco into the new Kit Kat Klub. His challenge was to create an intimate setting in a venue for 900 people. *Far left:* A team of a dozen painters, mostly from the Cobalt Scenic Studios, a scenic painting school, transforms Studio 54 into a new *Cabaret* venue. *Below:* Brill and Sam Mendes developed the set around a wall of three doors shown in Brill's original blueprint.

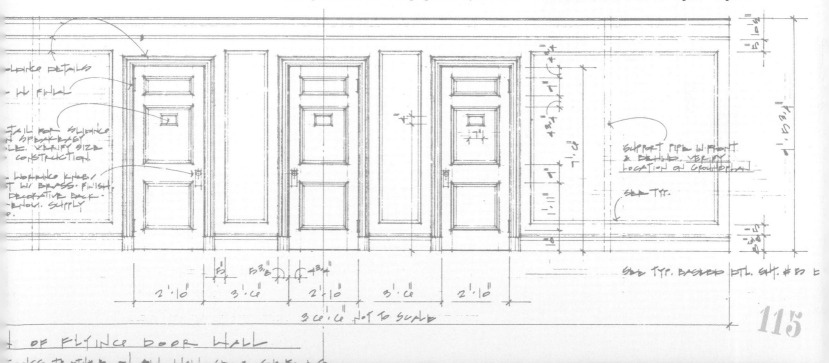

These original drawings by costume designer William Ivey Long show several different looks he created for Sally Bowles and Fraulein Kost. The short sweater and skirt outfit *(bottom left)* evolved into a Merry Widow corset and black leather jacket for the "Mein Herr" number. Many different fabrics *(far left and right)* were considered for the dresses.

W illiam Ivey Long created this
pattern *(right)* for Natasha
Richardson's signature corset. Constructed
of whale bones and three different kinds
of lace, the corset had to fit skin-tight,
cover all intimate body parts, and be
flexible yet durable enough to withstand
strenuous dancing. Though it looks as
though the women on stage are in their
underwear, underneath their corsets, bras,
panties, and garter belts, they wore two
pairs of underwear, including bras with
microphones sewn into the seams.

Long describes how he designed the Cabaret wardrobe as a process of "deconstruction." He began by dressing the actors in a full costume *(below)* and then eliminating one piece of clothing at a time until he achieved the desired effect noted by the red dots. Alan Cumming's trademark harness *(above and right)* was constructed by pinning together four pairs of suspenders.

Above: 1998 Tony Award winners Natasha Richardson and Alan Cumming accepting their awards on stage and (*below*) backstage. *Right:* Ron Rifkin. *Below Right:* Accepting the Roundabout's award for the Best Revival of a Musical are Ellen Richard, Managing Director, and Todd Haimes, Artistic Director.

TONY & OSCAR

CABARET, 1966-67.
Tony Awards:
Best Musical, Best Featured Actor in a Musical (Joel Grey), Best Featured Actress in a Musical (Peg Murray, who played Fräulein Kost), Best Director of a Musical (Hal Prince), Set Design (Boris Aronson), Costume Design (Patricia Zipprodt), Composer and Lyricist (John Kander and Fred Ebb), Choreography (Ronald Field).

CABARET, 1972.
Oscars:
Actress (Liza Minnelli), Supporting Actor (Joel Grey), Director (Bob Fosse), Cinematography (Geoffrey Unsworth), Art & Set Direction (Rolf Zehetbauer & Jurgen Kiebach, Herbert Strabel), Sound (Robert Knudson & David Hildyard), Scoring (Ralph Burns), Film Editing (David Bretherton). *Historical note: Cabaret is the only movie to win eight Oscars without being named Best Picture.*

CABARET, 1998.
Tony Awards:
Best Performance by a Leading Actor in a Musical (Alan Cumming), Best Performance by a Leading Actress in a Musical (Natasha Richardson), Best Performance by a Featured Actor in a Musical (Ron Rifkin), Best Revival of a Musical.

ROUNDABOUT at THE KIT KAT KLUB
TODD HAIMES, Artistic Director
ELLEN RICHARD, Managing Director
JULIA C. LEVY, Executive Director, External Affairs
present

NATASHA RICHARDSON   ALAN CUMMING
RON RIFKIN   MARY LOUISE WILSON
in

with
JOHN BENJAMIN HICKEY
DENIS O'HARE   MICHELE PAWK
VANCE AVERY   JOYCE CHITTICK   BRIAN DUGUAY   ERIN HILL
MICHAEL O'DONNELL   KRISTIN OLNESS   CHRISTINA PAWL
LEENYA RIDEOUT   LINDA ROMOFF   FRED ROSE   BILL SZOBODY

Book by JOE MASTEROFF   Lyrics by FRED EBB   Music by JOHN KANDER

Based on the play by JOHN VAN DRUTEN and stories by CHRISTOPHER ISHERWOOD

Set and Club Design by	Costume Design by	Lighting Design by	Sound Design by
ROBERT BRILL	WILLIAM IVEY LONG	PEGGY EISENHAUER & MIKE BALDASSARI	BRIAN RONAN

Orchestrations by MICHAEL GIBSON   Dance and Incidental Music Arranged by DAVID KRANE

Original Dance Music Arranged by DAVID BAKER   Musical Coordinator JOHN MONACO

Production Stage Manager PETER HANSON   Dialect Coach TIM MONICH

Associate Choreographer CYNTHIA ONRUBIA   Make-Up and Hair Design by RANDY HOUSTON MERCER

Casting JIM CARNAHAN & PAT McCORKLE, C.S.A.   Associate Director JENNIFER UPHOFF GRAY

General Manager SYDNEY DAVOLOS   Founding Director GENE FEIST

Press Representative BONEAU/BRYAN-BROWN   Director of Marketing DAVID B. STEFFEN

Musical Director PATRICK VACCARIELLO

Co-directed and Choreographed by ROB MARSHALL
Directed by SAM MENDES

Roundabout wishes to acknowledge a generous contribution by PACE Theatrical Group
Visit the Roundabout Website – www.roundabouttheatre.org

WHO'S WHO IN THE CAST

NATASHA RICHARDSON (*Sally Bowles*). Theater credits include: *Anna Christie* at the Roundabout (Tony and Drama Desk nominations for Best Actress; Outstanding Debut Award, Outer Critics Circle); *High Society*, West End; *The Seagull*, West End (London Drama Critics Award, Most Promising Newcomer*); A Midsummer Night's Dream; Hamlet* at the Young Vic. Television credits include: PBS' Great Performances "Suddenly Last Summer" directed by Sir Richard Eyre, the title role in TNT's "Zelda" (CableACE nomination). Film credits include: *Gothic, Patty Hearst, The Handmaid's Tale, The Comfort of Strangers* (London Evening Standard Award for Best Actress*), Widow's Peak, Nell* and *Parent Trap.*

ALAN CUMMING (*Emcee*) trained at the Royal Scottish Academy of Music and Drama. His Broadway debut, this performance has earned him the Tony, Drama Desk, Outer Critics Circle, Theatre World, FANY and New York Public Advocates Awards. Theatre (London): *Cabaret* (Donmar Warehouse, Olivier Award nom.), *Hamlet* (English Touring Theatre/Donmar Warehouse, Best Actor, TMA awards, Shakespeare Globe Award nom.), *La Bête* (Lyric Hammersmith, Olivier nom.), *Romeo and Juliet* (Royal National Theatre Studio), *Accidental Death of an Anarchist* (Royal Theatre, Olivier Award), *As You Like It, Singer* (RSC), *Conquest of the South Pole* (Royal National Court, Olivier nom.). Also seasons at the Traverse, and Royal Lyceum, Edinburgh; Tron, Glasgow; Dundee Rep, Bristol Old Vic and tours with Borderline, Theatre Workshop and Glasgow Citizens' TAG. Film: *Plunkett and Macleane, Spice World, Eyes Wide Shut, For My Baby, Buddy, Romy and Michele's High School Reunion, Emma, Goldeneye, Circle of Friends, Black Beauty, Second Best, Prague* (Best Actor, Atlantic Film Festival, Scottish BAFTA Best Film Actor nom.). TV includes: "Burn Your Phone" (which he also directed), "The Chemistry Lesson," "Mickey Love," "The Last Romantics," "Bernard and the Genie" (Top TV Newcomer, British Comedy Awards). Writing credits include the BBC2 sitcom "The High Life," the short film *Butter* (which he also directed), several "Victor and Barry" shows and two adaptations for the Royal National Theatre.

RON RIFKIN (*Herr Schultz*) received a 1998 Tony Award for his performance in this production of *Cabaret*. He originated the role of Isaac Geldhart in *The Substance of Fire* for which he received an Obie, Drama Desk, Lucille Lortel and L.A. Drama-Logue Award. He recreated the role to great acclaim in the film version. His list of NY., L.A. and regional theatre credits include *Three Hotels* (Drama Desk and Helen Hayes noms. and a second Lucille Lortel Award*), Three Sisters, American Clock, The Tenth Man, The Art of Dining, Goodbye People, Proposals* and *Rosebloom*. His most recent appearances on Broadway were in Arthur Miller's *Broken Glass* and Turgenev's *Month in the Country* (Roundabout). Films include *Husbands and Wives, Manhattan Murder Mystery, Wolf, Silent Running, Last Summer in the Hamptons, L.A. Confidential* and *The Negotiator.* Television films: "The Winds of War," "Evergreen," "Dress Grey," "Do You Remember Love." Television series: "Trials of Rosie O'Neil," "One Day at a Time" and "E.R."

MARY LOUISE WILSON (*Fräulein Schneider*) just completed a successful run Off-Broadway in *Full Gallop*, a play she co-authored with Mark Hampton. Her performance won an Obie and a Drama Desk Award. Prior runs include the Bay Street Theatre (Sag Harbor), The Old Globe (San Diego) and Manhattan Theatre Club. Broadway credits: *Show Boat, Fools, Prelude to a Kiss, Alice in Wonderland, Philadelphia Story, Royal Family, Gypsy, The Women* and Kander and Ebb's *Flora the Red Menace*. Recent Off-Broadway: *Flaubert's Latest, Baby with the Bathwater, Sister Mary Ignatius Explains...,* and *Buried Child*. Films: *Step-Mom, 24 Nights; Huck Finn, Mr. Wonderful, Green Card, Everybody Wins, She-Devil, Pet Cemetery, Zelig, Money Pit, Best Little Whorehouse, Teachers, Up the Sandbox, Klute.* Ms. Wilson has had articles published in *Playbill, The New York Times* and *American Theatre Magazine.*

JOHN BENJAMIN HICKEY (*Clifford Bradshaw*). Broadway: *Love! Valour! Compassion!* Off-Broadway: *Love! Valour! Compassion!* (Obie Award), *Blue Window* (MTC); *God's Heart, The Substance of Fire* (Lincoln Center); *The End of the Day, On the Bum* (Playwrights Horizons). Regional: *The Film Society, Dreading Thekla* (Williamstown); *Snakebit* (NY Stage & Film); *Valued Friends*

(Long Wharf); *New Music* (Cleveland Playhouse). TV: "Third Rock From the Sun," "Nothing Sacred," "Law & Order," "Molly Dodd." Film: *Love! Valour! Compassion!, The Ice Storm, Finding North, Eddie* and *Only You.*

DENIS O'HARE (*Ernst Ludwig*). Broadway: *Racing Demon* (LCT). Off-Broadway: *The Devils* (NYTW); *Silence, Cunning Exile; Woyzeck* (NYSF); *The Arabian Nights* (MTC); *Lonely Planet* (Circle Rep); *Hauptmann* (Cherry Lane). Regional: *Romeo and Juliet* (Center Stage); *Wonderful Tennessee* (McCarter); *Paddywack* (Long Wharf); *Dancing at Lughnasa* (Goodman & Arena). London (West End): *Never the Sinner.* In Chicago, Denis appeared in numerous productions including *Hauptmann* (Victory Gardens—Jeff Award), *Voice of the Prairie* (Wisdom Bridge—Jeff Award), *Lloyd's Prayer* (Remains), *The Iceman Cometh* (Goodman). TV: "New York Undercover," "Law and Order," "The Young Indiana Jones Chronicles." Film: *St. Patrick's Day, River Red.*

MICHELE PAWK (*Fräulein Kost*). Broadway: *Crazy For You* (Drama Desk nom.), *Triumph of Love, Mail*. Off-Broadway: *Hello Again, Merrily We Roll Along, John and Jen*. Regional theatre: premieres of *Oedipus: Private Eye, The Gig, Kudzu, Dirt*. Film: *Jeffrey, The Girl in the Watermelon* (Sundance Film Festival*), Flight of Black Angel*. Television: "Law & Order," "Shannon's Deal," "Dear John," "Golden Girls," "Quantum Leap," "FM," "L.A. Law." Recordings: cast albums of *Crazy For You, Hello Again* and the revival of *Merrily We Roll Along,* Varese Sarabande's *Lost in Boston III* and *Broadway Bound.*

VANCE AVERY (*Swing*). *Cabaret* marks Vance's Broadway debut. He was in the premiere Livent production of *Joseph...Dreamcoat* (Asher/ understudy to Donny Osmond). He was also invited to guest star in the first national tour. Along with numerous productions in Canada, Vance was an original cast member of *Les Misérables.*

JOYCE CHITTICK (*Frenchie, Gorilla*) At 17, Joyce toured the US with *Cats*. She recently appeared at The Public Theater as Bessye in Tony Kushner's adaptation of *A Dybbuk*. Broadway: *Once Upon a Mattress, Big, Tommy* and *Cats*.

125

WHO'S WHO IN THE CAST

BRIAN DUGUAY (*Victor*). Broadway debut. Brian has worked at several Off Off-Broadway theatres including the Greenwich House, the Duo, and the Judith Anderson where he was last seen playing the title role in *Dorian Gray*. New York directing credits include work at MCC, H.E.R.E., Center Stage and the Collective. He was a featured performer with the American Dancemachine (City Center & national tour), and has sung at Carnegie Hall with the Oratorio Society of New York.

ERIN HILL (*Lulu*) Broadway: Kate Mullins (orig. cast) in *Titanic*. Off-Broadway: *Rent* (NYTW), *Return to the Forbidden Planet* (Miranda), *Night of the Hunter* (Vineyard), *Between the Sheets* by Eduardo Machado (premiere), *Randy Newman's Faust* (Lincoln Center), *Honkytonk Highway* (Bistro Award: Outstanding Performer), *Home Fires* (Playhouse 91). Regional: Goodman, Syracuse Stage, La Jolla Playhouse, Goodspeed, George Street Playhouse, Pittsburgh CLO. Harpist: Carnegie Hall, *The Fantasticks* Off-Broadway. Also: Mint at New Dramatists in her sister Heather Hill's play *Smacking Mint*.

MICHAEL O'DONNELL (*Bobby*) returns to Broadway after appearing as Riff in the Westchester Broadway Theatre production of *West Side Story*. He was an original cast member of *Victor/ Victoria* and the Lincoln Center Theater revival of *Carousel*. National tours include *Jerome Robbins' Broadway*, *Brigadoon* and *The King and I*. Michael has also performed in the Radio City Christmas Spectacular and several ballet companies nationwide.

KRISTIN OLNESS (*Helga*) has choreographed and performed modern dance at various downtown spaces such as Theatre for the New City, Mulberry Street Theatre, Dia Center, as well as being co-choreographer and performer in China.

CHRISTINA PAWL (*Rosie*). Broadway: *Meet Me in St. Louis*. Regional: *Kiss Me Kate* (Berkshire Theatre Festival). European tours: *West Side Story*, *Oklahoma!* and touring with pop singer Nocera. Trumpet playing in *Who 'Da Funkit*. Solo singing engagement, MIE, Japan. Film: *Let It Be Me*, *Miracle on 34th Street* (re-make).

LEENYA RIDEOUT (*Texas*) Broadway debut. Off-Broadway: *Yiddle with a Fiddle*, *Portable Pioneer*, *Prairie Show*, and *Cowgirls*. Regionally she has performed such roles as Jenine-Kate in *Honkytonk Highway* at Florida Studio Theatre, Maria in *Sound of Music* and Julie in *Carousel*, and has toured internationally as Eliza Doolittle in *My Fair Lady*.

LINDA ROMOFF (*Swing*) was most recently seen on Broadway in *Victor/Victoria*. Other Broadway credits: Lincoln Center's *Carousel* and *Damn Yankees*. Linda also played Gloria Thorpe in the national tour of *Damn Yankees*.

FRED ROSE (*Herman, Customs Official, Max*) Broadway and national tour of Andrew Lloyd Webber's *The Phantom of the Opera* (Raoul u/s). Also in New York: Gallery Players' *Assassins* (Booth). Other favorites: Riverside Theatre, Fla., *1776* (Richard Henry Lee); Ascot Theatre, Denver, *George M!* (George), *Something's Afoot* (Geoffrey). Also in Colorado: *West Side Story* (Tony), *Show Boat* (Ravenal) and *Cabaret* (Emcee).

BILL SZOBODY (*Hans, Rudy, Bodyguard*) made his Broadway debut in *Dream*. Recently, he participated in the workshop of *Parade* for Livent. His regional credits include *Singin' in the Rain* (Westchester), *Crazy For You* (Northshore), *Strike Up The Band* and *Lucky in the Rain* (Goodspeed Opera House). Bill has also danced in the Radio City Christmas Spectacular.

ALEX BOWEN (*Boy Soprano*). Theatre credits: *The King and I*, *Beauty and the Beast*, *Whistle Down the Wind*. TV: "Another World," "Law & Order."

TAINA ENG (*Standby for Fräulein Schneider*). Broadway: *Look to the Lilies*, *Where's Charley?* (Tony nom.), *The Utter Glory of Morrissey Hall*, *Uncle Vanya*, *Strider*, *Nine*. Off Broadway: *Cheri*. National tours: *Irma La Douce* (opposite Denis Quilley), *Two by Two*, *Gigi*. Regional: *On Your Toes*, *Something's Afoot*, *The Tender Trap*, *Sound of Music*, *13 Rue de L'Amour*, *Zorba*, *A Little Night Music*, *I Hate Hamlet*, *Cabaret* (Barrymore Award). Film: *The Prodigal*, *39 Steps*, *Les Girls*, *The Bacchae*. TV: "The Great Wallendas," "Murder She Wrote." Soaps: "One Life to Live" "Guiding Light." Abroad: *West Side Story*, *A Little Night Music*, *Love Letters*.

BRUCE KATZMAN (*Standby for Herr Schultz*) has appeared in New York with the Manhattan Theatre Club, NY Shakespeare Festival, the National Actors Theatre, Soho Rep, NY Theatre Workshop, Gertrude Stein Repertory, and Cucaracha Warehouse Theatre. Film and TV credits include "Law and Order," "NY Undercover," "Late Night with David Letterman" and numerous daytime dramas.

JOE MASTEROFF (*Book*) has also been represented on Broadway on two occasions as a book-writer for the Jerry Bock-Sheldon Harnick musical *She Loves Me*, and on one occasion by the play *The Warm Peninsula*. In the near future, his new musical collaboration with composer Howard Marren, *Paramour*, based on Jean Anouilh's *The Waltz of the Toreadors*, will be presented at San Diego's Globe Theatre.

JOHN KANDER & FRED EBB (*Music, Lyrics*). Theatre: *Flora, the Red Menace*; *Cabaret*; *The Happy Time*; *Zorba*; *70, Girls, 70*; *Chicago*; *The Act*; *Woman of the Year*; *The Rink*; *And the World Goes 'Round—The Music of Kander and Ebb*; *Kiss of the Spider Woman*; *Steel Pier*; *The Skin of Our Teeth*. Films: *Cabaret*; *Lucky Lady*; *New York, New York*; *Funny Lady*; *Kramer vs. Kramer*; *A Matter of Time*; *Places in the Heart*; *French Postcards*; *Stepping Out*. TV: "Liza With a Z" (Liza Minnelli), "Goldie and Liza Together" (with Goldie Hawn), "Ol' Blue Eyes Is Back," "Baryshnikov on Broadway," "An Early Frost," "Liza in London."

SAM MENDES (*Director*) Most recently: *Cabaret* in New York, winning 4 Tony Awards, 4 Drama Desk Awards, 4 Outer Critics' Circle Awards and the New York Critic's Special Award. He has been Artistic Director of the Donmar Warehouse in London since 1992, where his productions have included: *Assassins* (Critics' Circle Award), *Translations*, *Cabaret* (Olivier Award nomination), *Glengarry Glen Ross*, *The Glass Menagerie* (also Comedy Theatre—Olivier Award; Critic's Circle Award), *Company* (also Alberry Theatre—Olivier Award; Critic's Circle Award), *Habeas Corpus*, *The Fix*, *The Front Page* and *The Blue Room*. Royal National Theatre: *The Sea*, *The Rise and Fall of Little Voice* (Olivier and *Evening Standard* Awards), *The Birthday Party* and *Othello* (Olivier Award nomination). Royal Shakespeare Company: *Troilus and Cressida*, *The Alchemist*, *Richard III* and *The Tempest* (Olivier Award nomination). West End: *Oliver!* (London Palladium—Olivier Award nomination), *London Assurance* (Chichester Festival Theatre/Theatre Royal Haymarket), *The Cherry Orchard* (Aldwych—Critic's Circle Award), *Kean*

WHO'S WHO IN THE CAST

(Old Vic—Olivier Award nomination), *The Plough and The Stars* (Young Vic).

ROB MARSHALL (*Co-Director, Choreographer*). Broadway: *Damn Yankees* (Tony nom., Outer Critics Circle Award, L.A. Drama Critics Award), *She Loves Me* (Tony nom., Outer Critics Circle Award, Drama Desk nom.), *Kiss of the Spider Woman* (Tony nom.), *Victor/Victoria* (Outer Critics nom.), *A Funny Thing...Forum* (Outer Critics nom.), *Company* (Outer Critics nom.), *Little Me*. Encores: *Promises, Promises* (Director/ Choreographer). London's West End: *Damn Yankees* (Olivier nom.), *She Loves Me* (Olivier nom.), *Kiss of the Spider Woman*. Off-Broadway: *The Petrified Prince* (Public Theatre). As Director: *Chicago*, Long Beach CLO (Drama-Logue Award), *Chess*, Paper Mill Playhouse; *Camelot, Brigadoon, South Pacific, Oliver,* Pittsburgh CLO. TV: Rodgers and Hammerstein's "Cinderella," ABC Wonderful World of Disney; Jerry Herman's "Mrs. Santa Claus" (Emmy nom.).

PATRICK VACCARIELLO (*Musical Director*) has been musical director on Broadway for *Victor/ Victoria, Cats, Joseph and the Amazing Technicolor Dreamcoat*. Internationally, he has served as musical supervisor for Sarah Brightman and Anthony Warlow on *The Music of Andrew Lloyd Webber* concert tour, as well as for top Chinese recording artist Fei Xiang on the *Broadway to China* album. Patrick was the supervisor for the national tour of *Cats* and has conducted at Carnegie Hall, Radio City Music Hall, numerous productions for the Goodspeed Opera House, the national tour of *Starlight Express* and the Broadway revival of *Take Me Along*. He recently served as musical director for the world premiere of *Whistle Down the Wind*.

ROBERT BRILL (*Set and Club Design*). Broadway: *Buried Child; The Rehearsal* (Roundabout, Drama Desk nom.). Off-Broadway: *God's Heart* (Lincoln Center), *Blue Window* (MTC), *A Park in Our House* (NYTW), *The Batting Cage* (Vine- yard). Regional: *An American In Paris* (Boston Ballet), *The House of Martin Guerre* (Goodman Theatre and Canadian Stage Company), *A Clockwork Orange* (Steppenwolf, Jefferson Award), *Betrayal*

and *Greensboro* (McCarter Theatre), Anna Deavere Smith's *Twilight: Los Angeles, 1992* (Mark Taper Forum and McCarter), John Steinbeck's *East of Eden* (Western Stage), Minnesota Opera, The Guthrie, Old Globe Theatre, Oregon Shakespeare Festival, and numerous productions for La Jolla Playhouse, including *Having Our Say, The Good Person of Setzuan* and *Fortinbras*. He is a founding member of San Diego-based Sledgehammer Theatre.

WILLIAM IVEY LONG (*Costume Design*) Credits include: *The Civil War, Annie Get Your Gun, The Mystery of Irma Vep, Cabaret, Chicago* (New York, London, Mel- bourne, Vienna, Stockholm) *1776, Smokey Joe's Café, Crazy for You* (Tony, Dora, Outer Critics' Awards), *Guys and Dolls* (Drama Desk Award), Madison Square Garden's annual *A Christmas Carol, Six Degrees of Separation, Assassins*, 1991 Obie Award for Outstanding Achievement, *Lend Me a Tenor* (Drama Desk, Outer Critics' Circle Awards), *Nine* (Tony, Drama Desk, Maharam Awards), Robert Wilson's *Hamletmachine*, Leonard Bernstein's *A Quiet Place, Trouble in Tahiti*, and *The Lost Colony*, Mick Jagger for the Rolling Stones "Steel Wheels" tour, Siegfried and Roy at the Mirage Hotel, Paul Taylor, Twyla Tharp, Peter Martins, and Susan Stroman.

PEGGY EISENHAUER (*Lighting Design*) is currently represented on Broadway by *Bring in 'Da Noise, Bring in 'Da Funk* for which she received the 1996 Tony and Drama Desk awards with Jules Fisher. In 1997 she received dual Tony nominations for *Ragtime* and *Cabaret*. Other designs include *Victor/ Victoria, Boys Choir of Harlem Live on Broadway, Twilight: Los Angeles 1992, Catskills on Broadway,* and *Tommy Tune Tonite!* For Broadway Cares/Equity Fights Aids, she designed *Betty Buckley at Carnegie Hall*, and *Sweet Charity* at Avery Fisher Hall. In the music industry she has created concert production designs for Whitney Houston, Crosby, Stills and Nash, Fishbone, Neil Young, and Tracy Chapman.

MIKE BALDASSARI (*Lighting Design*) received Tony, Drama Desk and Outer Critics Award nominations for Best Lighting as Co-Designer of *Cabaret*. He was also nominated for an Emmy Award for Lighting Direction of *Garth Brooks Live From Central Park*.

Other designs include Savion Glover's *Not Your Ordinary Tappers* and national tours of *The King and I, Dial "M" For Murder* and *Tommy Tune Moonlighting*. As the American Associate Designer he has imported to Broadway: *The Judas Kiss, The King & I, An Ideal Husband, Racing Demon, Indiscretions, Hamlet, An Inspector Calls*, and *Dancing at Lughnasa*. TV designs include VH-1's "Eight Track Flashback," and MTV News' "Video Music Awards."

BRIAN RONAN (*Sound Design*) Road companies: *42nd Street, Cats* and *Les Misérables*. Production sound engineer for *Shogun, The Secret Garden, Guys and Dolls, The Red Shoes, Damn Yankees* and *Rent*. Brian is the associate designer for *Smokey Joe's Cafe* and *Beauty and the Beast* tour. Broadway designs: *Busker Alley, State Fair, Triumph of Love, You're A Good Man Charlie Brown*, and *Little Me*.

MICHAEL GIBSON (*Orchestrations*) has orchestrated many shows, on Broadway and off. For Kander and Ebb he has scored *Woman of the Year, The Rink, Kiss of the Spider Woman, Steel Pier* and the new musical *Over & Over*. His other shows include *Anything Goes, My One and Only*, and 21 consecutive Christmas shows at Radio City Music Hall. He has received 2 Tony nominations for *Cabaret* and *Steel Pier* and was voted the Drama Desk Award for *My One and Only*. His orchestration of the film *Grease* earned him a platinum album. For symphony orchestra, Mr. Gibson has arranged and orchestrated suites from *Cabaret, Chicago*, and *Kiss of the Spider Woman*, along with an entire evening of the works of Duke Ellington to mark the imminent Ellington centennial.

DAVID KRANE (*Dance & Incidental Music*) had three shows running in 1996, *Showboat, Victor/Victoria,* and *Big*, and again in 1998 with *Ragtime, Cabaret*, and *Little Me*. He has just created new dance and incidental music for the newly conceived *Oklahoma!* for London's National Theatre. Past shows include *Kiss of the Spider Woman, Damn Yankees, She Loves Me* and *The World Goes 'Round* (both orchestrations, Drama Desk nominee). For Television: Dance music for "Mrs. Santa Claus," and for "Cinderella."

WHO'S WHO IN THE CAST

TIM MONICH (*Dialect Coach*) has worked on numerous theatre and film productions. For the Roundabout: *Old Times, Candida, Anna Christie* and *The Deep Blue Sea.* Faculty of the Juilliard Theater Center (1975-87.)

CYNTHIA ONRUBIA (*Associate Choreographer*) has peformed in and/or Assistant or Associate Choreographed on Broadway; *A Chorus Line* (at age 15), Bob Fosse's *Dancin'* (& National Tour), *Gotta Go Disco, Cats* (created *Victoria*), *Song & Dance* (& National Tour), *Jerome Robbins' Broadway* (& National Tour), *Metro, The Goodbye Girl, Damn Yankees, Victor/Victoria, Cabaret* (& National Tour), and was Associate Director/Choreographer on *Little Me.* Other credits: *Fortune* (off-broadway), *Carousel* (Kennedy Center), Michael Bennet's workshop *Scandal, Pal Joey* (Boston), City Center Encore's *Promises Promises, Lil' Abner, Chita Rivera,* and *All That Jazz.* Films: *The Jade Man, Night Passage, Everyone Says I Love You,* Tim Robbins' *The Cradle Will Rock,* and has choreographed for ABC TV's "One Life to Live."

RANDY HOUSTON MERCER (*Make-up and Hair Design*) has worked internationally in fashion, film, theatre and television. Recent films include personal make-up artist to Barbra Streisand for *The Mirror Has Two Faces,* key and personal make-up artist to Sir Anthony Hopkins for *Meet Joe Black.* Broadway designs include *Titanic, Sunset Boulevard, Chicago, Big, Smokey Joe's Cafe, Guys and Dolls, Crazy for You, Heidi Chronicles* and the almost Broadway production of *Whistle Down the Wind.* Randy has keyed many television shows and received a 1996 Emmy nomination for Outstanding Make-up. The Make-up and Hair for Broadway Bares is also designed by Mr. Mercer.

JIM CARNAHAN (*Casting*) also serves as Roundabout's Artistic Associate. For Roundabout, Jim has cast *The Deep Blue Sea, A View From the Bridge, 1776* (and subsequent move), *The Rehearsal, All My Sons, Three Sisters.* He has also done New York casting for the films *The Apostle* and *Bulworth,* as well as a Diane English pilot.

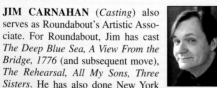

JENNIFER UPHOFF GRAY (*Associate Director*) is also the associate director of *The Blue Room* and was assistant director of *The Life, Death Defying Acts* and *Das Barbecu.* Her own productions have been seen at the Ensemble Studio Theater, HERE, Playwrights Horizons and the Chunchon International Theater Festival in South Korea. She holds a degree in drama from Harvard University and is a member of the Lincoln Center Theater Directors' Lab.

McCORKLE CASTING, LTD. (Pat McCorkle C.S.A.). Broadway: *A Doll's House, Misalliance, An Ideal Husband, Summer and Smoke, State Fair, Buried Child, Company, The Glass Menagerie, She Loves Me, Blood Brothers, The Kentucky Cycle* and *A Few Good Men.* Off-Broadway: *As Bees in Honey Drown, Radio Gals, Old Wicked Songs, Mrs. Klein, Travels With My Aunt, Driving Miss Daisy.* Film: *Eaters of the Dead, Madeline, Die Hard With A Vengeance* and *School Ties.* TV: AMC's "Remember Wenn?" and *Paramour,* the HBO "Lifestories" series, Showtime's "The Joe Torre Story" and PBS' "Ghostwriter."

PETER HANSON (*Production Stage Manager*). *Damn Yankees* (London, national tour, Broadway); *Encores!* At City Center: *Promises, Promises* and *The Boys From Syracuse; Blues in the Night* (national and Japanese tours); *Tamara* (Off-Broadway and Italy); *Steel Magnolias* (Off-Broadway); *Jeeves Takes Charge* (London, national tours, Off-Broadway); *Murder Among Friends* (national tour); *Oh! Calcutta!* (Broadway and national tour); Manhattan Theatre Club, Phoenix Theatre, six summers at the Totem Pole Playhouse.

JOHN MONACO (*Music Coordinator*) is a veteran of the musical theatre. He has been music coordinator for more than 100 Broadway musicals, has performed in more than 40 Broadway shows and has had the privilege of working with Richard Rodgers, John Kander, Jule Styne, Elmer Bernstein, Harvey Schmidt, Philip Springer, George Forrest, Robert Wright, Richard Sherman, Larry Grossman, Stephen Flaherty and many others.

GENE FEIST (*Founding Director, Roundabout Theatre*), since founding Roundabout in 1965, has been intimately involved as producer-director for more than 150 productions. For Broadway, he directed *The Play's the Thing* (1973), and produced *A Taste of Honey* (1981) and the Tony Award-winning revival of *Joe Egg* (1984). He sent *The Winslow Boy* and *A Raisin in the Sun* on national tour. Among the produced plays he has written are *James Joyce's Dublin, Jocasta and Oedipus, Wretched the Lionhearted, A Toy for the Clowns* and *Building Blocks.* He has provided distinguished adaptations of the works of Feydeau, Ibsen, Chekhov and Strindberg. Most recently, Mr. Feist produced a festival of Israeli plays at the Public Theater. A WW II Army Air Force veteran, he holds degrees from Carnegie-Mellon and New York Universities. Member: Dramatist's Guild, Society of Stage Directors and Choreographers, League of American Theatres and Producers. He is the recipient of the 1996 Lucille Lortel Foundation's Lifetime Achieve-ment Award.

THE DONMAR WAREHOUSE began life as a producing house under the artistic direction of Sam Mendes in October 1992. Within months the theatre asserted itself as a pioneer in London's performing arts community and established its identity both nationally and internationally. A maverick theatre, deliberately embracing a diverse body of work, the Donmar has originated 27 productions combining contemporary classics and musicals, in addition to mounting three seasons devoted exclusively to new writing. In six years, 14 plays and musicals have received their World or British premieres and seven plays their London premieres, with Donmar productions nominated for 35 Laurence Olivier Awards, winning ten, as well as receiving two *Evening Standard* Awards and six Critics' Circle Awards. In 1993 the Donmar was awarded *The Times* Critic's Award for "epitomising all that is best and boldest about British cultural life." Early in 1998 Sam Mendes developed his Donmar-originated production of *Cabaret* for the Roundabout Theater Company on Broadway, the first in a number of major collaborative projects with US theatres. Later that year Associate Director David Leveaux recreated his Donmar production of *Nine* in Buenos Aires, while back in London the Donmar presented the London premiere of *How I Learned to Drive* in association with the Vineyard Theater. Most recently the Donmar joined forces with the McCarter Theater, Princeton, who recreated Leveaux's Donmar production of *Electra,* which will be playing concurrently with *The Blue Room* and *Cabaret* in New York. At the conclusion of its sixth year of operation, The Donmar Warehouse will have three productions playing on Broadway.

ROUNDABOUT THEATRE COMPANY

Since its founding in 1965, Roundabout Theatre Company has grown from a small 150-seat theatre in a converted supermarket basement to become one of America's most significant producers of theatre. The not-for-profit, subscription-based company is committed to producing definitive interpretations of classic plays and musicals, ensuring that audiences and artists alike have access to high quality, professional stagings of important works that might not otherwise be presented in a purely commercial environment. Production highlights include *Joe Egg* (Tony, Drama Desk and Outer Critics Circle Awards for Outstanding Revival), *Anna Christie* (Tony, Drama Desk and Outer Critics Circle Awards for Outstanding Revival), *She Loves Me* (Outer Critics Circle, Drama Desk and Olivier Awards for Outstanding Revival of a Musical), *1776* (Tony, Drama Desk, Outer Critics Circle Nominations for Best Revival of a Musical), *A View From the Bridge* (Tony, Drama Desk, Outer Critics Circle Awards for Best Revival), and *Cabaret* (Tony, Drama Desk, Outer Critics Circle Awards for Best Revival of a Musical). Roundabout has garnered 51 Tony nominations, 49 Drama Desk nominations and 51 Outer Critics Circle nominations. In recent years, Roundabout has expanded its mission to include the production of new plays by great writers of the present day. Roundabout opened the company's Off-Broadway Laura Pels Theatre with the American premiere of *Moonlight* and Brian Friel's *Molly Sweeney* (Outer Critics Circle Award for Outstanding Off-Broadway Play). In 1998, Roundabout premiered its first commissioned play, Beth Henley's *Impossible Marriage*, starring Holly Hunter. Roundabout is recognized as the premiere classic theatre company in the country and continues to lead the way in innovative audience development and broad-reaching education programs.

BOARD OF DIRECTORS

Christian C. Yegen, *Chairman*
President, Yegen Companies

Mary Cirillo, *Vice Chairman*
Executive Vice President and
Managing Director, Bankers Trust

Todd Haimes, *President*
Artistic Director
Roundabout Theatre Company

Lawrence Kaplen, *Secretary*
Writer

Leslie Bains
Executive Vice President
Republic National Bank of New York

Samuel R. Chapin
Managing Director
Merrill Lynch & Co.

Robert G. Donnalley, Jr.
Retired, CPA

Douglas Durst
President, The Durst Organization

Gene R. Korf
Attorney, Korf & Rosenblatt

Kevin A. McCabe
Senior Vice President
The Chase Manhattan Bank

John P. McGarry, Jr.
President, Young & Rubicam Inc.

Douglas J. Mello
President, Large Business Services
North, Bell Atlantic Corporation

Cathryn C. Palmieri
Managing Director
Investment Management Practice
Korn/Ferry International

Laura Pels
President, The Laura Pels Foundation

Christopher Plummer
Actor

Barbara L. Rambo
Group Executive Vice President
Bank of America

David B. Rickard
Senior Vice President and Chief
Financial Officer, RJR Nabisco, Inc.

Jason Robards
Actor

Steven A. Sanders
Attorney, Beckman, Millman & Sanders

Donna J. Slade
Philanthropist

Barbara Schaps Thomas
Senior Vice President
& Chief Financial Officer
Time Warner Sports/HBO Sports

Anita Waxman
Producer, Alexis Productions

Patricia Wolpert
General Manager, System Sales
IBM Latin America

ADVISORY COUNCIL

Emery Westfall, *Chairman*
Retired, NYNEX Corporation

F. Murray Abraham

Jed Bernstein
Executive Director
League of American Theatres
and Producers

Gary K. Duberstein
Managing Director
Greenway Partners, L.P.

Ernest Ginsberg
Board Chairman Emeritus
Vice Chairman
Republic National Bank

Robert T. Greig
Attorney,
Cleary, Gottlieb, Steen and Hamilton

Charles Grodin

Samuel H. Hagler
Marketing Consultant

Irwin E. Kaplan
Retired, Datronics, Inc.

Stephen Lang

Frank Langella

Michael Littler
Vice President and General Manager
Millennium • Broadway

Carol Makovich
Vice President

Worldwide Communications
RJR Nabisco, Inc.

Honorable Anthony D. Marshall

Marsha Mason

Helen Mirren

Bruce Mitchell

Stanley H. Moger
President, SFM Entertainment

Charles B. Moss, Jr.
President, Moss Intertainment

Liam Neeson

Harold Oertell
Secretary/Treasurer
Milberg Factors, Inc.

Natasha Richardson

Ron Rifkin

Robert S. Roath
Retired, RJR Nabisco, Inc.

Florence Rosen
Executive Vice President
Rosen Associates Management Corp.

Robert A. Rosen
Chairman/CEO, Rosen Associates
Management Corp.

Lesley Sanders
Vice President, Process Improvement
Citibank, N.A.

Robert N. Sellar
Senior Vice President, Marketing
The Villager

Mary Steenburgen

Frank Skillern
Retired, American Express

Rebecca Sullivan
Producer

Yolanda R. Turocy
Vice President, Goldman, Sachs & Co.

Barry C. Waldorf
Managing Director
U. S. Trust Company of New York

Tony Walton

Robert F. Works
Managing Director, LaSalle Partners

ACKNOWLEDGEMENTS

The publishers wish to thank Alan Cumming and *Scotland on Sunday* for permission to reprint the diary of Alan Cumming on pages 103-104. And, the following people who helped to make this book a reality: Joe Masteroff; John Kander & Fred Ebb; Sam Mendes; Rob Marshall; William Ivey Long; Robert Brill; Alan Cumming; Natasha Richardson; Gilbert Parker of William Morris; Sam Cohn, Arlene Donovan, Maarten Kooij, and Paul Martino of International Creative Management; Adrian Bryan-Brown, Erin Dunn and Lisa Arkin of Boneau/Bryan-Brown; Robert Garlock of PMK; Kevin Smith of *Playbill*; photographers Joan Marcus and Rivka Katvan; David Steffen, Jason P. McLaughlin, and, especially, Elyse Cogan and Ellen Richard at the Roundabout Theatre.

PICTURE IDENTIFICATION & CREDITS

JOAN MARCUS (JM) is a New York-based photographer who specializes in photographing the performing arts.

RIVKA KATVAN (RK) is a New York City photographer who has been shooting Broadway backstage for the past 20 years

Page 1 Alan Cumming (RK)
2-3 John Benjamin Hickey (RK)
4-5 Natasha Richardson (RK)
6-7 cast (JM)
8-9 Alan Cumming (JM)
10-11 cast (JM)
12-13 Christina Pawl & Alan Cumming (JM)
14-15 Michele Pawk & Alan Cumming (JM)
16 Joyce Chittick (JM)
18 & 19 Alan Cumming (JM)
21 John Benjamin Hickey & Denis O'Hare (JM)
22 Joyce Chittick & Alan Cumming (JM)
23 John Benjamin Hickey & Denis O'Hare (JM)
25 Mary Louise Wilson (JM)
28 John Benjamin Hickey (JM)
29 Mary Louise Wilson (JM)
30 Natasha Richardson & Alan Cumming (JM)
35 Natasha Richardson & John Benjamin Hickey (JM)
37 John Benjamin Hickey & Michael O'Donnell (JM)
38, 39, 44-45 Natasha Richardson (JM)

48 Michael O'Donnell (JM)
49 Erin Hill (JM)
50 Michael O'Donnell (JM)
52 Michael O'Donnell, Alan Cumming & Erin Hill (JM)
54 Alan Cumming & Erin Hill (JM)
55 Mary Louise Wilson & Michele Pawk (JM)
57 Mary Louise Wilson (JM)
58-59 Christina Pawl, Joyce Chittick, Erin Hill (JM)
61 Alan Cumming (JM)
64 Natasha Richardson (JM)
67 Alan Cumming & Erin Hill (JM)
68 Alan Cumming, Joyce Chittick (kneeling), Erin Hill (standing) (JM)
73 Alan Cumming (JM)
74 Natasha Richardson, John Benjamin Hickey, Ron Rifkin, Mary Louise Wilson (JM)
77 Denis O'Hare, Mary Louise Wilson (JM)
78 Michele Pawk & Denis O'Hare (JM)
78-79 cast (JM)
80-81 (Foreground) Denis O'Hare, Brian Duguay (Background) Michael O'Donnell, Kristin Olness (JM)
82-83 Christina Pawl, Alan Cumming, Erin Hill, Michele Pawk (JM)
83 Leenya Rideout, Alan Cumming (JM)
85 Alan Cumming (JM)
86 Joyce Chittick, Alan Cumming (JM)
90 Ron Rifkin, Mary Louise Wilson (JM)
93 Alan Cumming (JM)

95 Natasha Richardson (JM)
98 Alan Cumming, John Benjamin Hickey (JM)
100-101 Leenya Rideout (RK)
102, 103, 105 Alan Cumming (RK)
106 Natasha Richardson & Alan Cumming (RK); Natasha Richardson (RK)
107 Natasha Richardson (RK)
108 (L-R) Leenya Rideout, Joyce Chittick (RK)
109 Alan Cumming (both) (RK)
110 Ron Rifkin, Michele Pawk, Denis O'Hare (RK)
111 Patrick Vaccariello, Mary Louise Wilson, John Benjamin Hickey (RK)
112 (left) Vance Avery, Michael O'Donnell, Erin Hill, Linda Romoff, Joyce Chittick (RK); (top right) Michael O'Donnell (RK); (bottom right); Christina Pawl (RK)
113 Michele Pawk (RK)
114-115 Photos by Robert Brill
116-117 Art by William Ivey Long
118 Natasha Richardson (RK); art by William Ivey Long
119 Joyce Chittick, Alan Cumming, Kristin Olness (JM); Alan Cumming, Michael O'Donnell (Photos by William Ivey Long)
120 (Clockwise from left) Natasha Richardson (Steve Shevett); Alan Cumming (Steve Shevett); Ron Rifkin (RK); Ellen Richard & Todd Haimes (Steve Shevett); Alan Cumming & Natasha Richardson (RK)
122 Photo of the cabaret at Studio 54 by Rivka Katvan
124-126 Bio Photos courtesy of the artists

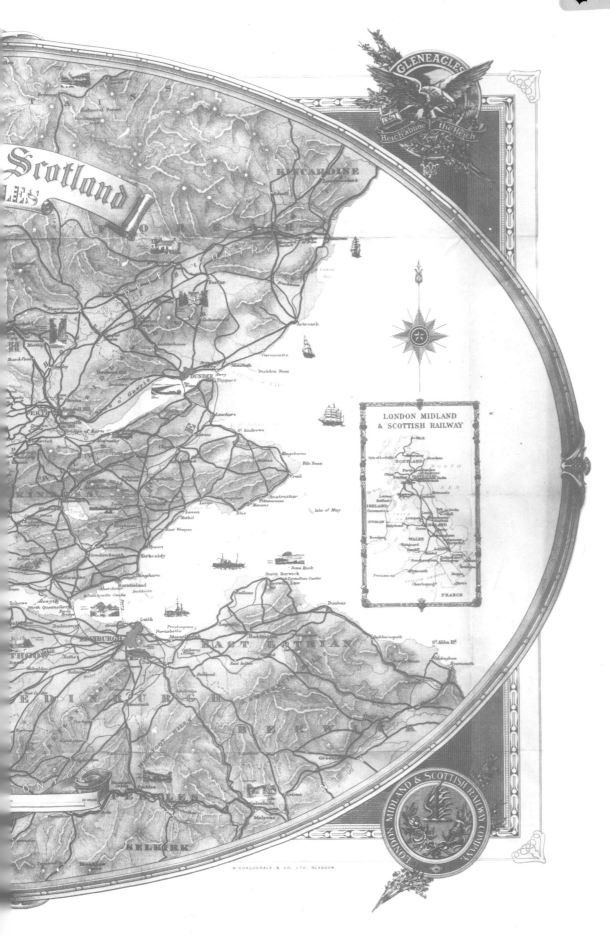

L.M.S. MISCELLANY

A Pictorial Record of the Company's Activities

in the Public Eye and Behind the Scenes

by

H. N. Twells

Oxford Publishing Company · Oxford

ACKNOWLEDGEMENTS

The preparation of this book has been greatly assisted by a number of fellow members of the LMS Society and others, who have loaned material and photographs from their own collections, supplied information and edited parts of the draft manuscript in an effort to ensure accuracy.

In particular, my thanks are due to John Alsop, Roy Anderson, Smokey Bourne, Bob Essery, Don Field, Greg Fox, John Hinchliffe, David Jenkinson, Don Rowland, Peter Tatlow, David Tee and Graham Warburton of the LMS Society, whilst Mike Brooks has very generously supplied material from his collection of LMS publicity items, and his records of naming ceremonies. Barry Handford, too, loaned some interesting LMS ticket issues, and Michael Stewart copies of his vast collection of LMS advertising tickets. Gordon Coltas, George Ellis and Vic Forster have each supplied photographs from their archives, and there are, of course, a number of other people to whom I am grateful for assistance.

It is pleasing to know that the vast collection of photographs taken by the official photographers for the LM&SR is now safely in the National Collection housed at the National Railway Museum, York. Until relatively recently, the plates and negatives were in the custody of British Railways at various centres, and I, along with many others, were then able to obtain copies for our own records. As well as these, a number of prints have been included by kind permission of the Keeper of the National Railway Museum and are Crown copyright, and this brings me to an important point.

A great deal of assistance in locating particular prints, and in proof reading and checking the manuscript, has been provided by John Edgington, Technical Information Officer at the museum, and a former employee of the LMS. His name is synonymous with railway history books, and it is a surprise when he is not mentioned in the acknowledgements. To John, my sincere appreciation for his efforts and encouragement.

Finally, my thanks to my understanding wife — Gill, for putting up with me and my typewriter.

Printed and Bound in the City of Oxford

Published by:
Oxford Publishing Co.,
8 The Roundway,
Headington, Oxford

The front of a folded map which was given to American tourists booking through the LMS Representative Office in New York, or through the Company's Passenger Agents in other American cities. The map shows the LMS network with lines radiating to Plymouth, Southampton, and other non-LMS towns, and there is no mention that these routes are operated by the other companies.

CONTENTS

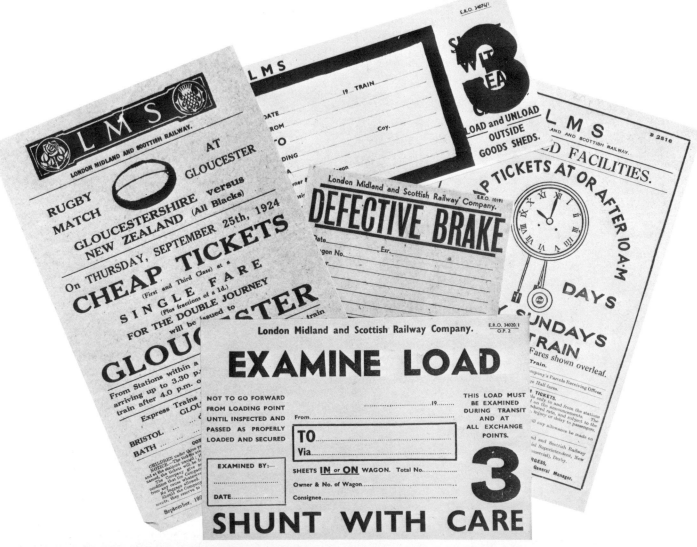

INTRODUCTION

The London Midland & Scottish Railway Company Limited was born a giant, at one second past midnight on the morning of 1st January 1923, and this fact is well-known to most if not all those who have taken an interest in its operations since that moment in time.

The fact that it was the largest joint stock corporation operating a railway anywhere in the world, is also well known, and if one were to delve through the mountain of paper which would produce the answer, it is likely that it could also lay claim to the title of the largest company in the world, irrespective of activity, in 1923 and for some years thereafter. It is more than thirty two years since the LM&SR ceased to exist in a Company identity, but it was then in 1948 a mere change in corporate identity with much of the LMS practices, continuing for many years into nationalisation.

With a wide spread of operations which ultimately led to the movement of passengers and freight traffic, there is much about the Company which has all but been lost in the passage of time, and it was this thought and interest in the non-rail side of the LMS which gave rise to this volume, *LMS Miscellany*. It would be impossible to even mention every aspect of the LMS operation in a volume of this kind, and therefore I have concentrated on providing some information on some of the important features of the Company which were to most people 'behind the scenes activity'. This was the side the public did not normally see, and included also are some of the points the public have perhaps forgotten, due to the passage of time.

I consider myself fortunate in having known the LMS, and I am told that at the age of 12 months I made my first journey from Swadlincote to Coalville and return — needless to say, this and other very early journeys in the late 1930s and early war years are beyond recollection, but I can remember travelling during the late war years from the Burton area to the Lancashire holiday resorts. Journeys from Lichfield (Trent Valley) through Crewe to Blackpool and Southport, Burton to Derby and others taking in Leicester, Birmingham and Tutbury are vividly etched forever in my mind. The streamlined 'Coronations' in grimy black, oily red Compounds and the swirl of steam and smoke were all part of a fascinating scene which impressed me as a youngster, and gave rise to my interest in this great company — an interest and a love for the LMS which I hope will show through in the pages which follow.

It is perhaps necessary to add further dimensions to the claim that it was the largest railway company, and whilst statistics can be made to prove any point, there are some figures which cannot escape inclusion:

(For ease of reference, the 1935 figures are quoted, since this date is almost the half-way stage in the Company's existence)

The Company's total authorised capital was:			£439,134,358	
and the total capital issued was:			£413,778,857	
Total receipts for 1935 amounted to			£71,814,564	
and after expenditure, Net Revenue was:			£13,027,525	
and after dividends etc. the surplus was:			£113,972	
The Company employed 38.26% of all railway				
employees in Great Britain	Males	212,423		
	Females	9,797		
	Total:	222,220		*580,766* *

	Miles	Chains	
The total mileage of running lines was, in single track terms:	13,366	17	
and there were sidings totalling:	6,015	49	
Total single track mileage:	19,381	66	

The total locomotive fleet, including 9 diesels was:	7,894	*20,359* *
The total number of passengers which the Company could accommodate, at any one time, at 31.12.1935 was:	1,054,750	*2,541,786* *
And the total mileage run by the Company's engines during 1935 was:	222,043,565	
Total passenger journeys for 1935 were:	442,809,870	*1,238,606,207* *

* Figures in italics are those of all railway companies in Great Britain.

This brief résumé of statistics serves to illustrate the sheer size of the LMS in its own right, and its dominant position in Great Britain. The image of the Company is perhaps mostly related to many of the areas through which the Company ran and where most of its traffic originated from, the industrial areas of the Midlands, Potteries, Lancashire and around Glasgow, rather than the picturesque countryside of the Peak or Lake District.

Many of the Company's activities have already been covered in book and magazine form over the years, and therefore I have aimed not to include repetitive material, but to augment these works with fresh material. There is still a mountain of information on the Company which will form the basis for further research activity, and it is hoped that this too will form another volume of this nature in due course.

I hope that every reader will find something of interest in this collection of photographs, and that the collection as a whole, will represent a broad résumé of the activities of this great undertaking, still affectionately known as 'The LMS'.

The small insets advertising different aspects of the Company's services are copies of those which regularly featured in the pages of the LMS Timetables, usually in areas of tables where there were no trains listed. What was the LMS — to use the early slogan, it was 'The Best Way' to travel after 1922 (or before on the Midland Railway who also used this slogan), and in the minds of many thousands of enthusiasts and others, the LMS is still alive. Nostalgia, yes, but we as enthusiasts, owe a great deal to past and present generations in the sphere of railway history, and it is important too, to recognise that we must play our part for the benefit of future generations, to perpetuate the memory of this and other great companies.

This has been the chief aim of The LMS Society which was founded in 1963 to co-ordinate research into the Company activity, and through the members to make available such information for the benefit of others, whether in book form, magazine articles or lectures, and much has been disseminated already.

H. N. Twells,
Chesterfield,
March 1982

The London, Midland & Scottish Railway Company Limited was formed through the grouping of railways under the Railways Act 1921, and embraced the following eight constituent and twenty-seven subsidiary companies:-

CONSTITUENT COMPANIES

London & North Western
Midland
* Lancashire & Yorkshire
North Staffordshire

Furness
Caledonian
Glasgow & South Western
Highland

SUBSIDIARY COMPANIES

Arbroath & Forfar
Brechin & Edzell District
Callander & Oban
Cathcart District
Charnwood Forest
Cleator & Workington Junction
Cockermouth, Keswick & Penrith
* Dearne Valley
Dornoch Light
Dundee & Newtyle
Harborne
Killin
Knott End
Lanarkshire & Ayrshire
Leek & Manifold Valley Light

Maryport & Carlisle
Mold & Denbigh Junction
North & South Western Junction
* North London
Portpatrick & Wigtownshire Junction
Shropshire Union Railways & Canal
Solway Junction
Stratford-upon-Avon & Midland Junction
Tottenham & Forest Gate
Wick & Lybster Light
Wirral
Yorkshire Dales (Skipton to Grassington)

The three companies listed were incorporated with the L&NWR Company as from 1st January 1922.

The LM&SR were also substantial shareholders in a number of joint lines:-

		Length of Line	
	LMS Shareholding	Miles	Chains
Cheshire Lines	1/3	143	49
Great Central & Midland Joint Lines	1/2	39	23
Great Central & North Staffs Joint Lines	1/2	10	77
Great Central, Hull & Barnsley and Midland Joint Line	1/3	4	77
Manchester South Junction & Altrincham Railway	1/2	9	13
Methley Joint Line	1/3	5	58
Midland & Great Northern Joint Railways	1/2	183	26
Oldham, Ashton and Guide Bridge Junction	1/2	6	16
Severn & Wye and Severn Bridge Joint Line	1/2	41	6
Somerset & Dorset Joint Line	1/2	105	40
South Yorkshire Joint Line	2/5	29	69
Whitechapel & Bow Railway	1/2	2	4
Total length of jointly owned and jointly leased lines		**581**	**58**

In Ireland the LMS were represented as follows:-

Half share in County Donegal Railways (total length 110 miles 8 chains)
Northern Counties Railway wholly owned — 280 miles 52 chains*
A minority shareholding in the Great Northern Railway (Ireland)
A minority shareholding in the Great Southern Railways
Dundalk, Newry & Greenore Railway — operated from 1933 by GNR

5ft 3in gauge — 202 miles 59 chains
3ft gauge — 77 miles 73 chains

The LMS were also shareholders in the following:-

Great Western Railway
London and North Eastern Railway
London Electric Railway to 30.6.33
London Passenger Transport Board from 1.7.33

These are taken from official statistical records covering the period 1923 to 1936, and there were other investments in companies unconnected with railways. The LMS also had substantial shareholdings in a number of omnibus companies spread over most of Scotland, and much of England and Wales, and the names of these are to be found in a future book *LMS Road Vehicles* which includes information of the LMS Road Motor Omnibus activities.

Plate 1   The British Railways stand at the British Industries Fair in 1939. Whilst each railway company presented its own stand at certain events, the principal companies combined their efforts when it came to being present at national events such as the BIF (as it was known). The message of all the companies was to attract business to the railways particularly from the roads which had seen a period of expansion from the early 1920s. This was chiefly to the loss of the railways, both as regards freight and passenger traffic. By 1939 many of the smaller publicity items issued by the railway companies had been printed to be applicable to any one or more of the companies. Nevertheless, individual identities were preserved by the use of posters from each company's standard range and representatives from each of the big four, from both the passenger and commercial departments would be in attendance to deal with enquiries. Advertising abroad was also undertaken jointly by the companies in certain locations, in New York and other centres in North America, in Paris and at exhibition locations, and on board certain transatlantic liners. Indeed, the LMS was proud of the fact that a railway ticket could be purchased in mid-Atlantic. With interchangeability of tickets, through routes for freight and other common features, it was financially beneficial to all the companies to co-operate in presenting a combined stand at large exhibitions.

National Railway Museum

Exhibition Stand

Plate 2   The LMS stand built Driscoll Bros. Ltd., of Manchester the Bolton Civic Week 1929. In addi to publicity material there is a interesting display of railway and models built by Bassett-Lowke Ltd LMS models, of course.

National Railway Muse

The LMS Research Department, Derby

For ten years the research work carried out by the LMS staff was done at various centres which were under Departmental Control, until that is, the formation of a Scientific Research Department at Derby. In 1933 the chemical and paint laboratories, together with textile and metallurgical laboratories formed the nucleus of the new organisation and further sections were added dealing with engineering research and physics.

Two committees were overlords of the LMS research activities and the Research Department worked closely with the various Government research establishments and research associations, and extra-mural investigations were conducted with the university laboratories.

A Scientific Research Committee of the LMS Board of Directors regularly monitored the various research activities being undertaken in the Company's laboratories and centres, and with the advent of the new Research Department the many avenues of interest were now more easily co-ordinated and reviewed. A further Advisory Committee composed of eminent outside scientists and the Chief Technical Officers of the Company considered the general policy towards research in general.

A research manager was supported by a chief metallurgist, textile technologist, a paint technologist and engineering research officer, all with their laboratories at Derby. In addition, the chief chemist was based at Euston with control over chemical laboratories at Derby, Crewe, Horwich and St. Rollox.

Staff of the new Research Department numbered around 150, of whom some 60 were usually scientific graduates with experience in other research laboratories prior to joining the LMS. With a close liaison maintained with the universities, an inter-change of staff took place in areas of mutual interest. With the establishment of this Research Department the gathering of information could be co-ordinated and duplication minimised. Advice on a variety of matters to the various operating departments of the railway was always available.

The Chemical Section of the Research Department was responsible for a wide range of subjects, and some of these were of great importance to the efficient operation of the railway. Much time, spread over many years, was devoted to measuring the thermal efficiency of a locomotive boiler in use, and if one remembers the tests carried out after the demise of the LMS, by British Railways on various locomotives during the 1950s at the Rugby Test Plant, then this subject can have few rivals for research duration. The steam locomotive boiler was merely a coal burning machine, but it was harnessing of maximum power from a measured portion of fuel, at the optimum level of efficiency which was the ultimate goal. With so many variables in types of boiler, qualities of fuel, condition of the heating surfaces and chemical composition of waters found in different parts of the country, it is hardly surprising that no precise single answer has ever emerged. The LMS Chemical Research Section merely added their contributions on this subject to those undertaken by their forbears and contemporaries in the other railway companies of the time. Not all the work was done in laboratories, but theories and practices were transferred to actual locomotives working under strict test conditions on the open road, with dynamometer recordings adding to other recordings and observations made during the journey from the footplate. Research into the thermal efficiency of the locomotive boiler continued throughout the LMS period and in 1937 the Company, jointly with the LNER, took a decision to set up the locomotive testing plant to be located at Rugby, but the outbreak of war in 1939 prevented its completion. Its purpose was to simulate actual running conditions and enable a more careful and accurate analysis of locomotive performance to be recorded. The nationalised British Railways inherited the Testing Plant and opened it in October 1948, some eleven years after it was planned.

Half a million pounds sterling was the cost to the LMS for the purchase and application of paint each year, and the purpose was to protect assets which had a much higher value in the Company's balance sheet. The L&NWR had set up a small laboratory in 1920 at Wolverton to look into the chemical properties of paint and until 1930 its research work had continued. In 1930 it was transferred and amalgamated with a parallel operation which had existed at Derby and this later became a part of the new Research Department. A Paints Standardisation Committee existed to control not only the quality of materials used,

but to agree the basic formulae which the Company required to be used. These formulae were compiled to enable all the paint manufacturers who supplied the Company to meet the Company's requirements which had been determined by the results of laboratory and in-use tests.

The Paint Laboratory was concerned with most aspects of the Company's activities, having regard to the fact that if a wrong type of paint was used for a particular purpose, then corrosion or decay could cost the Company heavily. It was organised into three sections. The first dealt with the routine testing of samples of paint supplied by the trade, and more than 4,000 samples were dealt with annually. Routine tests were a check that the LMS specifications were being adhered to, and close liaison was maintained with the stores and various departments using the paints. A further section was devoted to processes of paint application and in-use tests, and to unusual problems which may have been encountered in differing atmospheric conditions. Outdoor exposure tests were carried out by using panels painted with various materials under test and special test racks were situated at Derby, and at the Menai Bridge to give a choice of climatic and atmospheric test conditions. These tests were extensive with as many as 1,000 panels under exposure at any one time: the panels were inclined at a 45° angle facing due south. In addition, accelerated tests were carried out using a cylindrical machine known as a 'Weathermometer', which could in six weeks, simulate outdoor tests of sunlight and water which would naturally take up to twelve months to achieve.

The third section was concerned with research into new materials and the use of substitutes for specified ingredients. Special paint formulae were required, for instance, for application to the Company's steamers, and special anti-fouling paints were used. One particular contribution from the Paint Laboratory work was a waxing composition which acted as a cleaner and preservative, and was periodically applied to all the Company's locomotive stock, and to the more modern carriages.

The Textile Research Station had been set up originally by the Midland Railway at Derby in 1910, and it was another section whose work was connected with every department of the Company. Whilst one would correctly recognise the use of textiles in carriages, or on furniture, a fare-paying passenger could not ordinarily receive a ticket without first a date being applied using a cotton inked ribbon, and between every chair and sleeper there was a felt pad cushion. A wide variety of textiles was in use by all the railway companies and it is perhaps surprising that even as late as 1935, the LMS was the only railway company with its own laboratory devoted to research work into textiles and their use. As with the other aspects of the Research Department already mentioned, the Textile Section contributed much to the knowledge and improvement of the wearing properties of the wide variety of textiles used, and such was the thoroughness of the tests, that exposure tests of 100 hours constant duration were necessary to determine tendencies to fade, before materials were considered satisfactory for use. Special apparatus to simulate normal wear, humid conditions and the effect of sunlight all contributed to this unique department's activities.

The metallurgical and engineering research sections were other important aspects of the Research Department's function and wide-ranging tests were always under way. With the suspicions of war in the late 1930s, amongst tests undertaken were a series to determine the effect of a bullet fired at the cylinder casing of a locomotive, no doubt to determine whether a missile fired with high velocity would have any material effect on the cylinder. The outcome of these tests, however, is not known.

With the desire for higher speeds and the move towards streamlining locomotives to cut down resistance from winds and air disturbance, wind tunnel tests were carried out on scale models, the results of which would then guide the designers in choosing the final form to be built. The accompanying two plates have been included, since they show a model subjected to wind tests to determine the final profile of the 'Coronation' Streamlined Pacifics.

Other aspects of research are too numerous to mention in this potted record of the Research Department's activities, but these notes will serve to include one of the lesser known departments of the LMS railway amongst the more important aspect of operations.

In addition to experimental and research work undertaken in the various company laboratories, there was a considerable number of experimental projects carried out in 'in traffic' conditions, and amongst these was the series of tests of the pneumatic tyred railcars built by the Coventry Pneumatic Railcar Company, a subsidiary of Armstrong Siddeley Motors Ltd., in 1936. The LMS co-operated in this test venture after having earlier allowed the Michelin Tyre Company facilities to test one of their prototype pneumatic-tyred railcars. Michelin railcars were already in service with French Railways and the petrol engined unit brought to this country was the subject of much attention both on the LMS and the GWR.

The Coventry railcars were equipped to run on the Michelin patented pneumatic railcar tyres of the type used on Michelin's own test vehicle. In addition to this innovation there were a number of other new ideas incorporated into these vehicles. The use of aluminium for the body sections considerably reduced the total weight to around 9½ tons. Each vehicle was 54 ft in length with seating capacity for 56 passengers; considerably higher than Michelin's own railcar capacity; and in addition, a luggage compartment which was designed to take up to 15 cwt of passengers or similar luggage. Only one of the eight-wheeled bogies was powered, with an Armstrong Siddeley 12 cylinder 'V' petrol engine and this was sufficient to allow speeds in excess of 60 mph. The Coventry Railcar Co. also designed and constructed self-change, or 'automatic' in modern terms, gearboxes. Perhaps the most intriguing feature of these railcars was the safety devices fitted to the wheels. All sixteen wheels were fitted with a tyre pressure gauge, which in the event of a loss of pressure, would activate an audible warning device in the driver's high-level cab. Each railcar was provided with the necessary jacks and spanners for use in such an emergency, and it was claimed that a tyre-change could be completed in a few minutes. The faulty axle would be jacked clear of the rail, the six bolts holding the outside rim were released to enable the tyre to be replaced, and within a short time the railcar could continue in use. The tyre-failure rate was favourably low, with one failure recorded in each 37,700 miles average. Other features included dual braking systems, one manual for use in case of emergency and for parking when the compressor was not in use, and a power system operated by compressed air for normal use. These Coventry rail-

cars were built with the intention that orders would be taken from the British companies after trials had been completed, as well as hoping to attract interest from railway companies abroad. The LMS did not buy these vehicles, but they were used over varying stretches of line in the Midlands and there were advantages in using this type of unit over lines where small numbers of passengers were carried.

The LMS had in 1928 converted some early electric stock to form a four-car diesel railcar set, but this unit was under-powered and was not in service for long. In 1933, three 40 seat Leyland four-wheel railcars were purchased by the Company and although they were tested in various areas, including a special test trip over Shap, they were not popular and were relegated to local work in Hamilton.

Another experimental diesel railcar unit was built in 1938. A three-car unit with seating for 162 passengers, it bore a strong resemblance at either end to the modern design of the Coventry railcars, but it proved rather less reliable than had been expected and it remained out-of-use during the war years.

It is appropriate to include a reference to another passenger carrying vehicle which was purchased by the LMS, and which also came within the realms of being an experimental vehicle. Whether it can be considered as a railcar, or as a road motor omnibus, is not really the point, for it served as both. The Karrier Road Rail vehicle was an experiment to combine the advantages of rail travel with those of the road motor omnibus. The LNER had a Karrier Road-Rail vehicle with motor lorry body, but the LMS were very interested in the possibilities which this passenger vehicle presented. It was in the event another relatively short-lived experiment and it was used between the Welcombe Hotel in Stratford-on-Avon which the Company owned, and along the Stratford-on-Avon and Midland Junction Railway to Blisworth. Specially prepared areas were provided at Blisworth and Stratford Goods Yard with the road surface level with the rails to allow the interchange from road to rail wheels and vice versa, to enable the vehicle to turn and to continue its journey.

These experiments were but a few of the many undertaken by the LMS and they serve to illustrate the efforts that this Company, and others, were taking to assess alternatives to the steam locomotive and steam railcars. The accompanying plates are examples of these vehicles.

Plate 6   The second Coventry Pneumatic Tyred Railcar in service at Leamington Spa (Avenue) Station in 1937. The high-level driving position came within the standard loading gauge and was a space saver. Access to the luggage compartment was through the roller shutters.

J. Coltas

Plate 7   No. 1, in passenger service at Leamington Spa (Avenue) Station. Note the rounded front end with passenger windows, as opposed to the driving end which incorporated an air intake grille, visible in the previous plate.

J. Coltas

Plate 5   The Michelin Pneumatic Rail-car on LMS metals at Coventry in April, 1932. The front-end appearance followed continental road-motor design for the period, although this unit does present a heavy and possibly cumbersome appearance.

National Railway Museum

Plate 8   The Karrier Road-Rail vehicle in demonstration service on the Hemel Hempstead branch soon after delivery to the LMS. In this view the normal road wheels can be seen outside the flanged rail wheels, and upon arriving at the end of the rail section of each journey, the rail wheels were raised and at the same time the road wheels were lowered by means of eccentric mechanism. The change-over was completed within a matter of minutes. The two round slots, one on each side of the radiator, were provided to take a pair of buffers on a metal frame, but it is believed the buffers were seldom used. Indeed, the life of this vehicle as a passenger carrier was short-lived, entering service on 1st April 1932 and after a few months on 2nd July 1932, it was withdrawn from this service. It was certainly a novel vehicle which added a great deal of interest to the railway scene in the Stratford area, albeit for a short time.

Author's Collection

Plate 9   The Ro-Rail Bus, as it became known, is seen here in Cravens Works in Sheffield prior to delivery to the LMS. Livery was crimson lake with white roof, and the Company letters were applied by hand by Cravens paint shop staff and were not the normal Company pattern. There were other omnibus vehicles built by Cravens for the LMS and all carried similar pattern lettering. Although it is not readily apparent, entrance doors were provided to both sides of the vehicle.

Cravens Tasker

Fire Trains Arrangements

Railway Fire Trains were a feature of the LMS not often seen by the average passenger, despite the fact that there were six in total located at the principal workshops.

The pre-group companies had established fire trains as mobile fire stations in the late 19th century, as a further means towards reducing losses caused through fires which were beyond the average local fire brigade of the time, usually a horse drawn four wheel appliance. Fire fighting equipment was provided at virtually all stations, goods yards, signal cabins and other locations, varying in sophistication from the sand and water buckets to manual pumps, but a wide array of equipment provided for the fire train was superior to most local installations. The fire train was available to attend the more major fires and although there was invariably a delay before the train arrived at the scene of the fire, the local brigade could be relieved or assisted to extinguish the fire. The salvage operations or the damping-down of the fire would often take some time and the fire train, being Company owned, could remain at the scene for however long was deemed necessary and the additional expense was minimal. The Company would of course be charged by the local brigade for prolonged services of this nature, so this was further justification for the maintenance of fire trains.

The fire trains were signalled as express passenger trains on both the outward and return journeys and were given priority over other trains using the same line. Since speed was of great importance, the first available locomotive had to be provided and coupled to the fire train, and it is on record that the train could be despatched within a very short space of time — minutes — from the time the call for assistance was received. They were manned by railway workshop employees on a round-the-clock basis, who were fully trained in fire techniques and were part of the workshop fire brigade team. In addition to attendance at building fires, they were also called to lineside fires where it was often impossible for the local road brigade to reach the scene, and to railway accidents where there was a danger from the gas lit carriages, although most of these had disappeared by 1923.

The fire train areas overlapped at first in line with the pre-group interests, and from June 1924 adjustments to areas were made. Further adjustment to boundaries was made in July 1926 and the following areas were formed:-

WOLVERTON

Old L&NW line, London to Nuneaton and Leamington (both inclusive) and all branches south thereof. Joint line stations south of Melton Mowbray (inclusive). All old L&NW Passenger and Goods Stations in London area. Old SMJ line.

DERBY

London Tilbury and Southend line. The old Midland Main line and branches, between London and Cudworth, except Hereford and Brecon and Swansea Vale branches. Old L&NW line Wichnor Junction to Birmingham via Sutton Coldfield and via Walsall (Witton or Soho Road lines) and to Dudley (inclusive) via South Staffordshire line. The South Leicestershire branch to Nuneaton LNW and Ashby and Nuneaton Joint lines and the Loughborough branch. The LNW line Ashbourne and Buxton to Stockport but not including Stockport itself. The former North Staffordshire Railway line east of Stoke, not including Stoke, and the Churnet Valley line.

CREWE

The former LNW main lines and branches Nuneaton and Leamington (but excluding both towns station areas) to Euxton Junction, but excluding the junction, via Trent Valley and Birmingham lines. All the old L&NW lines, including joint lines and branches, south of a line Holyhead, Liverpool, Wigan, Adlington Junction (LU line), Bolton, Eccles Junction and Manchester London Road, including all the points mentioned and up to, but not including, Stalybridge, except where the Wolverton and Derby fire trains areas are shown as responsible. The Clifton Hall branch. The old NSR line west of a line, and including Macclesfield, Stoke and Colwich. The old Midland Hereford and Brecon and Swansea Vale lines.

HORWICH

Old L&YR line west of Manchester, Castleton, but excluding both these stations, but including Bacup, Burnley and Colne. The former LNW main line and branches, Euxton Junction (including the junction) to and including Carlisle, and all lines west of the line between Carnforth to Carlisle. The old Midland main line and branches, including Hellifield itself to Carlisle.

NEWTON HEATH

The old L&YR line east of the Horwich area, old LNW line and branches east of and including Stalybridge, Manchester Exchange Station and to, but not including, Eccles Junction. The old Midland main line and branches between Cudworth and Hellifield but excluding both points, but including Ancoats.

The arrangements for **SCOTLAND** were one fire train to be stabled at St. Rollox to provide cover for all lines north of the border.

The fire train usually consisted of a brake third carriage of pre-group origin, either short bogie stock or 6 wheel variety, for carrying firemen to the scene, a water tank wagon and a van containing the fire engine, usually a static pump, hoses and the full range of fire fighting equipment. Livery would probably have been post office red with white or yellow lettering to distinguish the train from breakdown trains or normal freight trains when in use.

The fire train at Horwich was allowed to stand in the forefront of the main offices and was always coupled to an in-steam locomotive, an L&Y tradition continued during the LMS period.

On occasions, owners of private property adjoining the railway could call upon the fire train for assistance, and either the local authority or the individual would recompense the railway for services rendered.

By early 1935, the Wolverton and Newton Heath fire trains had been disbanded and their areas merged in a general re-arrangement of the remaining fire train areas in England and Wales.

The revised areas were as follows:-

Mechanical Engineer — HORWICH

All stations Gretna and south thereof to a line including Liverpool Dock Stations, Allerton, Appleton, Moore, Styall, Handforth, Poynton, Disley, Barnsley, Cudworth, Grimethorpe, (DVR), Askern Junction, Goole, Hull; the Axholme Joint Railway was also included in this division, also the premises at Donegal Quay, Belfast were included in this division.

Works Superintendent, CME Department — CREWE

All stations south of the Central Division, Liverpool-Disley line, including Garston Dock and west of a line including Alton, Uttoxeter, Lichfield, Tamworth, Market Bosworth, Croft, Broughton Astley, Lubenham, Clipston, Northampton, Roade, Ridgmont, Dunstable and Boxmoor; the Dundalk, Newry and Greenore Railway, also premises at Dublin and Kingstown were included in this division.

Works Superintendent, CME Department — DERBY

All stations south of the Central Division, Liverpool-Hull line, and east and south of the Western Division Disley-Boxmoor line.

SCOTLAND
Mechanical Engineer, St. Rollox — GLASGOW

All stations north of Gretna.

During the war years, in addition to the Horwich locomotive in-steam arrangement, the Crewe fire train was also stabled with a locomotive ready for the road, since the threat to railway property was much more menacing from the hostilities. The fire trains were also in use as part of the general war effort, assisting local brigades in fighting fires close to railway property.

With the development of the road motor fire appliance between the wars and during the 1939-45 conflict, the role of the fire trains was gradually diminished. Local authority brigades were better equipped with faster machines on a more widespread scale, and the distances a fire train could be required to travel to the scene of a fire was progressively more of a handicap, but the advantages of access and time commitment still weighed heavily in their favour. By 1947, the operational areas of the trains had been reduced, and they were, by this time, intended to be used only within a reasonable distance of their stations to supplement or substitute for the local NFS (National Fire Service) brigade. Detailed general instructions on fire fighting were contained in the General Appendix to the Working Timetables, but the Fire Regulations issued by the Home Secretary had also to be observed.

One aspect of fire prevention at the lineside covered by the Railway Fire Acts of Parliament, 1905 and 1923, provided that every railway company, including the LMS, was liable for damage to forests, plantations, woods, orchards, market and nursery gardens, agricultural land

continued from previous page

and fences and crops thereon resulting from sparks from locomotives. Gangers working on the line had to cut down all undergrowth which could be a source of danger in a spark fire. Many of these hazards were in remote areas and inaccessible by road, and if the local gang of permanent way men were unable to quench the outbreak, then the incident could have demanded the calling of the Area fire train.

The accompanying photographs feature the Horwich fire train in 1936.

Plate 10 The Horwich fire train in its usual 'on-call' location on 5th May 1936, with the team of nine men posed alongside. The ex L&Y locomotive heads a 4,740 gallon tank wagon No. 167068, with roof mounted monitor fitted van No. 168989 and six wheel coach No. 168990.

National Railway Museum

Plate 11 The 5th May 1936 was obviously a demonstration day at Horwich, since it would be no small task to display an array of equipment the likes of which is shown in this official photograph. The Coventry Climax trailer pump of 500 gallons per minute capacity, is surrounded by a variety of rigid and flexible hoses, handpumps, standpipes for connection to water mains, extinguishers and floodlights. The two boxes in the foreground carried the All Service Gas Masks which the two firemen display. The two further cans to the left foreground were fuel supplies for the pump itself. It is on record that the Horwich train was on its way, within four minutes of the call being received, to a fire at the Alexandria Dock, Liverpool on 21st September 1940, and it arrived seventy three minutes later.

National Railway Museum

late 12 The covered van with Coventry
imax pump in position and hoses
tached, ready for connection to the
000 gallon water tank valves. Other
ms of equipment carried in this van
re ropes, extinguishers and protective
othing, which can be seen hanging in
e rear of the van.

National Railway Museum

Plate 13 The firemen's riding coach with hose and other equipment storage beneath the side seats. The guard's compartment is seen through the open door at the rear of the vehicle, and the centre table was probably out of a redundant saloon.

National Railway Museum

Plate 14 This view of fire fighting equipment on the deviation line at Crewe Locomotive Works features the Crewe train behind the two road appliances. A 4,740 gallon tank, formerly used in the Newton Heath fire train and similar to the Horwich vehicle, is provided and between this and the Class 2P locomotive is another tank vehicle converted from a redundant tender. The livery of the Crewe train is red, but the lettering is yellow or gold shaded black.

The two road motors are CNK 496, a Dennis New World Pump with ladder escape, and GAR 333, a Ford Thames vehicle fitted with a Sulzer pump, one of three of this type stationed at Crewe Works during the war years. The LMS crest on the Dennis engine has a maroon background to the LMS Company lettering.

Real Photographs

Road Fire Vehicles

In addition to fire trains, the LMS provided fire fighting equipment of one sort or another at most locations throughout the system, and this equipment included fire engines at certain locations. At Crewe, several road motor engines were provided primarily for use within the railway workshops but also in large areas of the town where the railway still owned large numbers of dwellings, schools, a gas works and a hospital. Assistance was also given to the town brigade when required.

At Horwich and Wolverton, two towns which owe their origins to the advent of the railways, the LMS not only provided the fire brigade for their own premises, but also were the local brigade turning out to whatever fire or other incident happened in the town area. The town authority at Horwich provided the LMS brigade with a road motor fire engine complete with pump and fire escape ladder and also an auxiliary water pump tender, and these were renewed at intervals as more modern and sophisticated equipment became available. The Wolverton brigade was equipped by the LMS and prior to 1923 by the LNWR, and here the appliances comprised a fire engine with pump and escape ladder, a motor water tender and a trailer pump.

The Wolverton council compensated the LMS for the use of the brigade and also paid for the services of the men whenever they were called to fires in the town. These arrangements were considered to be of mutual benefit to both parties – the LMS brigades gained greater experience from town involvement and the local authorities in turn benefited from being able to draw on a well trained brigade at a lower cost than would normally have been the case.

In addition to these points in the system, the LMS provided road motor appliances at important high risk locations, and in the ensuing two photographs the fire engine provided at Holyhead is shown. Holyhead was an important point on the LMS system and with dock warehouses and other more elaborate passenger ship facilities, there was a need for adequate fire appliances. This Fordson Thames vehicle with Sulzer pump was very similar to the one shown in an earlier plate at Crewe, but with a different locker arrangement from the body. This type of vehicle was also provided at other points on the LMS system.

Plate 15 GAR 333 being taken away after being replaced by British Rail.

Real Photographs

Plate 16 This photograph was taken on 18th July 1947, possibly when delivery of this vehicle took place to Holyhead, although the vehicle carries a pre-war registration number.

National Railway Museum

Road Transport Operations

Whilst the road vehicle activities of the LMS Railway Company are the subject of a separate volume entitled *LMS Road Vehicles* (to be published later), the author has no wish to duplicate those contents, the road transport operation of the LMS was so large a section of the Company as to merit a further selection of photographs in these pages.

There has always been something very basic about a horse and cart, and if one looks back from the twilight of horse transport, the 1950s and early 1960s, it is soon evident that little or no new developments of the types of horse vehicle in use had occurred since the turn of the century. The two most important features were perhaps the railway companies building their own vehicles to ensure more standardisation of vehicles, and interchangeability of parts etc. in the late 1890s, and the arrival of pneumatic tyred lightweight vehicles in the mid-1930s. Not much else changed and those horse drawn vehicles which were built by the LMS were to designs which had their origins with the pre-group companies.

The LMS horse stud was the largest in the country, and even as late as 1946 owned 6,168 out of a total 'railway stud' of over 9,000. This was only a third less than the stud total taken over from the constituent companies in 1923, and it is therefore clear that the LMS Railway Company placed great reliance on its horse transport operations.

It is true, of course, that throughout the LMS period road motor vehicles were coming more and more to the fore. Speedy collection and delivery of freight was what the private transport sector could offer and they were in direct competition with the railways for the available traffic. Whilst the road motor fleet owned by the LMS was expanded, for much of the time the horse drawn operations maintained their numbers and position, although the LMS was the only one of the four major railway companies to do this.

Whether it be horse drawn or road motor, the aim was the cartage of traffic to and from the railway and with the fierce competition offering rates which undercut the railways, traffic was lost. The railways sought, and gained through Act of Parliament, powers to enable them to compete for pure road traffic at competitive rates, and in direct competition with those who had set up years earlier to attract traffic which had for a very long time been rail-borne. One of the principal planks in the railway companies' argument against unfair competition, was the fact that they had considerable overheads to maintain the railways, whereas the road operator was not responsible for road upkeep, and could therefore offer low rates to attract business. Be that as it may, the LMS road transport activities were responsible for an annual carried tonnage of around 12 million tons and by the mid-1930s, an annual figure of around 80 million packages and parcels also.

The accompanying photographs are of typical vehicles which saw everyday service with the Company, and although there were a number of types which were confined to city and large town depots, there were many types which were used in large and small locations throughout the length and breadth of the LM&SR Company's territory. In some locations where other companies also provided rail services, it would not be uncommon to see horse drawn and road motor vehicles bearing both companies' initials, particularly from the early 1930s when duplicated fleets were unnecessary and undesirable in fighting the road competition. Jointly lettered vehicles usually had one side and either the front or rear lettering with one company's initials leading, and the other side and fore or aft with alternated lettering, to avoid any 'unintended' advantage.

Quite apart from the freight operations of road transport, the LMS also indulged in the passenger road vehicle operation as tramway owners and a very limited bus service in the early years. The two tramways, the Wolverton and Stony Stratford Steam Tramway in Buckinghamshire and the Burton and Ashby Light Railway which traversed a line through three Midland counties, were in decline as they came into LMS ownership and with road passenger competition from motor omnibuses affecting both lines, they were closed in 1926 and 1927 respectively.

With no more than three omnibuses in 1927, the Company could not be considered serious motor bus operators, but their intentions were most earnest. Along with other railway companies they were campaigning for a new Road Transport Act which would enable them to meet the competition from the passenger omnibuses. The 1928 LMS Road Transport Act was passed in August, and thus commenced a period of investment in establishing the LMS as a force in motor omnibus operations. Integration with rail passenger services as a means to overcome direct road competition was the aim, although the company was empowered to set up in direct competition to any road operator, save local authority transport departments within their own area boundaries. Again, it must be pointed out that the detailed account of this side of the LMS is to be found in *LMS Road Vehicles*, and the photographs in this volume are representative only.

With road transport so important a part of the LMS in all four aspects detailed here, a back-up staff was required to ensure these vehicles functioned when required.

Within the Chief Operating Manager's Department, a Horse Superintendent was appointed to look after the horses owned by the Company and to be responsible for all matters relating to their welfare and availability for work. Stables were provided wherever horses were required, and, in the larger centres, the stable buildings occupied large areas and some were on more than one level and included hospital wards for sick animals.

The road motor operations were controlled by the Road Motor Engineer and his principal assistant, and five District Road Motor Engineers based at Birmingham, Blackburn, Bradford, Manchester and Kentish Town in London. Self-contained road motor workshops were at these locations and they were equipped to undertake all forms of maintenance and repairs, and in addition to these centres, there were a number of subsidiary repair depots which could carry out routine inspections and minor repairs. Training of motor drivers was also carried out by the LMS staff at four regional schools which were set up in 1936 under the direction of an experienced instructor.

The LMS fleet numbered around 10,000 vehicles, trailers and motor-driven appliances just prior to nationalisation at the end of 1947, and high mileages were commonplace. Insofar as the trams were concerned, the depots at Wolverton and at Swadlincote undertook routine maintenance, and a single horse drawn tower trolley was used for overhead wire work on the Burton and Ashby Light Railway.

The omnibus activities were, suffice it to say, carried out in a variety of forms: direct LMS services; in joint operations with four municipal authorities; as outright owners, for one year, of the Crosville Motor Services Ltd., in North Wales; and on a share-participation basis in established companies such as Ribble, Midland Red and others. Only in the case of direct LMS services were the Company responsible for day to day maintenance and repairs, the others all coming under the control of the operating authority.

This summary is intended only as a preface to the road vehicle photographs which follow, and more information on this interesting part of the LMS operation is to be found in the Road Vehicle book previously mentioned.

Plate 17 There were several variations of lettering applied to horse drawn vehicles in the early period of the LMS, and by late 1923 the Company had settled on a full lettering style as depicted in this picture of a Type 33, 3¼ ton dray, and for all similar vehicles.

National Railway Museum

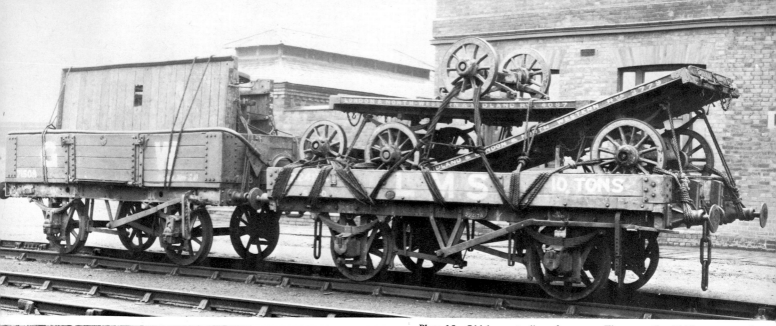

Plate 18 Old horse trolleys for scrap. Those on the LMS wagon are letter for joint L&NWR and MR use, with the companies' names alternating. LN first on the offside and Midland first on the nearside in accordance with t normal practice for jointly lettered vehicles.

National Railway Museu

Plate 19 A number of pre-group vans lined up awaiting the start of t Regents Park Horse Parade. The first vehicle is one allocated for use at t Horse Department Stables at Camden, whilst the tilt vans carry a variety advertising panels. These parades were an annual feature in most cities a towns and were often held in support of local hospital funds. LMS carte and their horses were regularly amongst the prize winners at these even reflecting the high standards demanded by the Company in all respects the care of the horses.

Real Photograp

Horse Drawn Vehicle

Plate 20 A photograph taken for demonstration and advertising purposes to show the ease with which an open container can be taken from the customer's premises to the railway wagon for onward transit. This print also serves to illustrate the lettering applied to the rear of horse drawn drays through the LMS period, although the full stops between the letters were soon omitted, and the number carried on the rear axle bearer was usually shown in a larger form.

R. J. Essery

Plate 21 Two of the tilt vans, in close-up, awaiting the start of the Rege. Park Parade.

Real Photograp

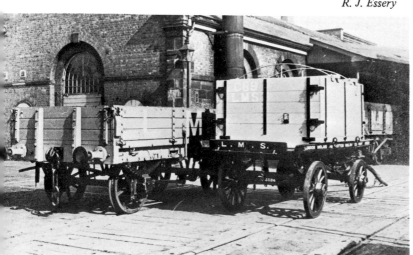

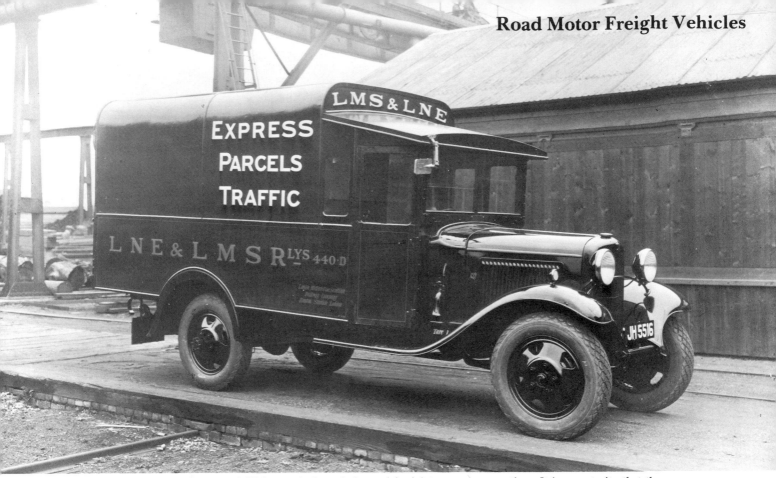

Plate 22   A Fordson 2 ton parcels van with Wolverton bodywork, lettered for joint company operations. It is a great pity that there are no colour photographs of vehicles such as this, for there could have been few more splendid railway items than this crimson and black lorry, fully lined out in gold and with gold-shaded insignia. The paint date is 27th September 1933, and the lettering on the black van top was white. This type of van was used in the towns and cities where a large proportion of the parcels traffic carried on the LMS originated.

National Railway Museum

Plate 23   ANK 193, a 3 ton Karrier 'Cob' Mechanical Horse and low-loading parcels van trailer, lettered for joint parcels work in an area where the LMS & Great Western Railway both served. The van body is fitted with an access door, the lower half to be dropped to form a flat platform onto which the vanboy could place parcels and cartons for the carter to remove and deliver. The top half merely folded round flat to the van front. Another type which was allocated for city work. The fleet number suffix 'G' is for the Mechanical Horse fleet and 'D' for parcels delivery van, and similarly on the van with the addition of the trailer, 'T'.

National Railway Museum

The Wolverton and Stony Stratford Tramway
and The Burton and Ashby Light Railway

THE TRAM, STONY STRATFORD.

Plate 24 The Wolverton and Stony Stratford Tramway had but a short life under LMS ownership and even when inherited from the L&NWR, the writing was on the wall. It was losing money on its short route mileage, and with mounting competition from the road motor buses along the same route, its closure came as no surprise to the local community, most of whom were employees of the LMS Carriage Works at Wolverton, and who, at one time or another, had used the line to travel to and from the Works. The General Strike brought about its closure in May 1926 and the equipment was sold, although there was a proposal that the line should be re-equipped for electric trams. This view of one of the tram engines and the bogie trailer car was taken at the Stony Stratford terminus, and both are in LMS livery with the small letters just visible on the cab side of the engine.

D. Tee Collection

Plate 25 (right upper) The Company's other tramway operation was carried on under the title of the Burton and Ashby Light Railway, and whilst the line ran between these two points in different counties, it also ran through South Derbyshire taking in the township of Swadlincote, the villages of Woodville, Newhall, Church Gresley and Castle Gresley. The central tram depot was at Swadlincote on land adjacent to the LMS single line which formed a loop off the main Burton to Leicester line. It had been Midland Railway territory, in fact the Midland Railway had taken great pride in the line, but by the time the LMS took over it was virtually doomed, again as a result of direct competition from local motor bus operators. There were twenty trams all built by the Brush Company of Loughborough, and all were on four wheel rigid frames. When it was first built, sections of the line were completed as separate railway sections, and all were combined to form the Burton and Ashby Light Railways. The LMS dropped the 's' and its title merely ended as Railway. In this view, the tram depot in Midland Road, Swadlincote, is shown in April 1913, at a time when most of the trams were in the second of the liveries and carried during the later Midland period of ownership.

National Railway Museum

Plate 26 (right lower) The first livery carried by the trams, and No. 13 is on one of the early trial runs prior to opening the line to the public in 1906. The tram has just come off one of the preserved sections through fields and is standing outside the Royal Oak, Newhall, between Burton and Swadlincote. Far from being a flat and operationally uninteresting line, the line took in several rather steep inclines and despite these, only one serious accident befell the Company when a tram ran backwards down Bearwood Hill, on a section of the track over which the Burton and Ashby trams were granted running rights by the Burton Corporation Tramways within the Borough boundary. The line was a feeder line to the railway, with termini at the Ashby, Castle Gresley and Burton Stations, and with passing stops at Woodville close to the railway station, and at Swadlincote. At the outset, the Midland Railway built a large bridge, in engineers' blue brick, adjacent to the Swadlincote Station to take the trams over the railway lines, and in fact this bridge is one of the few remaining reminders of the tramway which remains to this day in Swadlincote.

B. D. Mail

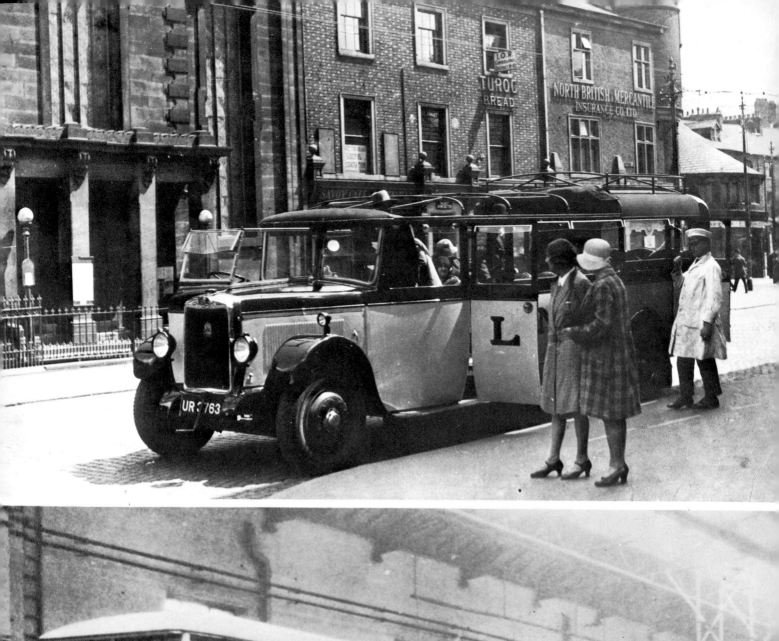

Plate 29 A line-up of Albion buses on 28th May 1929, in the Derby Carriage & Wagon Works, awaiting final fitting out before entering service in different parts of the country.

National Railway Museum

Motor Buses

◀ *Plate 27 (left upper)*   With the LMS as a motor bus operator with its own services, and as the owners of the Crosville Motor Company for one year, from 1st May 1929, and with operational interests in four Joint Omnibus Committees with local authority operators, a wide variety of vehicles carried some evidence of ownership by the LMS. Those vehicles owned directly by the Company carried the LMS initials, and were to be seen in various parts of the country. Services in the Hemel Hempstead and Harpenden areas were operated with company owned vehicles, and similarly some of the omnibuses used in the Sheffield Joint Omnibus Committee area were also company owned. The Crosville vehicles, delivered new to the Company, were emblazoned with a large oval device signifying LMS Crosville ownership, since the LMS continued the old established Crosville name. The vehicles used in the Todmorden JOC area, the Halifax JOC area in which the LMS had a third share interest along with the Corporation and the LNER, and those in the Huddersfield JOC area, all carried lettering reflecting the Joint Omnibus Committee ownership, although there were vehicles in each area which were solely owned by the local authorities. In Sheffield, the LMS again had a third share with the LNER and Corporation, and it was in this area that LMS vehicles were used principally on the Sheffield and Manchester routes. Other LMS vehicles were used in Scotland and Northern Ireland, and some Leyland coaches were operated on coach tours and sight-seeing excursions in the Yorkshire/Lancashire boundary areas and extending as far north as Carlisle and the Lakes. The LMS also invested in share ownership with a large number of the principal motor bus operators in Scotland, England and Wales, but these were not controlling interests and the vehicles operated by these companies never carried any indication that the railways were connected with them. Timetables and written material, however, did include a reference in the headings to the railway company's association. This Leyland coach is seen loading in Carlisle and the white-coated driver, traditional attire for those on the prestigious motor coach tours, would indicate this coach about to depart on a local tour. This vehicle was later absorbed into the Hebble fleet.

British Leyland

◀ *Plate 28 (left lower)*   Inside the Sheffield Corporation Works this 32 seater Leyland Lion with bodywork built at the Derby Carriage & Wagon Works was allocated to the category 'C' routes. Despite the sideboards carrying the LMSR name, the bodyside carried lettering for all three participants in the JOC. The fleet number, 14F, was the LMS fleet number, the 'F' being the LMS classification letter for omnibuses. The livery was crimson lake and white with gold and vermilion lining.

D. Ibbotson Collection

Workshops of the Company

All places served by the LMS services, but all places too where workshops owned by the Company were situated. Some were better known locations than others but all were equally important for the varying contributions to the LMS operations that they made.

EARLESTOWN
Primarily concerned with the construction and repairs to wagon stock, and the Company's containers. Total area 36 acres. 1,150 employees (1930).

INVERNESS
Formerly the workshops of the Highland Railway spread over approximately 8¾ acres and employing 163 (1930) on repairs to locomotives, carriages and wagons.

STOKE-ON-TRENT
A small works taken over from the North Staffordshire Railway Company and closed in 1927, and much of the 12 acres was sold to Robert Hyde & Sons Ltd., who remain owners to this day.

DERBY
One of the well known names in railway history, famous for locomotives as well as carriage and wagon building, for repairs to almost anything, and well over 200 acres of land and buildings giving employment to more than 7,200 in 1930. Also in Derby the LMS Signal and Telegraph Works.

HORWICH
81 acres used for the construction and repair of locomotives with 17 acres under cover. Just over 3,000 employees in 1930.

BOW
Formerly North London Railway Works occupying $3^1/_3$ acres and employing 172 in 1930, on locomotive repairs.

ST. ROLLOX
The largest workshops owned by the LMS in Scotland, with 9 of the 15 acres under cover. Famous for its construction and repair of locomotives with around 1,500 employees (1930).

CREWE
A legendary name whenever locomotive construction and repair is discussed. The principal works for express locomotive construction and repairs on the LMS and with 53 of the 160 acres built upon, giving work to more than 5,800 employees. In addition, there was a further 24 acres of land given over to carriage repairs, employing 320 (1930), whilst steel rails were rolled, and prefabricated wooden building sections were built.

BARASSIE
Carriages and wagons, and by 1930 only wagons, were repaired at this location by around 500 employees.

NEWTON HEATH
Carriages and wagons were constructed and repaired at this former Lancashire and Yorkshire Railway centre, the works occupying 45 acres and more than 1,660 employees worked there in 1930. The LMS Concrete Works was centralised here.

KILMARNOCK
A small locomotive workshop on approximately 4 acres with a staff of 130 in 1930 working on repairs only.

WOLVERTON
Still a legendary town in railway matters which has concentrated on achieving the finest standards of craftsmanship in carriage building. Virtually the whole town still depends to a great deal on the carriage and wagon works, and there were no less than 3,500 staff in 1930. The works occupied a total of 87 acres of which 35 were covered. In addition to C&W building it was also the principal Road Vehicle workshops for the LMS, both as regards horse vehicles and road motors. Large numbers of barrows and trolleys for platform use were constructed at Wolverton.

BARROW-IN-FURNESS
These former Furness Railway workshops were closed by the LMS in the late 1920s, but prior to this locomotives and wagons and the Company's steamers were repaired at Barrow, where the total area was approximately 19 acres.

There were other locations with works established to deal with specialised operations, but as these were chiefly concerned with the running department, and hence were not in the public eye, little attention was paid to them by most of those taking an interest in the LMS scene. Sheeting factories, a basket works, provender depots, a clothing factory, a sack depot for cleaning sacks after hire, and a clock and watch depot were located in different parts of the system. Whilst various activities have been generally described as 'locomotive repairs' or carriage and wagon workshops, the multitude of skilled trades required in each of the Company's workshops defies description, there were so many, and there were many departments within a single works which served other needs as well as the main works activity.

Since the earliest days of the railways, the companies had established their own workshops to deal with the construction of equipment and the progressive repairs, to both their own and private builders' equipment. Works had grown as the companies had expanded, and the machinery needed to cope with railway repairs was of a sophisticated and mainly heavy type. Forges and presses, turning shops and foundries, erecting shops and a paint shop, all were important sections of a workshop and in some cases, gas works and electricity generating stations were also attached to parts of the works to provide the necessary power. The LMS inherited a complete heavy engineering industry with specialist capacities, and continued to invest new machinery and techniques to improve their works' capabilities and effect efficient operations.

Workshop methods were examined, and where possible streamlined into progressive systems for repair of different components. Shopping of engines was organised on a 'Colourdex' basis, a system of coloured tabs from which the Chief Mechanical Engineer could ascertain quickly what the locomotive repair position was throughout the system. It was in three distinct phases; (i) engine numbers proposed for shops (ii) locomotives agreed for shops (iii) engines in the shops. There were coloured cards for different types of locomotive, i.e. passengers tender engines – yellow, passenger tanks – mauve, freight tender – green and freight tank – grey, which formed the key to the system, and after engines had been outshopped, a progressive record was maintained and if any particular examinations were required by the CME, then these were requested of the home shed. If a works visit was required to follow, then the engine would be entered on the 'Colourdex' display panel. Another innovation on the workshop scene was the inauguration, in 1936, of a 'Shadow Board' system for workshop tools. The background of the boards was dark and a painted representation of every tool was painted thereon in white, thus providing an immediate check of any tools which were in use. With more than 25,000 employees in LMS workshops, there was a requirement for new entrants to apprenticeships in all crafts and trades, and to ensure that all apprentices received a thorough grounding in their chosen craft. A standardised procedure was set up as 'The Progressive System of Workshop Training' in 1932. Each individual followed a predetermined schedule according to the trade or craft selected. A further development in apprentice training procedures took place in 1946, when approval was given to establish the Company's first Works Training School within the locomotive works at Derby. For the first year, an apprentice was classified as an apprentice trainee, whereupon he was then transferred to work in the main shops as a trade apprentice, with a programme organised to take in most of the activities connected with his main trade.

It would be extremely difficult to give a detailed account of all the workshop activities on a works by works basis, or of all trades, and the miscellaneous nature of this collection of photographs will serve to illustrate some of the activities one could have expected to find in the general workshops sphere.

Road Vehicle Department

Plate 30 The finishing section of the Road Motor Department at Wolverton with a wonderful line-up of newly-built Morris Commercial lorries receiving the finishing touches to the lettering. The LMS purchased considerable numbers of commercially made chassis and built their own bodies on to suit particular requirements.

National Railway Museum

Plate 31 The Road Motor shop at Wolverton with Karrier chassis in the course of receiving bodies. The nearest one to the camera is a rolling conveyor floor, whilst in the right foreground are two Fordson chassis awaiting parcels van bodies. In the background is part of the production area for bodies for motor vehicles and horse vehicles, and there are also parts of horse vehicles in the foreground.

National Railway Museum

Plate 32   The Road Vehicle shop at Wolverton on 22nd October 1937, with a very interesting collection of vehicles and equipment ready for allocation throughout the system. There is a mixture of horse vehicles to the left, with some newly built Standard Type 10 2¼ ton open vans forming part of Lot 982, a Lot of 150 ST 10s. The LMS purchased considerable numbers of Dennis chassis with cabs and they appeared with different sizes and types of body. They were known as the 'Flying Pig' type, and in this line it is interesting to note 2265-B is fitted with single rear wheels and heavy duty tyres all round. The second 'Flying Pig', No. 2367-B is lettered for the S&DJC, whilst at the far end of the line BNK 779 is lettered for LMS and LNE Joint operations. The Dennis chassis were 1½, 2, 2½ and 3 ton configurations. The right of centre is occupied by three Albions in front of another line of 'Flying Pigs'. All three are interesting in that the cab is not full width with nearside cab-side in line with the rear of the bonnet, possibly for carrying long steel rods etc. To the right there are several 4 wheel platform trolleys, a stable barrow and platform barrows of several different types.

National Railway Museum

Plate 33   Not a Company workshop, but the N(1 Erection Bay, Road Vehicle Department c Charles Roberts & Co. Ltd., at Horbury Junctio near Wakefield, with vehicles in varying stages o construction for the LMS. The two numbere(trailers, 21552 and 21553 are fitted with soli(tyres for heavy operations behind a tractor unit.

Author's Collectio

Plate 34 The Sewing shop at Wolverton with female employees practising their skills to produce blinds for carriage windows and also linen items and serviettes etc.

National Railway Museum

Plate 35 Van bodies under construction at Wolverton. It will be noted that the vertical external wood planking is backed by horizontal planking on the inside. The wooden panels were prefabricated and then fitted into the metal framing.

National Railway Museum

Wagon and Van Construction

Cell Shop

Plate 36 A general view of the Cell shop at Wolverto
Prior to 1927 there had been a small cell manufacturing u
at Wolverton, but with increased demand for cells, as the co
version programme from gas lighting was accelerated, t
Wolverton Cell department was enlarged to provide t
additional capacity necessary. The use of electric lighting
carriages brought a requirement for dynamos, regulators a
electric cells or batteries. Most carriages had 12 such cells b
others carried up to 24, and with an electrically lit carria
stock in excess of 16,000, there were approximately 195,0
cells to be maintained and renewed when life expired, as w
as the construction of new cells for the carriage building pr
gramme. This specialised unit was centred on Wolverton w
a capacity to produce 700 new cells and overhaul and servi
around 2,000 cells per week. The manufacture of the ce
involved acids and a variety of processes, and in this vi
large numbers of completed cells are shown, and to the l
the carboys which were used for distilled water and acid.

National Railway Museu

Timber Shop

Plate 37 The mechanised sawmill with standard lengths of timber being cut. The Company
was a large user of timber of all types, both
hard and soft wood, and in addition to using
new timber, reprocessing of reclaimed timbers
was carried out. The ducting from the circular
saws took much of the dust created away from
the machines and into containers for disposal.

National Railway Museum

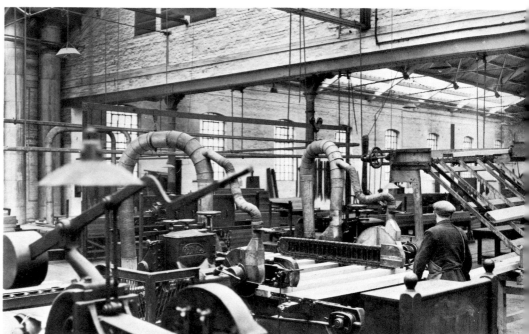

Lifting Shop

Plate 38 The Lifting shop at Derb
Carriage and Wagon Works with a Bai
Midland clerestory on temporary bogie
The tank with steam emitting is a bosh
for cleaning purposes.

Author's Collectio

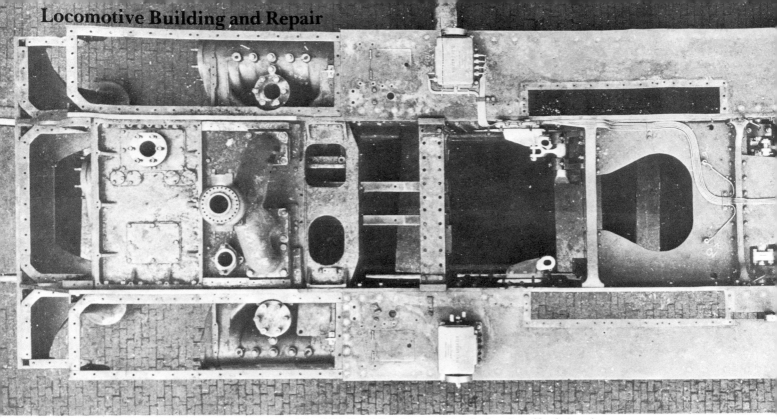

Four plates showing various stages in the construction of No. 6100 *Royal Scot* in preparation for its trip to North America.

Plate 39   A bird's eye view over the frames and footplating. The offside lubricator has the lubrication pipes in position.

R. J. Essery

Plate 40   The heat retaining asbestos boiler lagging being added to the boiler and firebox with boiler fittings fixed.

R. J. Essery

Plate 41   The lagged boiler has now been sheeted over and is almost ready for lowering onto the frames. The ashpan is shown to the right.

R. J. Essery

Plate 42   The engine nearing completion, hoisted in preparation for fitting the front bogie. It has been reported that No. 6152 and No. 6100 changed identities for the North American tour, but there is nothing to confirm this on the Engine History Cards. In the case of No. 6229 and No. 6220 for the 1939 tour to America the changed identities are recorded on the History Cards. Nevertheless No. 6100 was provided with a new boiler and tender for the tour, and it has been assumed the two 'Scots' exchanged frames.

R. J. Essery

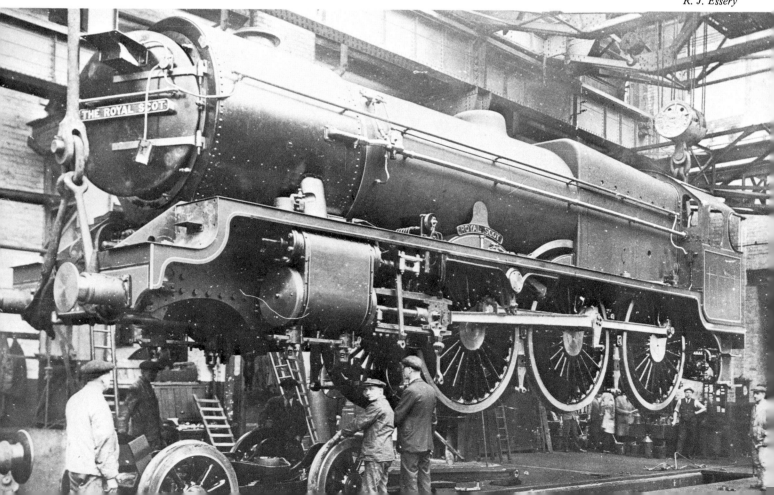

Plate 43   One of the small Johnson 0-4-0STs of Midland origin, minus its wheels, in Derby Works.

J. Coltas

Plate 44   Crewe Works sheet metal shop with the streamlined casing for one of the 'Coronation' Pacifics being formed on a wooden framework from the patternmakers.

National Railway Museum

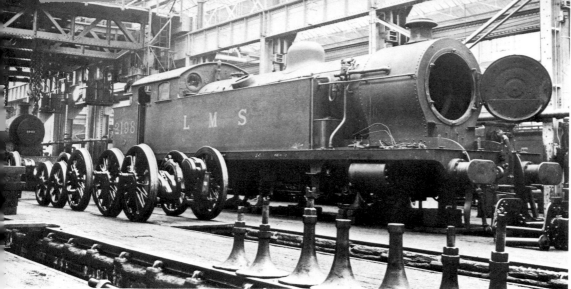

Plate 45 Ex-London, Tilbury & Southend Railway 4-6-4T, No. 2198, in Derby Works in 1931. This locomotive was re-numbered from No. 2106 in 1928/9, one of a class of eight such locomotives. The jacks in the foreground are of the type used to support the frames when the wheels were removed.

J. Coltas

Plate 46 A 'Patriot' locomotive under construction in 1933. No. 6018 with the name *Private W. Wood, V.C.* in place. It is interesting that the name is in position during construction, for there are records which fix the date for the naming of this locomotive as 1936. It was later renumbered 5536.

J. Coltas

Plate 47 No. 6399 *Fury*, the experimental high-pressure locomotive, completed in 1929 at the North British Works, Glasgow, seen here inside Derby Works in 1932. The design resembled the 'Royal Scot' class as regards the frames, but this engine was a three cylinder compound, one high-pressure cylinder located in between the frames with the low-pressure cylinders in the conventional outside position. The locomotive was not a successful one, and soon after completion its life was marred by a burst tube which killed one man and injured another. There are comparatively few photographs of this engine and it was later rebuilt as No. 6170 and named *British Legion*.

J. Coltas

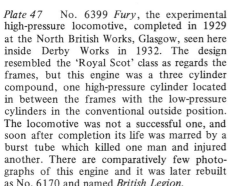

Tarpaulin Sheet Works

Plate 48   Trent was noted for its Junction station, and the fact that it was situated more than a mile from Long Eaton, the nearest town. Nevertheless it was also an important centre for the LMS in that the Tarpaulin Sheet Works were just to the west of the station, close to the main Derby-Trent lines. The Sheet Works had been located here by the Midland Railway, at a point which was said to be at the centre of the Midland system, as early as 1848. The sheets for wagons and road vehicles were made from grey canvas of English or Scottish weaving. Several of the 36 or 42 inch wide strips were sewn together to make up the required size, before they were automatically brushed with a waterproofing mixture, each side being treated to three coats. Lettering and numbering were painted on, together with the date of issue, and a post-date to indicate when the sheet was to be examined and re-conditioned if necessary. This latter mark was painted in red. Manilla cords were then tied to the prepared and reinforced holes, 16 in all, before the finished sheet was sprinkled with sand or sawdust, or treated with soapstone, to prevent sticking in transit. In the early years of the LMS, wagon sheets were dark grey or black, whilst those for road vehicles were finished with Brunswick Green dressing. The Sheet Works had space to hang more than 2,500 sheets, and there was a regular workload of reconditioning and new sheets, as the normal lifespan of a wagon sheet was no more than five years. In this view, taken on 24th October 1933 in the sheet sewing room, the strips of canvas are being hemmed prior to being sewn together to form the larger sheets.

National Railway Museum

Plate 49   The No. 1 Sheet Examining Berth at Trent, where men are preparing to hoist a sheet for examination and such repair as may be necessary. In addition to Trent, there were other Sheeting Factories located at St. Helens Junction, Manchester (Osborne Street) and Glasgow, with a total workforce of more than 500.

National Railway Museum

Sack Department

Plate 50 Trent Junction was also the home of the LMS Sack Depot, and here staff were employed on cleaning and repairing the Company's stock of grain sacks which, in 1947, exceeded 1½ million. Sacks were hired to brewers, farmers and others to enable them to despatch quantities of grain which did not justify, or require, the special bulk grain vans owned by the Company. Cleaning was done by fan suction after which they were examined and repaired as necessary. June 1925 in the Sack Repairing Room at Trent.

National Railway Museum

Clothing Factory

Plate 51 A hive of acitivity in the Machine Room of the Company's Clothing factory situated at Osborne Street, Manchester in February 1934. Up-to-date machinery and methods enabled this factory to produce approximately one third of the total uniform clothing supplied free to the Company's staff.

National Railway Museum

Concrete Depot

Plate 52 The LMS Concrete Depot at Newton Heath in September 1941, with some of the mould materials in the foreground and a concrete beam about to be lifted. In the mid-1930s, the Company had developed the use of pre-case concrete for a variety of purposes. In 1938 they decided to concentrate production from a number of centres at one depot located at Newton Heath, in order to be able to co-ordinate and control the production of standard units and increase its use for renewal of bridges etc. A works employing around 150 men was under the control of the Resident Engineer for Newton Heath Depot, and a standard range of articles, including fencing and other posts, track bins, flags, copings, air raid shelters, cycle shelters etc., were amongst approximately fifty items being produced. The shortage of essential materials and growing restrictions imposed by the war, hastened the development and use of pre-cast concrete as a major structural material, and parts for locomotive shed roofs as well as pre-cast concrete sleepers were added to the range of products from the LMS Concrete Works.

National Railway Museum

Electric Power Stations

These will be recognised more easily as a necessary part of the railway scene, as producers of power to the electrified sections of the network. In 1923 there were five Generating Stations supplying current for traction purposes, producing no less than 105 million units of electricity in that year. By 1930 two of these had been closed, at Heysham and at Swadlincote, but unit production exceeded 136 million for that year. The Company also owned, in 1923, a further 43 Generating Stations, with an output of 31 million units, but by 1930 the number had been reduced to 22 stations and output down to 21 million units. The largest single station was that at Stonebridge Park which supplied current for the electrified lines out of London Euston to Watford. A number of features determined the siting of this Generating Station in 1914/1915; it was close to the load centre of the Euston to Watford line, had easy access for coal supplies, and it was close to a series of artesian wells which drew water from a depth of around 500 ft. from supplies which permeated beneath the dense clay deposits on which London stands. Stonebridge Park produced nearly 79 million units of electricity in 1930, at 11,000 volts output, and one of the first concrete cooling towers - now familiar enough on the skyline - in the country, was constructed at this station. In addition there were eight wooden cooling towers with the whole of the station standing alongside a lake of water for cooling purposes. To meet the coal supply requirements, the Company purchased 30 large bogie hopper wagons, each with a capacity of 40 tons, for carrying coal from the East Midlands coalfield to Stonebridge Park.

Plate 53 Two of the generators at the Swadlincote Power Station which supplied current for the Burton & Ashby Light Railway tramway system in South Derbyshire. This station closed in February 1927, when the trams ceased operation.

National Railway Museum

Plate 54 A later day photograph of the Stonebridge Park Power Station resplendent in the wartime camouflage markings which were intended to disguise the appearance of the buildings and make them less vulnerable to airborne attack. The signal cabin is Stonebridge Power House box.

British Railways

Company Gas Works

GAS WORKS OWNED BY THE COMPANY AT CREWE AND WOLVERTON

It will perhaps surprise many readers to learn that the LMS were the owners and operators of quite large gas works which supplied the townships at Wolverton and Crewe, as well as the Company's own works at these places. These two towns were little more than villages or hamlets before the railway came to them, and the railway works, both of which were a part of the L&NWR, were responsible for providing work for the local population and for those who migrated to these towns in search of work with the railway. Large numbers of tied cottages were built and with no other local forms of power, the L&NWR built gas producing works to supply local needs as well as the works. These works came into LMS ownership along with the rest of the railway scene in 1923, and again it may be a surprise to learn that there were more than 12,000 private consumers at Crewe and over 2,750 at Wolverton. Annual output of gas at Wolverton was 86 million cubic feet, whilst Crewe produced more than three times this quantity, around 266 million cubic feet. Prepayment meters were installed in the majority of homes and a team of collectors had the task of emptying these, using two wheel handcarts to carry the heavy loads of coin which resulted.

The two gas works consumed more than 23,000 tons of coal each year, and this in turn produced not only the gas, but more than 16,000 tons of coke which the Company could use in the locomotive works and distribute to stations and depots. Other by-products included 22,000 gallons of tar, quantities of ammonia, sulphur, carbon and crude benzole, and even the ashes and clinker were sold.

The LMS re-organised Crewe Works in 1923 and installed up-to-date gas producing equipment and mechanical handling plant, and with all gas installations, there was a chemical laboratory to carry out the essential tests to determine the quality of the gas and by-products. In the town itself was a cash office and showroom from which consumers could order the latest gas appliances available. At Wolverton the works were rebuilt and extended in 1928, to cater for the increased demand.

Both gas works were absorbed into the Gas Corporation.

Plate 55 The Retort House gallery at Wolverton Gas Works with t mechanical coal handling plant at the end of the track.
National Railway Museu

Plate 56 The Gas Control Room at Wolverton Gas Works showing t pumps and valves used to control the supply to the eleven miles of ma pipes serving the town and small villages close to the town.
National Railway Museu

Plate 57   A general view of the pressure vessels and timbers being withdrawn after treatment, taken at Beeston in October 1929.

National Railway Museum

There were several creosote depots which supplied sleepers, crossing timbers, telegraph poles and various other timbers. More than a million sleepers were required for track renewal purposes each year as part of the regular care and maintenance procedures, and around 150 employees staffed the various depots. At the Beeston Creosote Works on the outskirts of Nottingham, new plant was installed giving more efficient and economical operation towards producing more than 365,000 new sleepers per year. The timbers were pickled in creosote in pressure cylinders, which ensured the heart of each timber was impregnated right through. The largest single item consumed by the plant was 1 million gallons of creosote per year.

◀ *Plate 58*   Machines were installed for automatic boring of sleepers.

National Railway Museum

◀ *Plate 59*   After treatment, the sleepers were returned to the workshops to allow the chairs to be machine screwed, as depicted in this view.

National Railway Museum

Permanent Way Activities

Plate 60   Another general view of Beeston yard with vast quantities of sleepers around. The small trucks to the left are the ones used for stacking the sleepers on to be drawn through the pressure vessels for impregnation.

National Railway Museum

Plate 61   The finished chaired sleepers being used in this extension to the locomotive yard at Wellingborough in 1930. The rail-built buffer stops do not bear any evidence to suggest that the method used by the Midland Railway to anchor this type of stop has been used. The Midland method was a complete track section to be placed beneath the running track and the buffer stop frame was bolted to both track sections.

National Railway Museum

Civil Engineers Work

Plate 62 Another major structural operation was the widening of the lines south of Ambergate Station on the former North Midland route from Derby. This required the excavation of the old tunnel through rock formation. The enormity of the task can be seen in this view of the excavations looking south, the old tunnel lining having been uncovered as the stone was outcropped. The parabolic shape of the brick lining was stronger than a circular construction, and one should perhaps add that the workmanship uncovered here was a credit to those early craftsmen — remember the lining was put in from the inside!

G. Fox Collection

Winter Experiments

Plate 63 A scene during the snowfalls of 1947 along the Ashbourne to Buxton line. A jet engine has been mounted on a four wheel wagon and tests were carried out to determine the suitability of the jet engine for snow clearance. In many parts of the system heavy snowfalls were commonplace, particularly in the more remote parts of Scotland, and apart from causing severe damage to ground equipment and lineside posts, the Company was always concerned with movement of trains in these conditions. The sheer volume of snow, in drifts, demanded very high resources of power from the conventional snowploughs, and with the wartime development of the jet engine came a source of blast power from the exhaust which could blow the snow from the line.

G. Fox Collection

Morning 'Brolly' Turn

Plate 65 (below) 'All Change', and literally so for many. Here LMS staff have had another bumper day on emptying a train – is yours amongst them?

Author's Collection

Plate 64 (above) Ratcatchers were employed by the Company in an effort to reduce the menace of the rodent, and were located at various points throughout the Company. They were called in to assist Station Masters and Goods Agents where serious infestation occurred, and could not be handled on a local basis. Stations and depots were supplied with poisons and cages, and staff were encouraged to keep cats, but in areas where goods and foodstuffs were stored, special precautions were necessary. A great amount of damage was done to merchandise and also to property, caused by the burrowing and gnawing of the rodent, and in addition to the official courses of action, some employees enjoyed using ferrets and dogs for sport with rats as a means of keeping the pest down. It must be said, however, that the Company's goods premises were often old, and once the vermin were established it was as much as could be done to control them without any real hope of completely eradicating them. The rat was a national problem, and the Ministry of Agriculture and Fisheries regularly drew attention to the need to control the pest, and one week per year was declared 'National Rat Week', as a means of intensifying the fight to destroy the menace of the rat. This plate displays the equipment used by the Crewe Ratcatchers, and a measure of their success.

British Railways

Ratcatchers Department

Locomotive Naming Ceremony

Naming ceremonies were considered to be special occasions, and this was another aspect of the railway scene which the LMS considered had useful advertising potential. At first, the LMS selected names for locomotives including those carrying regimental names in the first series of 'Royal Scots'. Later, however, when some of the old locomotive names carried by the 'Scots' were being replaced, the Company approached the regiments for permission to use the title, although in many cases the regiments had asked to be honoured by having a locomotive carry their name. The naming of some of the 'Coronation' Class Pacifics with city names was performed at special ceremonies in the cities so honoured, although not all achieved this distinction with Lord Mayor and civic dignatories in attendance. Nameplates were cast by the LMS workshops, but regimental shields and plates were made by specialist outside firms, and in the case of the plates fitted to No. 6170 *British Legion*,

they were made in a period of 12 days by Firmin & Sons Ltd., in Birmingham. The correspondence relating to *British Legion* states that the tight time allowance meant that overtime would have to be permitted if the plates were to be ready in time, and an additional charge for overtime would have to be made beyond the quoted price of £9. 12s. 6d. each plate. They were ready on time and the final cost to the LMS was £30 for the two plates.

The naming ceremony of No. 5504 *Royal Signals* took place at Euston Station on Saturday, 10th April 1937, with a full military programme.

The Regular Army Division of the Signals Regiment were present together with the regimental band and territorial and cadet units from the London area. Since very few naming ceremonies have been included in published material, the detailed arrangements for No. 5504 are reproduced here.

L.M.S. LOCOMOTIVE No. 5504 "ROYAL SIGNALS"
****

MILITARY PROGRAMME FOR NAMING CEREMONY

AT

EUSTON, SATURDAY, 10th APRIL, 1937.
==================================

1.0 p.m.	Troops forming the Guard of London Corps Signals, T.A. and S.R. arrive at Fulham House.
1.30 p.m.	Guard falls in, sizes and embusses.
2.15 p.m.	Guard debusses at Euston War Memorial. Band debusses at Euston War Memorial. Representative detachments arrive under their own unit arrangements at Euston Station and report to R.S.M. Evelyn, London Corps Signals, on No. 1 Platform.
2.30 p.m.	Guard and Band form up in line at the Euston War Memorial facing west. Guard Commander inspects the parade.
2.40 p.m.	Guard (with band playing) marches in column of fours to Platform No. 1, Euston Station.
2.45 p.m.	Guard forms line opposite and parallel to the engine and opens order.
	The Band takes up a position facing inward on the right flank of the Guard.
	Representative parties from other units fall in in single rank behind the Guard and on the left flank of the Guard facing inwards.
	The parade dresses, stands at ease and stands easy under the orders of the Commander of the Guard.
2.55 p.m.	The Colonel Commandant of the Corps, and the representative of the L.M.S. Railway and the principal guests arrive on No. 1 Platform.
	The Guard Commander calls the whole parade to attention and gives the following commands –
	"Guard, Slope Arms". "General Salute, Present Arms".
	The band plays a General Salute.
	The Guard Commander gives the order to slope arms.
3.0 p.m.	The Colonel Commandant, accompanied by the representative of the L.M.S. Railway, the Officer Commanding, The London Corps Signals, the Adjutant of The London Corps Signals, and the Guard Commander, inspects the Guard.
	The Colonel Commandant and the L.M.S. representative mount the special platform near the name plate.
	The Guard Commander Orders the Guard to Order arms and the whole parade to stand easy. The principal guests form up on either side of the dais.
	The representative of the L.M.S. Railway welcomes the Royal Corps of Signals.

The Colonel Commandant replies.

The representative of the L.M.S. Railway formally invites the Colonel Commandant to unveil and christen the locomotive.

The Guard Commander calls the whole parade to attention and orders the Guard to slope arms.

The Colonel Commandant draws the curtains and says "I christen this engine, "Royal Signals"."

The band plays the march of the Royal Corps of Signals.

The Guard Commander orders the Guard to order arms and the whole parade to stand easy.

The principal guests inspect the engine.

The R.S.M. of The London Corps Signals marches the right guide of the Guard to a selected point on the road beside No. 1 Platform.

The Guard Commander calls the Guard and band to attention, gives the order to slope arms and move to the right in fours.

The Bandmaster orders the band to countermarch and halts facing the opposite direction.

The Guard Commander gives the order to quick march and Guard with band leading moving off down the platform to form up on the right marker in column of fours facing south. (Band does not play).

At the same time representative detachments about turn under orders of detchment commanders and form line on the edge of the road facing away from the engine, opening out to leave a space opposite the central splasher of the engine for the Colonel Commandant to take the salute.

The Guard marches past in fours, the band playing the Corps march.

The Guard falls out at Euston Square. Rifles are placed in the bus and any man wishing to do so may return to inspect the engine. (A guard must be left over the rifles).

DRESS.

Officers –	Service Dress with swords but not medals
Guard –	Service Dress – Review Order.
Band –	Full Dress
Representative Detachments –	Service Dress – Review Order without arms.

Plate 66   The general scene at Euston with a bank of floodlights lashed overhead.

Plate 67   The Colonel Commandant of the Royal Corps of Signals performing the christening ceremony.

Plate 68 After the ceremony, the Colonel Commandant poses with the footplate staff, Mr. W. A. Stanier and other military attendants.

M. Brooks Collection

Plate 69 A close up of a regimental crest of the Rifle Brigade, a carried by No. 6146 *The Rifle Brigade*. These were cast in gunmetal b outside specialists and incorporated the true details of the batt honours of the regiment.

M. Brooks Collectio

Plate 70 The naming of the last conver tional 'Royal Scot' class locomotive, No 6169 *The Boy Scout*. The ceremony wa carried out by the Chief Scout who seen alongside Sir Josiah Stamp an senior scout officials.

M. Brooks Collectio

Barrows and Trolleys

Each of the constituent companies had its own types of barrow and trolley for use at passenger and goods stations, although some were also used in the various workshops. It must be admitted that in some cases, company variations were minimal and to most travellers a two-wheel barrow was just that, give or take the odd few inches difference. The Midland and L&NWR each had large numbers of many different types, and the smaller companies either bought from them or from one of the private manufacturers such as Slingsbys or Tubewrights Ltd. Many of the pre-group types were perpetuated by the LMS until certain types were classed as LMS standardised designs. Even then, these standard types were open to individual interpretation, particularly in the case of the two-wheel large heavy barrow of Midland design, some of which were built at St. Rollox for use in Scotland. The old Caledonian end ironwork of their two-wheel barrow, which was not dissimilar to the Midland heavy barrow, was inclined at about 120° outwards from the flat, and when St. Rollox interpreted the LMS standard design drawing, it preferred the inclined ironwork of Caley pattern to the vertical LMS pattern. There were other examples. In addition to the standard types of barrow and trolley for platform use, there was an interesting array of special types to suit individual requirements, and some of these follow. Sack trucks and wheelbarrows also come into this category, and again there was a multitude of sizes and types. By 1923 brakes of one type or another had been fitted to the majority of 4-wheel trolleys and some of the heavy barrows, particularly where they were used up and down platform ramps. Basic construction was of wood with metal cornerplates and other fittings. A new design of trolley was developed in the early 1930s, employing an all-steel framework with wooden decking, and rubber tyres on cast wheels. With normal usage it is not surprising that there are still many pre-group and LMS barrows and trolleys in use today. Buffet trolleys for serving snacks and drinks from the platform were used at the principal stations and most of these originated from the constituent companies. The early 1930s saw some new buffet trolleys introduced to the key stations, such as Euston and Lime Street, and these had white or cream bodies with large pneumatic bi-cycle wheels, rather like the ice-cream pedal bicycles. Automation came to trolleys with the introduction of a 4-wheel electric truck in the late 1930s from Harbilt of Market Harborough, and the Lansing Bagnall 'Imp' mechanical tractor used in the early 1930s. The 'Imp' was a heavy duty petrol engined small unit which could easily pull a line of loaded trolleys about the station. The Harbilt battery unit was for similar use with the advantage of being much quieter. Livery was generally black for the motorised units with white lettering, although many of the sack trucks were finished in wagon grey with white lettering. Barrows and trolleys at most stations were finished in crimson lake, and buffet barrows were varnished wood finished. Allocation of these items was in accordance with the following table:-

Stations at which number of staff handling traffic is	Number of 2-wheel barrows small, medium & large and 4-wheel trolleys, small or large
1 – 5 men	One truck in excess of the number of men
6 – 9 men	Two trucks in excess of the number of men
10 and over	1 plus 10 trucks per maximum number of men handling traffic

and at stations with a total barrow or trolley stock in excess of 20, the name of the station was painted on. The barrows and trolleys which follow are typical of the many types used by the LMS.

Plate 71   A wheelbarrow being assembled in the Crewe Barrow Shop from a stock of machined parts, in July 1936.

National Railway Museum

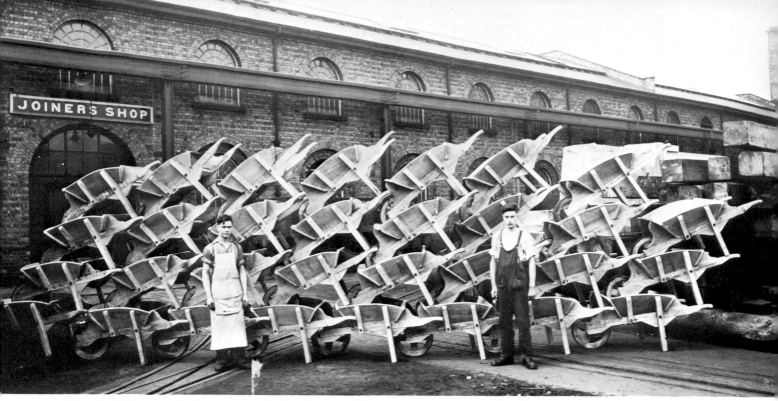

Plate 72 Thirty one wheelbarrows assembled by these two joiner apprentices in one working day. Before jig assembly and the machining of parts it would have taken almost 5½ hours for one barrow to be produced. Short production runs were obviously the order of the day, since even the LMS could not find a requirement for thirty one wheelbarrows a day for long.

National Railway Museum

Plate 73 Large numbers of this large barrow were built to a former L&NWR design. This example was one of the later modified types, having the axle retained on blocks instead of on a shaped side bar as was the earlier pattern, and riveted end ironwork instead of cast ironwork. Type No. 229.

Author's Collection

Plate 74 Sack truck, type 216, lettered for use by the Locomotive Department, Derby. This truck has been preserved by the Midland Railway Trust, Butterley.

Author's Collection

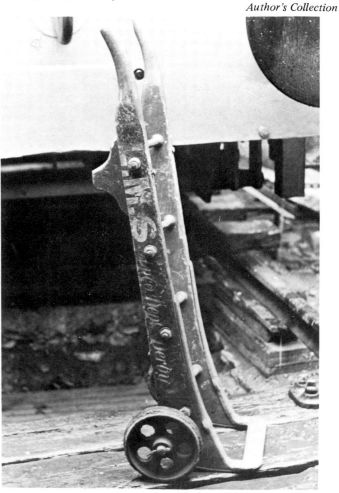

Plate 75 (above) A rather elegant rugs and pillow truck, type 212, built with panelled body and finished in coaching style. This example has also been preserved, in the Glasgow Museum of Transport. This one was to a Midland Railway design, although the L&NWR built similar trucks to slightly different measurements, as shown in the next illustration.

Author's Collection

Plate 76 (right) An example of the L&NWR design.

Author's Collection

Plate 77 This is a Street Orderlies cart or box cart of type 275, in this case being used for stable work. It will be noted that the end was hinged to enable the cart to be tipped or the load shovelled out.

National Railway Museum

Plate 78 A 4-wheel trolley, type 201, again a pure Midland trolley repainted in LMS livery. The handle did not last long and was soon replaced by the pattern shown in the next picture. Earlier examples had been fitted with disc wheels with either 5 or 6 holes and ribs on one side, but these were replaced by the spoked wheel, possibly because the spoked wheel would be lighter.

British Railways

Plate 79 Another type 201 trolley, but with a number of modifications to the basic design. The wheels were another type used for only a short period in the late 1930s, and the wheel irons were now made out of steel bar suitably twisted, instead of the earlier cast supports. There is a hinged tailboard which could be dropped onto the floor of a van and the roll-off flat with load transferred directly into or out of the van. The four chain fittings would allow the flat to be lifted by crane, or anchored once in position inside the vehicle.

British Railways

Lifting Appliances

The term 'lifting appliances' covers a wide range of items ranging from the breakdown cranes used at mishaps, to the small hand crane in the goods yard. It also includes wagon lifts, overhead cranes, jacks hoists and passenger lifts in hotels and at the LMS Headquarters at Euston House. On seeing a train of wagons loaded with merchandise of various shapes, sizes and weights, one seldom thinks of the means of loading the material for rail movement, and were it not for the availability of lifting appliances, a large proportion of the total volume of such traffic would not have been able to be moved by rail. The Chief Mechanical Engineer's Outdoor Machinery Department (ODM) was responsible for the provision and maintenance of all lifting appliances and it must be appreciated that whilst the larger cranes were steam operated, others were electrically or diesel powered, and there were many more which relied on nothing more than manual operation. One of the earliest forms of hoisting gear was a block and tackle, and the hand-operated crane was a natural development from this. More than 4,000 hand cranes of various types were in use in goods depots and at docksides and these were a satisfactory form of lifting appliance where the loads and traffic handled was limited. Manual or hydraulic operated luggage and goods lifts were located at many of the larger passenger and goods depots, although conversion to electric operation was carried out where demand justified the additional expense. Steam operated cranes were usually of the travelling type and the larger ones formed part of a breakdown train allocated to a locomotive shed for use in a prescribed area for breakdown work. The Engineer's Department were also users of these large cranes, and they would be brought into use where the erection or dismantling of permanent way materials, iron and steel-work was necessary.

Some 2,000 hydraulic lifting appliances were in use in goods depots and docks, ranging from the warehouse dock crane of 30 cwt capacity to a 50 ton hydraulic wharf crane. At Goole's West Dock, a 40 ton electrically operated crane was installed by the Company and used for automatic loading of coal onto ships, whilst in the Great Bridge goods yard at Wolverhampton the Company installed a 25 ton overhead crane with an electro-magnet attachment which speeded up the handling of scrap metals. Wagon lifts were installed at a number of the larger goods sheds to lift or lower wagons where the unloading and loading points were on a different level to the wagon reception sidings, and these lifts were located within the goods shed itself. In addition to the following photographs, there are a number of lifting appliances shown elsewhere in this volume, amongst the erecting shop subjects. Heavy overhead cranes were a regular feature in the erecting shop, with mechanical coal handling and ash disposal plants at motive power depots, and in some goods sheds.

Breakdown Cranes

Plate 80 The sheer bulk of this 40 ton steam crane built by Ransomes and Rapier in 1916 for the Midland Railway, is typified in this wartime picture of RS 1038/40. Although the jib is raised, the lifting capacity would be extremely limited, as the propping girders, which could be withdrawn from either side of the frames, were not extended. It will be noted however, that there are rail clamps at either end of the crane to give some additional stability. The crewman in the picture is wearing protective clothing against mustard gas attack.

British Railways

Plate 81 A Cowans 15 ton steam crane built in 1893 and allocated to the breakdown train at Wellingborough Depot. Cranes were kept in steam 24 hours a day and the breakdown train could be despatched from the depot just as soon as the gang, guard and locomotive were to hand, and it was a matter of honour that this should be in record time.

P. Tatlow Collection

Plate 82 The propping girders are seen extended in this staged scene during wartime on the Strathaven branch. This old Caledonian 'Dunalastair' 4-4-0 No. 14330 was used to demonstrate lifting and recovery techniques under gas attack.

P. Tatlow Collection

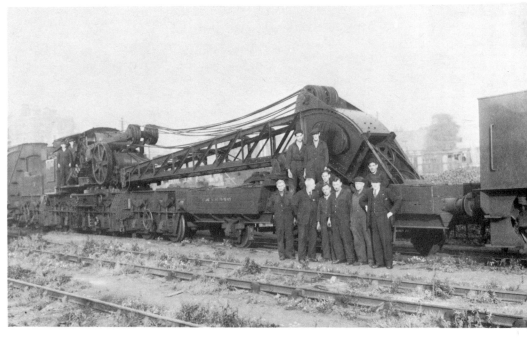

Plate 83 The Cravens 50 ton steam crane seen with the train crew at Willesden in 1945. This crane was originally built in 1931 as a 36 tonner and it was strengthened and up-rated to 50 tons just before the war and reallocated to Willesden from Newton Heath in 1939.

Real Photographs

Plate 84 A 36 ton breakdown crane demonstrating its lifting capabilities with propping girders extended.

British Railways

Plates 85 and *86*   Two old types of hand crane for goods yard use. The counterweight was positioned close to the king pin during travel in trains to even up the axle loads. Prior to lifting however, the counterweight would be moved to the outer end of the crane superstructure, where it more effectively balanced the load. The Furniture Container illustrates the point that these early cranes were unsuitable for this type of work.

British Railways

Plate 87 One of the new designs of hand operated cranes introduced in the mid-1930s by Cowans Sheldon of Carlisle. It had a capacity of 6½ tons and was eminently suitable for lifting road-rail containers, as shown in this illustration. Contrast this lifting appliance with the larger one in the background and note that this was not to lift more than 6 tons.

British Railways

Plate 88 One of a number of petrol electric cranes supplied by Walker Bros. of Wigan. It was capable of lifting a load of 6 tons with the jib in the position shown. The jib indicator marks the angles for the different weights above 3 tons. The markings indicate that this crane was used in Belfast.

A. G. Ellis

Plate 89 One of the dockside lifting slings which were capable of lifting quite heavy weights onto the decks of ships.

P. Tatlow Collection

THE LMS INVOLVEMENT WITH RAILWAY AIR SERVICES LTD.

The LMS Air Transport Act was passed by Parliament on 10th May, 1929, but almost five years elapsed before any active steps were taken to implement the powers granted to the Company. As with motor bus operations the LMS, and the other three main line companies, were alive to the possibility of competition from the developing private air network, and with shorter journey times possible by air, the competition could become a serious threat.

The main line companies were empowered to own and operate aircraft and to provide passenger and freight air services, in addition to organising and maintaining the full range of facilities required to support such an airline operation. The LMS along with the other companies and the then British Airways Ltd., merged to form a company under the title Railway Air Services Ltd., with the RAS Ltd. providing the aircraft and British Airways the flight and ground personnel and support services.

The Great Western Railway had already commenced its own flights in 1933, but these were brought into the RAS network, and other routes were determined by the railway 'zones' in the United Kingdom. The first LMS route was inaugurated on 20th August, 1934, between London and Belfast, with the London base at Croydon. At first the intermediate places served were Birmingham, Castle Bromwich, Manchester and Ronaldsway in the Isle of Man, but Belfast became an intermediate stop when the service was extended to Glasgow later in 1934. Additional intermediate calls were added later, first in 1935 Liverpool Speke Aerodrome, and in 1936 a request stop advertised for Stoke-on-Trent, calling at Meir Aerodrome on the outskirts of the city.

Passengers intending to use the Meir stop were required to give 24 hours notice of their intention when booking tickets, in order that the local representative who had been appointed the Railway Air Service Inspector could be advised the aircraft would call. One of the prizes at stake on this route was the GPO Royal Air Mail Contract and the LMS were successful in gaining this in 1934, lost for 1935, but regained from 1936 and retained thereafter.

Quite apart from RAS Ltd., the LMS and the Isle of Man Steam Packet Co. Ltd., subscribed additional capital to form the Manx Airway Section of Railway Air Services Ltd., and in April 1935, a new service was opened from Liverpool, via Squires Gate Airport, Blackpool, to the Isle of Man. Some two years later a re-arrangement of the Manx Airways led to a merger with the Blackpool and West Coast Air Services Ltd., and the reactivation of a company formed earlier as Isle of Man Air Services Ltd., and the LMS had a 1/3rd share in this undertaking. Other re-arrangements of interests took place which effectively brought the LMS a 50% share in two companies operating in Scotland, Scottish Airways Ltd., and Western Isles Airways Ltd. The four railway companies had been successful in their involvement with the developing air service network, inasmuch as through their controlling investment in RAS and the other companies, they operated more than 80% of the total United Kingdom internal air mileage.

The Railway Air interests were requisitioned for the war effort and all services were discontinued prior to the declaration of war. Services were allowed to recommence as the war progressed but it was not until late 1944 that civilian services were allowed over the London area. In 1947 the individual companies, including Railway Air Services Ltd., were merged into the newly formed British European Airways and the railway involvement ceased.

Tickets for the Railway Air Services were obtainable at any railway station and were fully interchangeable for all or part of each journey with rail services. Luggage could be sent in advance by any of the air routes, more costly than by rail service, and the holders of railway season tickets or bulk travel vouchers were allowed discounts on journeys by air.

The aircraft used were all supplied by the De-Havilland Aircraft Company of Hatfield, and as traffic increased additional aircraft were added to the fleet. Specifically allocated to the LMS services within the RAS were three D.H. 86 four-engine planes, each able to carry 10 passengers and a quantity of mail or luggage, along with an aircrew of one pilot and a first officer. It is interesting to note that these planes, known as the 'Dragon', were built from wood with a 3-ply wood panelling forming the fuselage. One D.H.89 was also allocated to the LMS by 1937.

Whilst the LMS was concerned with the competition it could face from air transport operators, and this led it into the air transport operation, the limited capacity available on each route, even with two services in each direction each day between London, Belfast and Glasgow, could hardly have been considered a major threat to the rail services. Nevertheless, the LMS took a leading part in the development of internal air services prior to the 1939 war, and a great deal of prestige was associated with their air transport involvement upon which it would be difficult to place a price.

FLY TO SAVE TIME.

AIR SERVICES are operated by RAILWAY AIR SERVICES LTD. on behalf of the LONDON MIDLAND AND SCOTTISH RAILWAY COMPANY between :

LONDON
BIRMINGHAM
STOKE-ON-TRENT
MANCHESTER
LIVERPOOL
BELFAST
GLASGOW

and on behalf of the LMS and ISLE OF MAN STEAM PACKET COMPANIES between :

MANCHESTER
LIVERPOOL
BLACKPOOL
ISLE OF MAN

"THE MANX AIRWAY."

The following are the Flying times between the places shown (aerodrome to aerodrome) in minutes :

	London	Birmingham	Stoke-on-Trent	Manchester	Liverpool	Blackpool	Isle of Man	Belfast	Glasgow
	Min.	Min.	Min.	Min.	Min.	Min.	Min.	Min.	Min.
LONDON (Croydon)	—	50	70	125	90	135	190	185	250
BIRMINGHAM (Castle Brom.)	50	—	15	70	35	80	135	130	195
STOKE-ON-TRENT (Meir)	70	15	—	50	15	60	115	110	175
MANCHESTER (Barton)	120	65	45	—	15	15	105	105	170
LIVERPOOL (Speke)	90	35	15	15	—	20	40	80	145
BLACKPOOL (Squires Gate)	—	—	—	15	15	—	35	90	160
ISLE OF MAN (Ronaldsway)	210	155	135	60	40	35	—	40	110
BELFAST (Aldergrove)	185	130	110	105	80	90	40	—	55
GLASGOW (Renfrew)	250	195	175	170	145	160	110	55	—

The Service will call at Birmingham (Castle Bromwich) and Stoke-on-Trent (Meir Aerodrome) for the conveyance of passengers to and from London, Belfast and Glasgow to Blackpool and the Isle of Man on 24 hours notice being given to any R.A.S. Booking Office.
Time tables subject to alterations and additions.
Full information respecting the conveyance of passengers and freight available at any undermentioned Office, where tickets can be obtained and seat reservations effected.

LONDON.
Euston House, Seymour Street, N.W.1
(Telephone : Museum 2900, Extn. 640).
Airway Terminus, Victoria Station, S.W.1.
(Telephone : Victoria 2211).
BIRMINGHAM.
New Street Station. (Telephone : Midland 2740.)
Snow Hill Station. (Telephone : Central 7944).
STOKE-ON-TRENT.
Stoke-on-Trent Station.
(Telephone : Hanley 4121).
MANCHESTER.
L.M.S. Office, 47, Piccadilly.
(Telephone : Central 0384).
Barton Airport. (Telephone : Eccles 1392).
BELFAST.
York Road Station. (Telephone : 44211).
11, Donegall Place. (Telephone : 44211).

BLACKPOOL.
Central Station. (Telephone : Blackpool 1243).
Squires Gate Aerodrome.
(Telephone : South Shore 41849).
ISLE OF MAN.
Isle of Man Steam Packet Co., Imperial Buildings,
Douglas. (Telephone : Douglas 1101).
L.M.S. Office, 7, Parade Street, Douglas.
(Telephone : Douglas 567).
L.M.S. and Isle of Man Steam Packet Companies,
Joint Office, Ronaldsway.
(Telephone : Castletown 120).
LIVERPOOL.
Lime Street Station.
(Telephone : Royal 2960, Extn. 61).
48, Castle Street. (Telephone : Bank 991).
11, James Street. (Telephone : Bank 8640).
GLASGOW.
Central Station. (Telephone : Douglas 2900).

Also at Imperial Airways, Airways House, Charles Street, Lower Regent Street, London, W.1,
(Telephone : Victoria 2211) ; and at Imperial Airways, Air Port of London, Croydon (Telephone : Croydon 4422) ; and at the principal travel agencies.
Any Railway Station or Town Office will also arrange for reservations to be effected and for tickets to be obtained if reasonable notice is given.

McCorquodale & Co. Ltd., Printers, London and Newton.

Plate 90 The LMS services with journey times as shown.
Author's Collection

EMERGENCY LANDINGS (Instructions to the Pilot)

Should it be necessary for the pilot to make an emergency landing at any point he will telephone, on landing, the nearest station. On receipt of the pilot's message, the station master is at once to make arrangements for one or more motor cars to proceed to the landing ground and take the passengers to the nearest railway station, giving the best connecting service to their destination, afterwards notifying the chief commercial manager and district passenger manager by wire. Passengers air tickets should be collected and ordinary first class single railway tickets issued free of charge to destination in exchange. The rail ticket must be accounted for in the usual way and the air tickets surrendered should be dealt with as warrants and sent to the chief accountant's department (audit section) in the usual way.

An account should be obtained from the motor car proprietors for the conveyance of the passengers, and this should be sent to the district passenger manager.

No charges should be collected from the passengers in these circumstances.

Plate 91   G-ACVY *Mercury* in flight, one of the four-engined D.H. 86B ten seat aircraft, somewhere over LMS territory.

British Railways

Plate 92 (right)   The Railway Air Services Ltd., pocket timetable for 1935, showing the routes it operated within the United Kingdom on behalf of the LMS and the other railway companies.

Author's Collection

RAILWAY AIR SERVICES LTD.
(and connecting services)

DIAGRAM OF ROUTES

The numbers correspond with the number of the time-table contained in this folder.

RAILWAY AIR SERVICES

GENERAL TIME TABLE

RAS

Plate 93 One of the early twin-engined D.H. 'Dragon Six', G-APCX at Croydon Airport in south London.

British Aerospace

Plate 94 One of the four-engined D.H.86B 'Dragon' express aircraft used on LMS services on the tarmac at Croydon.

British Railways

Plate 95 Speke Airport, Liverpool, with the aircraft in wartime camouflage livery, and windows blacked out. Note the military corporal checking the passengers onto the plane.

British Rail

Holidays on the LMS

In the spring of 1934, the LMS decided to get in on the camping scene, and 42 bogie corridor carriages were converted to provide accommodation which included three bedrooms, each with two berths, a living room, kitchen and bathroom. They were located in sidings in some of the beauty spots, including various points in Wales, in the Peak District of Derbyshire, on the Yorkshire Moors and in the Lake District. The camping holiday was increasing in popularity and the LMS venture was to create more holiday traffic to and from the locations of these carriages which were styled LMS Caravans. One of the conditions when booking was that four full summer fares must be taken, in addition to the rental, which in the first year was £3 per week with an extra 10/- (50p today) for bookings in July, August and September.

In the 1934 season, these 42 caravans proved popular with each one averaging ten weeks bookings. A further 28 caravans were added for the 1935 season and out of the total available, 30 were placed in Scotland and 8 in Ireland. To popularise the LMS Caravan after refurbishing for the 1935 season, many were placed on view at various stations throughout the system, the theme being 'A Novel Holiday'. For the 1936 season still more caravans were fitted out to bring the total up to 150, and bookings continued to rise as the popularity of this type of holiday increased. During 1937 many caravans were located at suitable sites in the London suburbs to provide accommodation for those travelling to the Coronation of King George VI and Queen Elizabeth, which was held early in May. Thereafter, the vehicles were returned to holiday locations. Popularity of these caravans continued up to the outbreak of war. The 1939 season saw a change of title for these holiday homes, and they were advertised as 'Camping Coach' holidays. Soon after the war had finished they were again made available for holiday use, and many of the pre-grouping carriages converted by the LMS continued to be used in the same manner by British Railways.

Caravans and Camping Coaches

Plate 96 Resplendent in fully lined out livery is this former L&NWR arc roof corridor third.

National Railway Museum

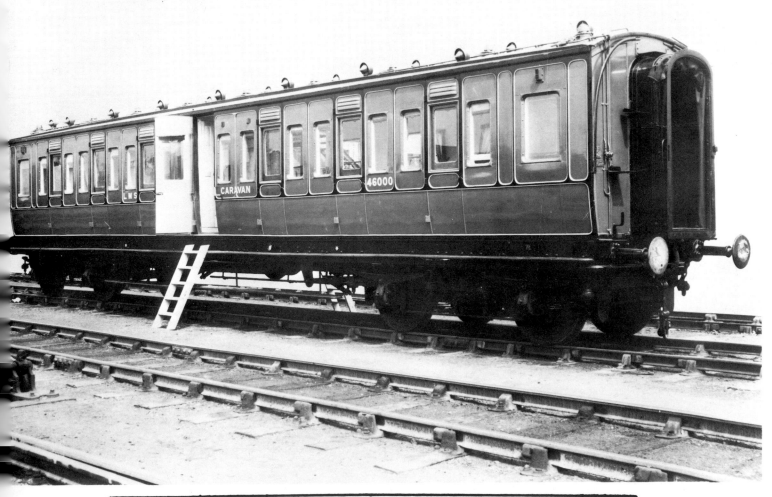

Plate 97 (above) New mattresses and crockery being added to the caravan inventory of this former Midland clerestory carriage, in Derby Works.

British Railways

Hotels

Plate 98 (left)   Holidays on the LMS could also be meant to include holidays LMS hotels, and the chain of hotels stretched throughout the country, mak the Company the largest hotel operators in Europe. There were 40 establishme in 1923 and whilst some were closed, others were opened, the most notable be the Gleneagles Hotel in Perthshire. Modernisation schemes were carried out several and at Leeds a completely new hotel was built during 1935/7 to rep! an earlier and outdated structure. By 1939 there were 28 hotels open and m; were requisitioned by the government for wartime purposes.

An interesting feature is that the broadcaster, Henry Hall, was Director of M for LMS hotels and the conductor of the dance orchestra at Gleneagles Ho and he later left the LMS to take up a position with the BBC. In addition hotels, the Company owned three golf courses and was co-owner, with Tho Cook & Sons Limited, of the holiday camp at Prestatyn in North Wales. Un the control of a Chief Hotels Superintendent, other establishments associa with the hotel trade included laundry operations, catering for the hotels and dining and sleeping cars, restaurants and even the responsibility for a pig farn Willesden. With so large an operation, and much of the preparation for dining services done in the London area, there were considerable quantities of w; food, vegetable peelings etc., to be disposed of daily, and what better way doing so than feeding a herd of pigs. Chickens were also kept at Willesden, ; from this enterprise a fair proportion of the pig meat requirements and chick and eggs were used in the Company's hotel business. A great deal of advertis exposure in timetables, on stations and in the Company's Holiday Guides taken by the hotel business and as all but one (Welcombe Hotel, Stratford-up Avon) of the establishments were close to a railway station, the convenie factor was great. This picture of the Entrance Lobby of Gleneagles Hotel shows part of the surrounding countryside and the famous golf course.

Author's Collect

Canals

One of the less well known activities of the LMS was its role as a canal owner and operator, and there were 13 lengths of waterway with a total mileage of 542. Canal haulage was a relatively cheap form of transportation which had played an important role in the industrial development of this country, and it is not surprising that the canals owned by the Company, all of which had been inherited from the constituent companies in 1923, were all in the industrial centres of the Midlands and North West, and Scotland.

The Company's canals were:-

England & Wales	Miles	Chains
Ashby	29	75
Coalport	1	17
Cromford	16	79
Huddersfield	23	49
Lancaster	73	47
Manchester, Bolton & Bury	15	76
Shropshire Union (bought 1923)	194	3
St. Helens	16	33
Trent & Mersey	117	28
Ulverston	1	28
Kensington (LMS 1/3rd share)		11
Sub Total =	490	46

Scotland		
Forth & Clyde	38	74
Monkland (closed 1934)	13	20
Grand Total =	542	60

The total tonnage conveyed in 1923 was 14,594,377, and in 1938 this had dropped to 12,951,746, but little over 1 million tons per annum actually originated on the LMS canals. The canal activities ran at a loss, the tolls received going nowhere near covering the expenses involved. The principal traffic was heavy goods, with coal, timber, various ores, iron, steel, earthenware, pottery and carpets being carried. Private craft including pleasure boats were permitted to use the waterways on payment of the tolls for each stretch, and whilst the accompanying pictures clearly evidence the LMS as a boat owner, the author has failed to discover just how many craft were owned by the Company.

CARTAGE

The LMS can cart your goods in town or rural areas cheaply and efficiently.

Ask the LMS Agent for particulars.

Plate 99   The canal basin at Albion with LMS boat No. 62.
Author's Collection

Plate 101 (above) Carpets for export are being loaded onto an LMS barge at the Kidderminster basin for a canal journey to Wolverhampton whereupon the consignment would be transferred to rail to continue it journey to the docks. The LMS Boatage Depot is in the background.
Author's Collection

Plate 100 (above) The canal alongside rail connection at St. Helens.
Author's Collection

Plate 102 (left) The Anderton Ca Lift which links the LMS Trent Mersey Canal and the River Weaver, opened in 1876 and could lower b from the canal level 50 feet above river in only 5 minutes. Although ow by the River Weaver Trust, the lift of great importance to the traffic u the LMS Canal.

British Railw

Plate 103 TSS Slieve Bawn, one of the cargo only vessels, leaving Holyhead for the Dublin North Wall Quay. This vessel, built by Wm. Denny Bros. in 1937 for the LMS, was withdrawn in the 1970s.
British Railways

LMS Steamer Services

Three important cross-channel routes across the Irish Sea, passenger services on the Clyde, a ferry service across the Thames estuary and summer services on several lakes and lochs, coupled with cargo services from Goole to a number of continental ports, gave the LMS a not inconsiderable share of sea traffic.

With a fleet in the mid-1930s of 65 ships having a gross tonnage exceeding 65,000, including several jointly owned vessels, the LMS house flag was a familiar sight in and around the shores of the British Isles. The house flag was a white cross on a red flag, with the LMS crest in the centre, and was flown on all vessels owned by the Company.

The pre-grouping companies and their forerunners had been operating the sea routes for a considerable period and there was competition on some of the routes, particularly the City of Dublin Steam Packet Company, but also between the Midland and the L&YR and LNWR joint services. One of the routes out of Fleetwood was discontinued and the LMS Irish services concentrated on three main routes, Holyhead to Kingston (for Dublin), Heysham to Belfast, and the short sea route between Stranraer and Larne.

Passenger services on the Clyde were an institution, being the longest established of all the services taken over by the LMS, and the river is reputed to have had by far the best steamer services in Britain. With the 1923 grouping, the Caledonian Steam Packet Company also became a part of the LMSR. Another Scottish operator, David MacBrayne Ltd., was acquired jointly with Coast Lines Ltd. in 1928 but continued to operate under the MacBrayne title, and a further acquisition was made in 1935 when Williamson-Buchanan became part of the LMS fleet.

The ferry service across the Thames Estuary between Tilbury and Gravesend was taken over from the London, Tilbury & Southend Railway who had been operators since 1862, although they are recorded also as having opened the service in 1850. Four steamers were taken over by the LMS for this very short service and two further ships were added in 1924 and 1927. Sailings were timed to connect with train services on the Tilbury line.

The inland steamer services were operated on the English lakes of Windermere and Coniston, and north of the border on Loch Awe and Loch Tay. Those on Windermere are perhaps more well known than the others, and the route is still operated today by two vessels built for the LMS, *TSMV Teal II* and *TSMV Swan II*. The Loch Awe steamers connected with LMS motor buses running from Oban at Ford Pier, which in turn connected with rail services at Oban, and the steamer

sailings of David MacBrayne Limited to Mull and other islands.

Cargo was of course carried on the Irish routes, but the principal cargo services were those acquired from the L&YR in the form of The Goole Steam Shipping Company, operating out of Goole Docks which are some 40 miles inland on the River Ouse. Regular services were operated from Goole to Copenhagen, Amsterdam, Rotterdam, Hamburg, Ghent, Antwerp and Dunkerque, and they also had operating agreements with Angleterre-Lorraine-Alsace S.A. de Navigation for a service between Tilbury and Dunkerque, and jointly with the LNER on the Hull-Zeebrugge service.

The Goole services were operated by the LMS until May 1935 when an arrangement was entered into to amalgamate with those of other Humber steamship companies, and from that date the services were operated by the Associated Humber Lines on behalf of the individual companies concerned.

There were still more vessels in the LMS fleet, but all were of a specialized nature and carried neither passengers nor cargo. Dredgers, hoppers and sundry craft were operated out of Garston Docks on the Mersey, and there was even one craft, *Garstonia*, a bucket dredger, which was a stationary steamcraft. The LMS also owned well-equipped docks and harbours, and although they do not naturally fall within the heading of this section, the Company's steamer services operated from them, and therefore they command inclusion. On the West Coast the docks owned by the Company were those at Holyhead, Garston, Fleetwood and Wyre Dock, Heysham, Barrow-in-Furness, Stranraer, Ayr, Troon and Bowling. Poplar Docks London, Grangemouth and South Alloa were owned on the East Coast, and in addition the LMS also owned up-to-date shipping and coaling appliances at Goole, Maryport, Swansea and at the General Terminus Quay at Glasgow. A very detailed account of the LMS Shipping fleet has been prepared by John Hinchliffe and is included in the *LMS Society Teach-In Notes, Volume 1*. This gives a ship-by-ship account of all the Company's vessels and is excellent additional information.

For the benefit of intending customers, the Company published an LMS Map of Europe showing the steamer services in and around the British Isles and linking the continent, together with a gazetteer of principal continental towns with the names of the main agents for merchandise traffic, as well as a list of agents in the principal continental towns who sold LMS railway tickets and steamship reservations.

Plate 104 The *TrSS Duchess of Hamilton*, one of the Clyde steamers built in 1932.

J. Edgington

Plate 105 The front of a pocket timetable detailing the principal train services linking with the steamer services to Ireland.

Author's Collection

Freight Handling

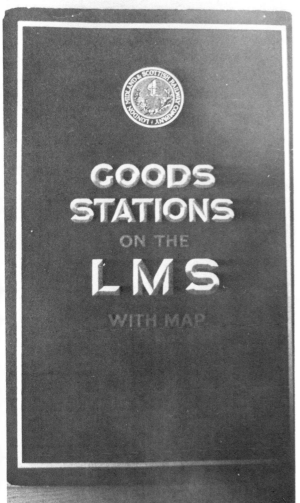

Plate 107 (above)   The former L&NWR goods shed at Rhyl, with a typical wooden hut built by the Company providing additional accommodation.

Real Photographs

Plate 106 (left)   Another LMS publication intended to assist traders in planning their delivery routes by rail. In addition to a list of towns with goods stations served by the LMS, there were advertisements offering LMS sites for works, ideal sites for new works, factories and bulk oil and spirit depots, close by or alongside the Company's rail routes, and assuring would-be takers of a good and reliable rail transportation system.

Author's Collection

Plate 108 The interior of Rugeley goods shed showing the type of lifting appliance often found in warehouses and depots.

Author's Collection

Plate 109 (above) Livestock was an extremely important commodity to the Company, and as will be well known, cattle docks were a common feature at a majority of the stations. For 1930, the numbers carried by the LMS make interesting reading:-

Cattle	1,870,601
Calves	188,544
Sheep	6,145,332
Pigs	722,076
Horses	24,377
Misc.	2,527

and a total equated tonnage of 1,252,520.

At a number of stations special facilities were available for the road conveyance of livestock in the Company's own fleet of specially equipped vehicles. In this plate it looks as though the lone cow is looking for a place behind the engine!

National Railway Museum

Plate 110 (left upper) The covered loading area for road vehicles at Camden in 1933.

Real Photographs

Plate 111 (left lower) A newly erected corrugated-sheet grain shed situated at Llandudno Junction. The timber framing supports a floor raised to wagon level, and as well as providing good ventilation for the structural timbers, is a discouragement to vermin.

British Railways

Plate 112 October 1938, the scene at Bristol St. Philip's goods depot, and an interesting view of the rope capstan used in goods depots for the movement of vans and wagons. In the foreground is a form of wagon transverser, upon which the vehicle was hauled and moved into another open road before being off-loaded.

National Railway Museum

Plate 113 A pair of six wheel carriages with interiors removed and doors locked up to form mobile warehouses, here parked in the Coventry goods yard on 16th May 1930. Traders could hire areas of the goods warehouses, with or without clerical assistance provided by railway staff, to enable their stocks to be kept close to the distribution area. However, a further service was provided by the Company in the form of a mobile warehouse and converted passenger or brake vans could be used in multiples to give the trader all the advantages of mobility of stock holding. 'Warehouses on wheels' were used as temporary storage vehicles, or to provide additional accommodation at short notice where existing fixed accommodation in warehouses was fully occupied. The trader was able to have his mobile warehouse moved from station to station as his sales campaign progressed. They were normally positioned in the goods yard with a parallel siding adjacent, to allow freight arriving to be unloaded direct into the mobile warehouse, and secured to await delivery. Vehicles are numbered 01836 and 01837.

National Railway Museum

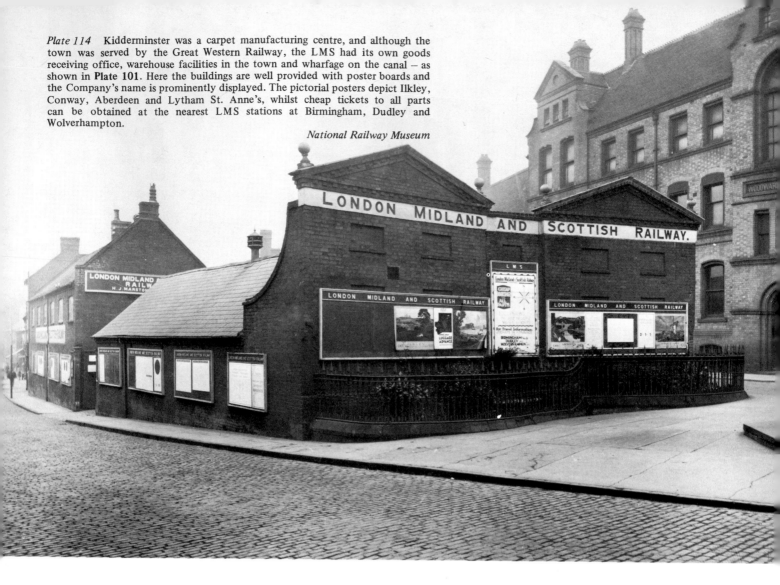

Plate 114 Kidderminster was a carpet manufacturing centre, and although the town was served by the Great Western Railway, the LMS had its own goods receiving office, warehouse facilities in the town and wharfage on the canal – as shown in **Plate 101**. Here the buildings are well provided with poster boards and the Company's name is prominently displayed. The pictorial posters depict Ilkley, Conway, Aberdeen and Lytham St. Anne's, whilst cheap tickets to all parts can be obtained at the nearest LMS stations at Birmingham, Dudley and Wolverhampton.

National Railway Museum

Passenger Stations

The total number of buildings at stations was considerable and well into five figures, but very few of these were actually built by the LMS, the majority having origins dating back into the pre-group period. There were almost as many different designs as there were stations, although some companies did achieve a measure of standardisation in stations constructed in the last 30 years before the amalgamation.

In a volume of this nature, one could not attempt to include examples of all the types of building, nor an example from each of the constituent companies, but it is possible to look at various features which have been a part of the station scene. Most station views have been taken, not for the station itself, but to record trains either stationary or passing through. The architecture of station buildings is covered in *LMS Architecture*, a volume dealing with the designs and materials used by the LMS and its constituent companies, and published by Oxford Publishing Company. It would, however, be impossible to re-create the British railway station scene in a series of pictures alone. What must for the future be but a memory, is the atmosphere of the station, and for the majority of those who used the railway station during the steam era, the damp, steamy, dirty and smelly aroma did not end too soon. The LMS has been glamorised in the years since it was absorbed into British Railways in 1948, until one could believe that it was a wonderful railway in every respect.

Past employees have their own recollections of their period of service, the badly lit stations, coal fires in waiting rooms and booking offices which would not throw out any heat, long periods of working inside in one's overcoat during winter, and of trains arriving blowing smoke and steam over the waiting passengers. The other railway companies were no different when it came to the conditions of the stations, and it would be wrong to tar every station with this depressing brush of conditions. Generally, the stations serving the cities and the towns, and those older stations in the suburbs, were not the best of places, but conversely there were many stations which were homely and clean and well cared for by the staff and a credit to the Company. The station staff were intensely loyal to the Company and by their own efforts, a cheery 'good morning' or 'hello' made the traveller feel welcome, and the Company encouraged staff to be as helpful as possible, believing that goodwill engendered in this way would bring further traffic to the Company. The public's contact with the railway was chiefly through the passenger or goods station staff, but the footplatemen were also a part of the station scene, particularly at the principal termini. Station activity at the large stations was intense and the measure of co-ordination achieved was fascinating, although the sceptic would scoff that it was nothing short of chaos. The fact was that the trains did run, the passengers by and large caught the right service, the freight did move, all achieved at times against the most adverse of factors, not least the dreadful effects and extremes of climate.

The atmosphere cannot be recreated, but the station scene has been captured in the accompanying pictures.

Plate 115 One of the new LMS stations was this one at Bowker Vale, between Heaton Park and Crumpsall on the Bury Bolton Street to Manchester Victoria electrified line, which was opened in 1938 to coincide with the introduction of the new winter timetable. Much of the construction was from pre-cast concrete sections made at the Newton Heath concrete works. One of the station features often overlooked was the platform surface, and yet there were a variety of finishes, some of which were characteristic of individual companies. The surface at Bowker Vale appears to be of shale and gravel with concrete edgings.

National Railway Museum

Plate 116 The roadside of the ex-ondon Tilbury & Southend Station at ast Ham.

British Railways

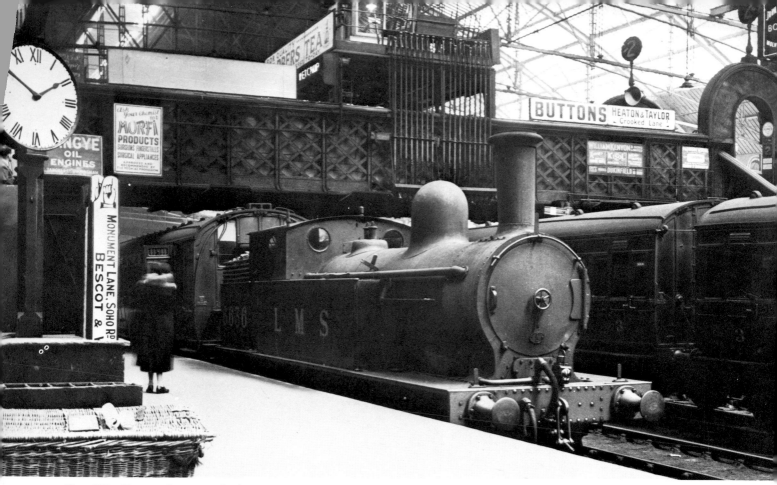

Plate 117 New Street Station, Birmingham in 1938, with ex-L&NWR 2-4-2T, No. 6636, at the head of a local train.

J. Coltas

Plate 118 Blackpool Talbot Road Station concourse in 1925, with a great number of interesting items making up the scene.

Real Photographs

Plate 119 One of the most unusual stations in the system, Trent Junction, more than a mile from the town of Long Eaton, but an important junction for the Erewash Valley, Leicester, Derby and Nottingham services. The island platform occupied a large area and was around 30 yards at its widest point. Now, alas, but a memory. The platform surface beneath the canopies was slabbed and the outer reaches shown here were tarmac.

Real Photographs

Plate 120 Euston Station arrival behind 'Claughton' No. 5999 *Vindictive* with a Bagnall 'Imp' tractor at the head of a train of barrows in 1934. This was a common sight at most large stations, particularly termini, where unaccompanied luggage and other items had to be emptied from the trains. Note the large slabs of York stone forming the platform, and note also, the deflectors above the train for deflecting smoke and soot particles.

Lansing Bagnall

Plate 121 A small country station, the first up the line from Stratford-upon-Avon to Blisworth, at Ettington. The platform edging is made up of ordinary bricks, one of the more unusual edgings.

M. Mitchell

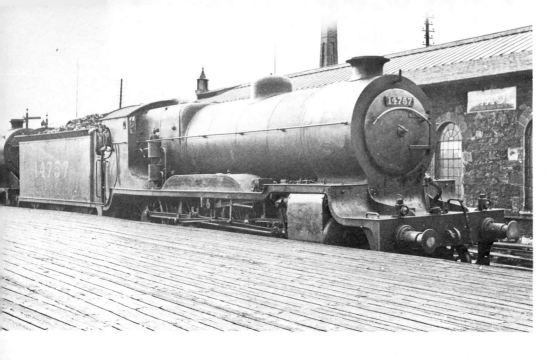

Plate 122 Inverness Station in 1931 with No. 14757. The platform here is formed from wooden planks suitably spaced to provide drainage for surface water, and laid longitudinally down the platform.

J. Coltas

Plate 123 A great deal further south, at Leamington Spa Avenue Station, another wooden plank platform, but this time laid across the platform. 'Patriot' Class No. 5523 is seen in 1936 prior to receiving the name *Bangor*.

J. Coltas

Plate 124 Clifton Mill Station, the first station out from Rugby on the Market Harborough line, in 1947, with Class 5, 4-6-0 locomotives, Nos. 5419 and 5430 heading an express. The station building was built from the wooden sections prefabricated at Crewe, whilst the platform is made up of bricks, edged by blue edgings with a diamond pattern cast into the surface to give grip underfoot.

J. Coltas

Station Garden Competitions

ate 125 Colourful station gardens were a part of the ene, particularly in the pre-1939 period, and competi- ons were organised in the various districts to select the rden for the title 'Best Kept Station Garden', and there as a great deal of rivalry between stations to take the ophy and other awards which were made by the ompany. In 1937 there were 401 stations entered for e national competition, and the staff were given every couragement to practise the gardening hobby on the ation premises. Passengers using these stations were ivileged, and appreciative comments made to the rail- ay personnel gave them pride and did much for odwill. This view of part of the garden at Verney nction was in fact taken in 1952, but there is little to ggest it is other than a typical LMS station garden.

J. Coltas

Plate 126 The smallest station on the LMS was this one at Blackwell Mill on the Midland branch line between Millersdale and Buxton, this view being taken on 9th November 1926, looking towards Buxton. The line coming in from the right was the Midland connection from the northern end of the main Manchester to Derby route, forming a triangle with the line from Millersdale. Blackwell village was one mile distant and it is believed these staggered platforms were put in for the benefit of Midland Railway employees who lived within the triangle of track mentioned. The signal cabin, just visible behind the signal holding the freight train, was Buxton Junction. Note the unusual telegraph poles and the stone building, which in fact was the only structure at this remote and little used station.

British Railways

Plate 127 (below) Scotland, and the station waiting room at Renton between Dumbarton and Balloch, with a paint date of 19th July 1939 recorded for all to see.

The late Dr. G. Stilley

Plate 128 (above) An early morning scene at Euston, with mail bags off-loaded from the early arrivals. A scene so typical of the pre-diesel era.

Author's Collection

Accidents

Despite strenuous efforts by everyone in the Company, accidents did occur, however unfortunate, and were a part of the railway scene. It was one aspect which the Company did not publicise, but accident damage to locomotives and rolling stock did reveal weaknesses in design and materials which enabled modifications and additional measures to be taken to make railway travel much safer. All the railway companies carried large numbers of passengers each day and as a mere relative statistic, the accident record compared very well to other forms of transport. In the day to day operational side of the railway there were many thousands of individual ingredients which helped to sustain the good working of the railway with the utmost reliability and safety, and it is perhaps ironic that many of the accidents were caused not by human failing, but by small parts which were insignificant themselves,

but important as a part of the works, or purely as a result of adverse weather conditions.

It is not necessary to dwell on each accident to be able to look at the behaviour of the rolling stock or track. For every accident causing fatal injuries to one or more individuals, there were others where injuries were not fatal. It is also true that a greater number of injuries were caused through movement of railway vehicles than through accidents to trains, and the LMS published a safety booklet which was issued to all staff, with illustrations of the correct and incorrect procedures for a variety of tasks: the uncoupling of trains, the opening of carriage doors and many others.

Plate 129 A crumpled front-end, probably the result of meeting buffer stops with more force than was necessary. No. 671 awaits repair at Buxton in August 1939.

J. Coltas

Plate 130 'Claughton' No. 5970 requiring attention after losing a rear wheel whilst racing at speed down Madeley Bank. The rear driving wheel axle broke and when the wheel was lost the engine retained the road, thus avoiding what could have been a disaster on a heavily used stretch of line. Who could argue with the very apt name for this majestic locomotive of the premier line – *Patience!* The cabside and valancing were buckled and no doubt other damage was found when she eventually entered the works.

The late G. Platt Collection

Plate 131 One of the famous L&NWR 4-4-0 engines, No. 5278 *Precursor* undergoing heavy repair following the derailment at Great Bridgford on 17th June 1932. This locomotive was heading the 7.23pm express from Crewe to Birmingham, and whilst crossing from the slow to the fast line became derailed, very similar circumstances to the Leighton Buzzard accident some fifteen months earlier.

J. Coltas

Plates 132 and *133*　　The year 1946 began disastrously for the LMS with this accident on 1st January at Lichfield Trent Valley Station on the North Western main line. In the early evening a local passenger train from Stafford, the 18.08 to Nuneaton was standing in the up platform to allow the 14.50 Fleetwood to London Broad Street fish train to pass on the up through road. Points at the north end of the station did not close completely when the road was reset for the 'fish' to run through, with the result that the 'fish' was diverted along the slow line and into the rear of the local passenger train. The impact was enormous and the wooden carriages forming the local train were reduced to matchwood, the whole train being pushed on through the station and into the sandtrap beyond the up slow line exit to the main line. These two pictures show the damage caused in the crash, with the bogie shorn from its mountings and the remains of one carriage pushed beneath the leading brake.

British Railways

Plate 134   Grendon, between Atherstone and Polesworth, was the location of this accident involving streamlined 'Coronation' Pacific No. 6244 *King George VI* and was caused by poor track condition in the immediate post war years. Speeds were reduced during and after the war because of the lack of maintenance due to various factors, but the leading bogie wheels left the track and forced the engine to her side and pulled seven of her coaches onto their sides. When the 'King' re-appeared after repair at Crewe, the streamlined casing had been discarded. For a considerable period the train involved, the 8.30 am Euston to Liverpool, had been the regular out working for No. 6202 turbomotive, and it was perhaps by chance that the turbomotive was not working the train on this occasion.

British Railways

Plate 135   Stanier flush-sided stock forming the Liverpool train.

British Railways

Plate 136   Dining car No. 36 with its underframe partly submerged in the ballast, and the sleepers reduced to mere matchwood.

British Railways

Plate 137   Soon after the derailment, ambulance and other staff are seen checking the overturned carriages.

British Railways

Plate 138 Although badly creased, this photograph shows that in April 1948, No. 6251 *City of Nottingham*, one of the 'Coronation' Pacifics has come to grief hauling the up West Coast postal at Winsford in Cheshire. Although it was after nationalisation, it involved LMS rolling stock, and the purpose of including this plate, is to show the disintegration of the ex-LNWR full brake between the leading vehicle, a GWR syphon and the leading postal sorting van which was of much stronger construction.

British Railways

Plate 139 'Royal Scot' Class locomotive No. 6114 *Coldstream Guardsman* was derailed on Sunday, 22nd March 1931, whilst diverting from the down fast to the down slow line at Leighton Buzzard to run round permanent way work which was being carried out on the fast line. A great deal of damage was caused but the London & North Western dining car, to the left of this picture, did not sustain the same measure of damage as some of the later carriages which were in this train formation. Speed through the crossover was the principal cause of this accident, and one must be thankful that some years later the much recalled passage of the test-run of the 'Coronation Scot' through the reverse crossover at the entrance to Crewe Station did not result in similar devastation.

National Railway Museum

Plate 140 One of the Motor Brake third driving carriages, on the Liverpool to Southport electric line, after suffering bomb blast damage during the wartime raids on the Merseyside area. Little damage other than the shattered windows is evident.

British Railways

Wartime

Plates 141 and 142 Two scenes of devastation after bomb attacks affecting LMS railway property. In the first plate, outside Sandhills (Bank Hall) Liverpool, the lorry beneath the 'Bass' advert carries the lettering 'Demolitions Engage Kenny'!

British Railways

Royal Travel

The Royal Train was a proud possession of the London Midland & Scottish Railway Company, even though the coaching stock was inherited from the London & North Western Railway. The finest examples of craftsmanship were exemplified in this one collection of carriages, and whenever it was in use it drew admiring glances from railwaymen and public alike.

The L&NWR livery was retained on this train until the outbreak of war in 1939 when it was repainted in the less conspicuous LMS crimson lake livery. In 1941 the LMS built three new special carriages for the Royal Train and these were fitted with armour plating protection as a precaution against war damage.

The traditional home of the Royal saloons has always been the Carriage Works at Wolverton, and this remains so to this day. The workings of the Royal Train, even on empty stock workings, was a closely guarded secret and only those employees directly connected with the passage of the train were given the information necessary to ensure its safe passage. As a result there are not so many photographs of the train en route, other than those by photographers who were per-

haps privy to the arrangements, or those who knew through Royal visit publicity in the vicinity of the destination.

The full train for overnight journeys between London and Scotland was often doubleheaded and standby engines were positioned at various locations along the route in case of problems with the train engine.

In addition to the personal staff of the Royal Family who were travelling, there were always a number of railwaymen travelling with the train. There were at least ten train attendants drawn from the Wolverton C&W staff available to ensure everything was working correctly, a guard and two skilled telegraphists and of course the enginemen. At either end of the journey the Stationmaster, and at the larger stations attired immaculately beneath a top hat, would meet the train and conduct the members of the Royal Family through the station to their waiting transport.

It is indeed a fitting tribute to the many skilled men who have worked on the train, both in constructing it in the early part of this century, and to those who have tended it since, that a number of the saloons should have been preserved for future generations as part of the National Collection in the Railway Museum at York.

Plate 143   Compounds 1176 and 1135 at the head of the Royal Train in the Beattock area during 1930.

Late G. Wilson Collection

Plate 144 (left) The Royal Train headed by 'Jubilee' Class No. 5587 *Baroda* and a sister engine on Brock Troughs in May 1936.

A. G. Ellis

Plate 145 (below) Passing Crewe, and displaying the Royal headcode of four lamps, is blue streamlined 'Coronation' Pacific No. 6222 *Queen Mary*. The first two carriages are LNER vehicles, with the second vehicle being the ECJS Royal Saloon. It is believed Queen Mary herself was fond of this saloon and it may well have been that on this occasion she was the Royal traveller, particularly as the locomotive being used was named in her honour.

Real Photographs

Plate 146 (below) The three Royal Saloons built by the LMS in 1941 at Wolverton. The three in order are power brake car with convertible sleeping accommodation, No. 31209, the King's Saloon, No. 798 and the Queen's Saloon, No. 799. A close look at the saloons of the King and Queen will reveal the protective armour plating on the doors, which were fitted with small look-out panels, the sliding shutters to the windows and the axlebox covers. Each of the Royal Saloons contained a suite of rooms, including lounge, bedroom and bathroom and an attendant's room and toilet with a double entrance lobby at both ends. The power brake car No. 31209 is still used in Royal Train formations, and the two LMS Royal Saloons are now happily preserved as part of the National Collection in the Railway Museum at York.

British Railways

Plate 147   The Queen's Saloon in the immediate post war LMS period after the armour plating had been removed.

National Railway Museum

Plate 148   The Queen's lounge in No. 799, reflecting the simple decorations and materials used during the war years.

National Railway Museum

Pullman Cars on the LMS

Although Pullman cars were running on LMS trains in Scotland, the Company were not the owners until December 1933 when they took over the total of 22 cars of varying origin. The Pullman Car Company of America had an agreement with the Caledonian Railway for these cars to be operated and they were advertised on particular services with a supplementary fare being charged.

In the early LMS years there were a number of interesting Pullman restaurant car workings, which included the 12.20pm Perth to Carstairs section workings of the 10.05am Aberdeen to Euston, the 1pm Aberdeen to London with the Pullman car taken from the train at Law Junction, and the 5.30pm working out of Glasgow to Carlisle. Return working from Carlisle was as part of the 11.45pm Euston-Glasgow sleeping car express, whilst the Aberdeen and Perth Pullmans returned north as part of the 10am ex-Euston which was split at Symington for Aberdeen etc.

They were also used as restaurant cars on services between Glasgow and Oban, Glasgow and Aviemore, Perth and Inverness. The observation car, a 57ft vehicle with movable armchairs for twenty two passengers, and built in 1914 by Cravens of Sheffield, was used between Glasgow and Oban. The outward working in the summer of 1935 was 9.45am ex-Glasgow arriving in Oban at 2.7pm with a return from Oban at 3.40pm, due Glasgow at 8.5pm. The *Maid of Morven* was allocated the LMS number of 209 and withdrawn in December 1937. Six of the Pullmans were built during the LMS period, three by Clayton in 1923 and three by Metro-Cammell in 1927.

The Pullman livery of umber and cream was replaced by LMS crimson lake with simplified lining, and the earlier names were not perpetuated, merely being lettered 'Dining Car'. Eleven of the twenty two cars lasted through into British Railways ownership.

The accompanying photographs are all pre-LMS period, although it is the livery which was carried until 1934.

Plate 149   The observation end of *Maid of Morven* — quite an impressive tail to any express, and well worth a supplementary fare.
Author's Collection

Plate 150 Maid of Morven soon after delivery from the Cravens Works in 1914.
Author's Collection

Plate 151 The individual armchair seating from which the real delights of the Oban route could be enjoyed.
Author's Collection

Plate 152 Another of the Cravens 1914 batch of cars, Flora Macdonald, which later became No. 206 the LMS numbering scheme, before final withdrawal came in October 1937. The car would appear to be coupled next to another Pullman on the right, and to a standard type of carriage just visible on the left.
Author's Collection

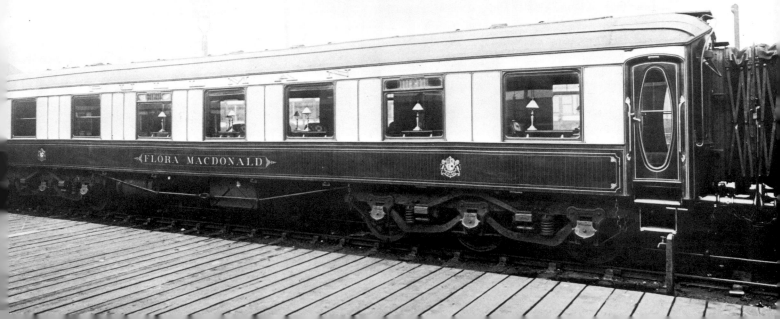

ARP and Ambulance Trains

Plates 153 and 154 (top and above) These two plates show the conversion [of] early LMS stock for use in ambulance trains during World War II. Double doo[rs] have been added to facilitate the use as a ward car, and apart from the numbe[r] there is little other lettering. No. 5503 was fitted out as a kitchen car.

British Railwa[ys]

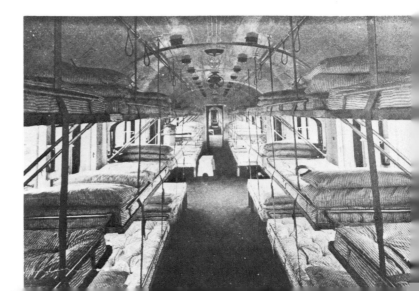

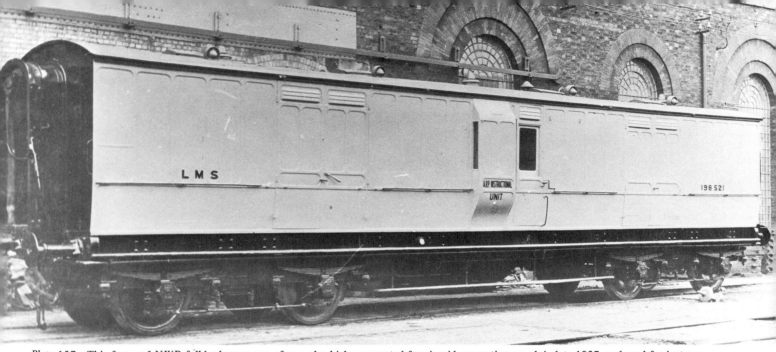

Plate 157 This former LNWR full brake was one of several vehicles converted for air raid precautions work in late 1937, and used for instructional purposes in all parts of the system. Two brakes formed an ARP unit, comprising one fitted out as a decontamination unit complete with air-locked compartments, giving an undressing room, bathroom with shower baths and a dressing room to enable the three phases of cleansing to be undertaken. The other brake was fitted out with a lecture theatre for an audience of 30, complete with a supply of gas masks and protective clothing. The two-coach units were used in the areas where staff would not easily be able to attend lectures at central points. The lectures and practical training were chiefly concerned with the effects of air raids, particularly the effects of poison gas and incendiary bombs. The Company envisaged that in the event of war breaking out, these units could be used in conjunction with breakdown trains which would be attending incidents.

Author's Collection

Plate 158 A wartime formation of carriages of LMS and LNWR origin, specially for the use of the Prime Minister, Rt. Hon. Winston Churchill. This is the only known photograph of this train, which because of the war hostilities was used under conditions of extreme secrecy in all parts of the country.

R. J. Essery Collection

Plate 156 (left) The interior of a ward car converted by the Midland Railway for use during the period of the First World War. Note the three levels of bed arrangement giving approximately thirty six beds per ward car.

Author's Collection

Plate 155 (far left) Air raid precautions were being prepared as early as 1937 and after war was declared the LMS issued each member of its staff with a copy of this handbook.

Author's Collection

Plate 159 Handbill advertising of Special Trains was, and still is, a p[...]lar form of mass communication, and this selection of nine is typic[...] the many thousands originated by the LMS Railway. In the early y[...] of the LMS, the full name of the company appeared beneath [...] initials in a panel flanked by the English Rose and Scottish Thistle[...] doubt as a means of emphasising the extent of the network. The d[...] to gradually change the heading style of the handbills is shown in [...] selection, the final heading being the elongated bean shape w[...] appeared in mid-1934 and continued in use until 1939. Poor qu[...] paper was usually the order of the day, but in a variety of colours [...] for the paper and ink used, with red, brown and black [...] predominating.

Because of the volumes required, printers throughout the cou[...] were used and whilst Bemrose of Derby, and McCorquodale'[...] Wolverton and London undertook much of the railway printing req[...]ments, smaller firms were very much in evidence for han[...] preparation. From an examination of handbills, it is clear that as w[...] the events of national appeal held at well known locations around [...] country, more localised fetes and shows, including special film pres[...]tions, were heavily supported by the LMS with special trains, or sp[...] fares to the location using existing timetabled services, again aime[...] maximising public support. One interesting point is that on an out[...] excursion journey passengers were only permitted to take small [...] luggage and luncheon baskets, whilst for the return journey they c[...] take with them goods etc. not exceeding 60lb in weight, free of ch[...]

To summarise the styles shown:

Top: *Left to Right* – 1931 – 1932 – 1933
Mid: *Left to Right* – 1939 – 1934 – 1927 (Sept)
Bot: *Left to Right* – 1927 (Jan) – 1937 – 1925

The reverse side often contained abbreviated announcements of future excursions, for instance those relating to a Football Match carried a preliminary announcement about special trains which would run to the F.A. Cup Final and suggesting early reservations be made – even though the teams competing were not then known at that date. In addition, the reverse side of handbills provided useful space for publicizing railway services available, and the LMS Road-Rail Containers for Furniture Removal was a regular feature. The names of booking agents where tickets could be purchased often appeared also, together with an invitation extended to obtain further details of facilities from the District Passenger Manager for the area served. Although a large number of each issue would fall on so called 'stony ground', the handbill as an advertising medium has been in use since long before the LMS came to be, and as we know, it is still a feature of the booking halls to this day.

Many gimmicks were also tried and for the 1935 Excursion programme, arrangements were made to exhibit Land Utilization Survey Maps at some 50 stations in England and Wales as an aid to walkers and hikers using rail services to reach their starting points, and to enable them to find a convenient station from which to commence the return journey.

Author's Collection

Shed Pass – MPDs

One of the highlights of a day on the railway scene was always a visit to a locomotive shed and invariably it provided a happy hunting ground for the train spotters, and every visit was different, with Sunday being the day when everyone knew the sheds would be full of engines. It was a part of the railway one never tired of visiting, no matter how often a visit to the local shed could be arranged, and at weekends and during school holidays, children, with parents trailing behind, would converge on places like Rugby, Crewe, Chester, Preston and Carlisle, Glasgow Central or Euston, or to the Midland line at Derby or Leeds, and time was the enemy for the day was never long enough. Armed with a shed pass, the 'well disciplined' group with the responsible parent would arrive at the Shedmaster's Office, 'running to time' . . . every time. One could never generalise to the extent of 'every shed's the same' because those on the main line were different to those local to home, and the abundance of 'namers' made it all so worth-while — the swansong for Dad on the way home and plans were in the embryo stage for the next visit. Those with cameras were full of anticipation at the prospect of being able to relive those special moments 'on shed', particularly where a friendly and co-operative driver had moved this or that engine for a better picture position — and many a driver or fitter did just that to oblige the youthful smiling face.

Train journeys were always carefully planned with the youngsters moving from side to side to be in the best position for each shed along the line, the likes of Millhouses, south of Sheffield, or Hasland further south beyond Chesterfield, or on the main line, Nuneaton or Stafford, or even the shed at Oxenholme. They were railway journeys 'par excellence', and the soot and smoke did not matter a jot.

Alas, the steam shed is no longer with us and the children of today are unable to savour the real atmosphere of a Crewe North, or a Toton in the heyday of steam. Nostalgia, on the part of the author, yes, maybe, but it was a part of the steam railway scene which can never be properly recreated. The Preserved Steam Centres are doing a splendid job and it is true that many are occupying what were 'real' steam sheds, but the difference is it is all so predictable, we know which locomotives will be on shed, with a small number in steam. The difference was that you went to a shed wondering what engines you'd find, and most would be in steam. That was the steam MPD, and in the accompanying photographs, scenes so typical of the MPD have been selected to evoke some of the memories for those who were around at that time, and to illustrate what the LMS shed scene looked like.

First, however, we should remember that the Motive Power Depot was a servicing centre for a variety of locomotives which were working in the area of a particular shed, and a base for an allocation of engines which was balanced to suit the type of traffic which originated also in that area.

Vast amounts of capital were tied up in the buildings and equipment provided at the locomotive sheds throughout the system, and virtually all the LMS sheds were received from the constituent companies in more or less complete form. Locomotive sheds were provided where there was a need to maintain and service engines, usually a traffic centre or at a junction station. The locomotive shed and all it entailed

was popularly referred to by railwaymen as the 'running department', particularly by those on the old L&NWR, since that was its prime function, to keep engines running.

There was a wide variety of pre-group procedures, and methods of operation differed between sheds and it was not easy in the early years for standardised procedures to be introduced into the Motive Power Department by the LMS. The multiplicity of spare parts which were required to keep 10,300 locomotives, spread through 393 different classes, was enormous and efficiency in the sheds was hampered if a locomotive was out of traffic awaiting spares to arrive. The layout of many locomotive depots was not on an organised basis to allow speedy servicing of engines between trips, and this again hampered the efficiency of operations.

With LMS engines running more than 230 million miles in total each year it was important that maximum efficiency was achieved, and the motive power depot was an important feature in the life of the locomotive stock. Various studies were undertaken and detailed analysis of the workings of certain depots were prepared in order to achieve a basis for standardising and improving the availability of locomotives, achieving increased efficiency, and in general improvements began in 1932.

The main shed operation was one of servicing and this was organised on the following system:-

    i) Coal and water, if possible by mechanical means
    ii) Ashpit work
    iii) Turning
    iv) Locomotive stabled in shed, or placed in preparation pits ready for further duty

Where shed track layouts did not permit the locomotive a smooth passage, changes were made in order to achieve more efficient operational patterns. Running repairs were carried out as necessary in between trips, based on the driver's report made on completion of the last trip. The LMS installed new machinery in the form of lathes, drilling machines etc. and equipment to speed up repairs, and in addition, new mechanical coal plants and ash disposal equipment was installed at a number of the busier motive power depots.

At most depots the servicing sequence was always underway as locomotives arrived and departed at regular intervals to meet traffic requirements, and the continuing activity was one of the major attractions of the MPDs.

The first modernisation schemes were approved in 1933 and involved 47 installations. As the scheme progressed and enthusiasm amongst staff grew, a Motive Power League was organised in 1935 for the whole of the line, based at first on 29 motive power areas, and later on 32 areas. Points were awarded according to the number of casualties causing locomotives to require attention and affecting the availability for traffic, and friendly rivalry developed between areas as the league progressed. It was a means of motivation directed to achieve greater efficiency, and to foster a pride in one's work.

LONDON MIDLAND AND SCOTTISH RAILWAY COMPANY.

E.R.O. 49086

DISTRICT PASSENGER MANAGER'S OFFICE, MANCHESTER

Telephone—
Telegrams—

YOUR REFERENCE

OUR REFERENCE

D/37939/291

9th July 1946

Dear Sir,

    In accordance with your request, I have been pleased to arrange for your visit to the undermentioned Motive Power Depot on the date and at the time shewn.

    On arrival at the Motive Power Depot, this permit should be presented immediately and a responsible member of the staff will conduct you round.

    In the interests of safety, no person under 16 years of age will be allowed to visit a Motive Power Depot unless accompanied by an adult, and the visit will terminate before the hours of darkness. The only luggage permitted in the Motive Power Depot will be cameras, and photographs may be taken for private collection only.

    Acceptance of this permission will constitute an agreement to relieve the Company in the event of any personal injury or loss of or damage to property being sustained on the Company's premises.

    I hope you have an instructive and enjoyable visit.

Motive Power Depot to be visited	Date	Time	No. of Persons (Males only)
Saltley	21.7.46	-	One

D.F.Tee Esq.,
8 Cloister Road,
Heaton Mersey,
Stockport.

Yours faithfully,

For H. E. BAILEY

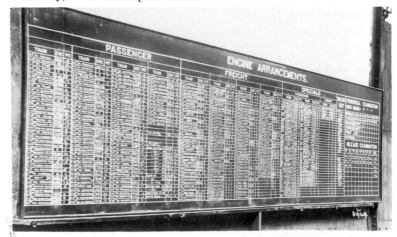

Plate 161 At all locomotive depots an Engine Arrangements Board gave details of which locomotive would work a particular turn, and where on shed the locomotive was positioned. A crew signing on would see which engine was rostered for their turn, and similarly any engines requiring periodical or mileage examinations, wash-outs or other attention, would be marked up appropriately. Obviously the size of the board suited the number of turns from the shed.

Real Photographs

Plate 163 The picturesque surroundings of
Kyle of Lochalsh shed with an interesting trio
of former Highland Railway engines. No. 14398
Ben Alder of the 'Small Ben' 4-4-0 Class, and
two of the Skye Bogie 4-4-0s Nos. 14283 and
14282.

A. G. Ellis

Plate 164 Crewe North, on 7th May 1939,
with 'Coronation' Class No. 6225 *Duchess of
Gloucester* and 'Jubilee' Class No. 5629 *Straits
Settlements* stabled in the yard. An interesting
view of the details at the rear of the tender, an
unusual viewpoint.

A. G. Ellis Collection

Plate 165 'Garratt' Class No. 4981 at
Cricklewood on 17th August 1935, with
another of the class to the left. These locomotives worked the Midland main line coal trains
from Derbyshire pits via Toton to London, and
also through Trent to the Derby to Birmingham
line, which they joined at Stenson Junction.
They were a common site at the Motive Power
Depots of Cricklewood, Wellingborough, Toton
and Hasland.

A. G. Ellis

Plate 166 Ex-L&YR 0-8-0 No. 12826 leaving Agecroft shed with 'Garratt' No. 4972 being hauled dead in October 1930, after the centenary celebrations of the opening of the Liverpool and Manchester Railway which had included exhibitions of locomotives and rolling stock at both the Liverpool and Manchester ends of the Railway. The 'Garratt' has a fixed coal bunker which was replaced some two years later with a 9 ton rotary coal bunker.

A. G. Ellis

Plate 167 The newly completed mechanical coaling plant installed at shed 19A Sheffield Grimesthorpe by Dempsters, giving two 150 ton bunkers over two coaling roads. 19A was the final LMS shed code reference introduced in 1935, and prior this date, Sheffield was coded 25 under both the Midland Railway and the LMS Midland Division arrangements.

National Railway Museum

Plate 168 One of the sheds which did not feature in the sights of many camera-men, Westhouses, just to the east of the northern end of the Erewash Valley main line. This view was taken in 1951, and though it is a BR scene it differs little from what would have been seen in the LMS period and includes virtually all the buildings of this MPD.

Author's Collection

Plate 169 Kentish Town, Midland Division shed 16, which became 14B in the 1935 reorganisation. No. 7249 is on the wagon slope to the former Midland Railway coaling plant, and the shed yard is in the process of some reorganisation. This view was taken on 7th February 1939.

National Railway Museum

◀ *Plate 170 (left)* The ash disposal plant at Toton MPD on 9th June 1932, with ash hopper wagons being discharged direct into waiting wagons. Removal of ash from locomotive smokeboxes and ashpans at the end of a duty could occupy up to 30 minutes and once removed the hot ash had to be disposed of as quickly and efficiently as possible, particularly since ash could be a hazard to shed staff. From the ashpit the material fell into a hopper from which the ash wagons or skips, as they were sometimes called, were hoisted to be tipped as shown in this plate. A later advancement was the addition of pneumatic ash extraction equipment, and through vacuum suction the ashes were removed from the locomotives and piped to a hopper ready for disposal into wagons.

National Railway Museum

te 171 Inside Kentish Town shed during numbering in May 1934. The bunker side of this 3P k engine carries the new number 28, whilst the smoke- door number has still to be changed. Many of this ss were fitted with condensing apparatus and whilst the side view is clearly detailed, the following plate shows additions to the nearside, of another Kentish Town ine.

V. Forster Collection

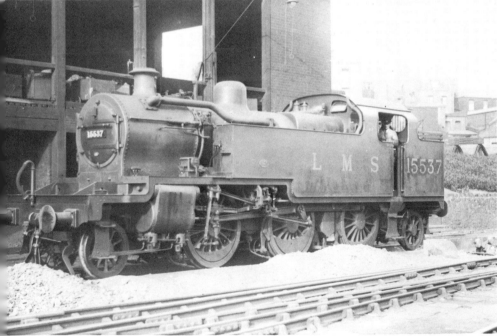

Plate 172 (left) No. 15537 at the coaling stage, showing for the benefit of modellers the nearside of a condensing locomotive.

V. Forster Collection

Plate 173 (right) Stanier 2-6-4T No. 2554 being watered at Saltley shed in June 1936.

V. Forster Collection

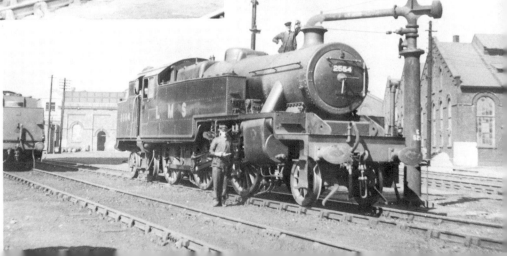

Plate 174 A general scene outside Leeds, with engines in the early LMS livery style.

A. G. Ellis

Plate 175 (right) Buxton Midland MPD with Class 4F, No. 4258, beneath the sheer legs used for lifting one end of the locomotive to release an axle for attention.

A. G. Ellis

Plate 176 (below) Policemen are on duty at the former L&Y shed at Agecroft, in an effort to forestall any would-be saboteurs during the General Strike in 1926.

A. G. Ellis

Plate 177 One of the 'Hughes' 4-6-0 Class No. 10472 taking water at Crewe in July 1933. The LNWR high-level water tank is partly in the picture and a coke burner with long chimney is seen immediately beneath.

J. Coltas

Plate 178 The stone built engine sheds at Perth in 1930, with Crab No. 13183 and Compounds Nos. 1144 and 921 coaled and ready for duty.

J. Coltas

Plate 179 No. 14395 *Loch Garve* alongside the coaling stage at Inverness Motive Power Depot in 1931.

J. Coltas

Plate 180 No. 14010, formerly No. 123 of the Caledonian Railway at Perth shed in 1930. Built in 1886, this locomotive was close to retirement and apart from some local passenger and light express train duties between Perth and Dundee, she was also regarded as the Officers Inspection Saloon locomotive on the Northern Division of the LMS. She is shown in the livery which replaced her Caledonian blue livery in June 1924. She has since been restored to Caledonian livery and preserved in the Glasgow Museum of Transport.

Author's Collection

Plate 181 The former L&NWR coaling and water tower at Bescot MPD in 1931 with a 'Cauliflower' Class No. 8592 taking on water. Note the coal chute just to the right of the engineman on the tender. The former Midland & L&NWR coaling towers required a great deal of manual work to move the coal and this was a time consuming part of servicing the engines.

J. Coltas

te 182 LMS Compound No. 1119 looking
her splendid in a sunlit crimson lake livery.
Author's Collection

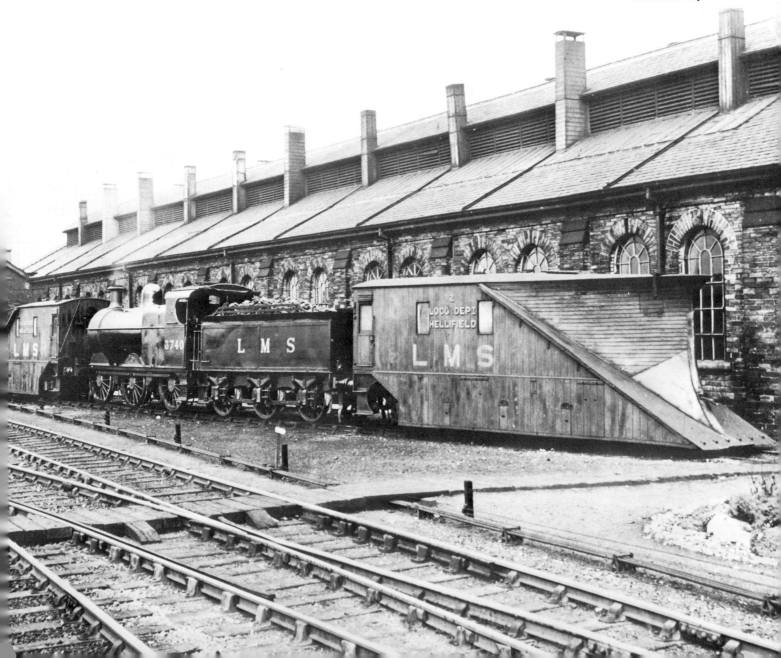

Plate 183 The two specially built bogie snowploughs maintained at Hellifield MPD, for use on the Settle & Carlisle main line. Built in 1909 by the Midland, they were withdrawn around 1930. The livery is believed to have been crimson, which would soon have become weathered, with white lettering for Company initials, and it would appear the Loco Dept Hellifield lettering was shaded and therefore possibly gold shaded black. A very informative article and drawing by fellow LMS Society member, David Jenkinson, appeared in the December 1965 *Model Railway News* magazine – this is mentioned with the railway modeller in mind.

British Railways

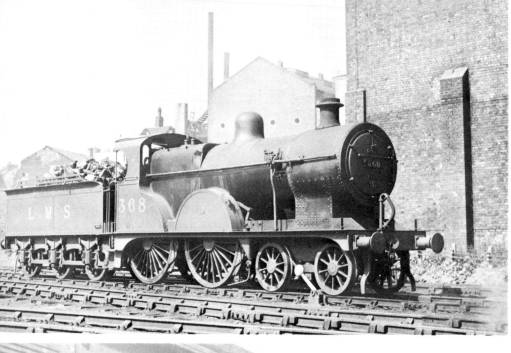

Plate 184 (above) The LNWR practice of allocating a locomotive to each of the District Engineers and replacing the number with a cast plate, was continued on the Western Division of the LMS. The 2-4-0 seen here is plated Engineer Watford, with the Engineer's six wheeled inspection saloon attached.

National Railway Museum

Plate 185 Former Midland 4-4-0 Class 2P No. 368 in the yard at Kentish Town in June 1935, a rather pleasing outline in this pose.

V. Forster Collection

Plate 186 (left) No. 5643, a 'Jubilee' as yet without its name *Rodney*, on Derby shed in 1936. It is fitted with indicator shelters as a prelude to undergoing test runs. The window was for the benefit of the man who rode inside the shelter monitoring the recording instruments: without doubt an exhilarating experience when travelling at speed.

V. Forster Collection

Traffic on the LMS

To most people the principal fascination of the railway scene was watching express trains rush past, or in observing the scene from the end of a platform. It was this fascination which led to the majority of photographers concentrating their cameras on trains and locomotives, with express passenger engines proving the most popular subjects. On some of the lesser known lines interesting combinations of locomotives, carriages and wagons were just as fascinating, but they did not draw the cameraman to the same extent because there was little glamour about the line, the locomotive or its train. All were, however, just as important to the well-being of the railway as the principal expresses and the following plates have been selected, first of all because they appeal to the author, and for that reason I make no apology for the selection, and secondly, because there are aspects of each picture which provide interesting detail information for those who model the LMS.

For Urgent
Consignments
Consign Your Goods
under the
"GREEN
ARROW
SERVICE"

Ask the LMS Agent
for particulars

For Specially
Controlled Passenger
Train Transit
and Delivery Consign
Your Parcels
under the
" BLUE
ARROW
SERVICE "

Ask the L M S Station
Master for particulars.

Send
YOUR
Consignments
by the
"C. O. D."
Service

The L M S Agent will give
you full particulars.

Plate 187 The outer end of the platforms at Glasgow St. Enoch Station, at Easter 1931, with one of the former Glasgow and South Western Railway 'Manson' 4-4-0 engines taking water from the high-level storage tanks, which was not of the usual rectangular pattern. Prior to the 1939 war, the ends of buildings and roof tile areas were often used for advertising purposes and many of these were easily seen from passing trains. The water column and signal gantry with banner repeaters are other points of interest for the modeller.

J. Coltas

Plate 188 A peaceful scene at Evercreech Junction on the Somerset and Dorset Joint Railway, with former S&D 0-6-0 carrying one of the numbers previously allocated to one of the Midland 'Johnson' engines which had been withdrawn. This two coach formation was typical of the local passenger trains on this line. The water column appears to serve one line only, with a further platform mounted column at the end of the nearside platform.

D. Field

Plate 189 The 'Fowler' 2-6-4T engine which had the distinction of carrying the name *The Prince* in honour of HRH the Prince of Wales' visit to Derby Works. The name was in painted letters and was carried until 1933. When first built, the locomotive was outshopped with 14 in letters and 10 in numbers, but these were changed to 14 in numbers later on. *The Prince* is here standing at one of the down platforms at Stafford on 1st March 1930, and at this early date appears to have lost her red lining.

D. F. Tee Collection

Plate 190 Another Somerset and Dorset scene this time at Bath, with former Midland Railway 0-4-4T at the head of non-corridor stock. These tank locomotives saw service in many parts of the system on local passenger work and were fitted for push-pull operation.

D. Field Collection

Plate 191   The first of the crimson and gold 'Coronation' streamlined engines, No. 6225 *Duchess of Gloucester* awaiting her turn of duty at Shrewsbury. She was a majestic sight and few locomotives can claim to rival the magnificent lines of this class – a personal view and I suspect one held by many others.

A. G. Ellis Collection

Plate 192   Easter Monday 1931. No. 14117, formerly of the Glasgow & South Western Railway, is about to leave Glasgow St. Enoch Station. A picture full of the atmosphere of the period.

J. Coltas

Plate 193   A Maryport and Carlisle Railway 0-6-0 No. 12488 at Carlisle. The first wagon behind the tender is of North British origin.

A. G. Ellis

Plate 194   The solitary member of the North Staffordshire Railway KT Class 4-4-0 No. 599, here seen at Llandudno soon after the grouping, possibly a return excursion working to the Potteries.

A. G. Ellis

Plate 195 (above) 0-6-0 No. 2898, one of two engines built originally for the Ottoman Railway in Turkey, but diverted to the London Tilbury and Southend Railway. They were absorbed into the Midland numbering sequence when the LTSR was taken over by the Midland, and retained their unique type of cab until withdrawal in the 1930s.

A. G. Ellis

Plate 196 The first Class 7F 0-8-0 No. 9500, a class of locomotive which looked immensely powerful and saw service chiefly in the Central and Western Divisions of the LMS.

A. G. Ellis Collection

Plate 197 Small boilered 'Claughton' 4-6-0 No. 5963 and 7F 0-8-0 No. 9527 at the head of a mixed freight near Berkhamsted on the ex-L&NWR main line in 1930. The first vehicle is an ex-L&NWR cattle wagon with small LMS letters on the top plank and the running number immediately beneath.

A. G. Ellis Collection

Plate 198 An interesting Caledonian combination, engine No. 14358 with the tender off sister engine No. 14354 doubleheading LMS Compound No. 1066 on the outskirts of Carlisle, with a mixed ten coach express.

A. G. Ellis

Plate 199 One of the 1935 Derby built 2-6-2 tanks at the head of a Sheffield train entering Chinley on 15th May 1938. The first three vehicles are an ex-L&YR centre corridor third, an ex-MR Bain corridor third and an ex-L&NWR arc roof carriage. The sleeper built sand box and wooden hut, the miniature corrugated upper quadrant arms on a Midland bracket post are details for the modeller. It is appropriate to notice the grimy condition of the signal posts — they did not stay a perfect white and black for very long and there were no cleaners for the things which did not move.

H. Townley

Plate 200 In 1929, one hundred specially built beer vans emerged from Derby Carriage & Wagon Works, primarily for the heavy beer traffic from Burton-on-Trent. Few photographs of these vans are known to exist, quite probably because the beer traffic to London St. Pancras, the route on which they were principally used, was overnight traffic. Beer traffic was loaded during the day and the breweries 0-4-0T locomotives took the loaded wagons down to the reception sidings ready for the evening departures to all parts of the country. Return empty workings to Burton were also likely to be overnight, with arrival at the various exchange sidings in time for the brewery engines to pick the wagons up for moving into the various ale loading bays. This 4F, No. 4432, is seen specially posed with a train of new beer vans on 11th December 1929, taking the Leicester line, off the main Derby to Burton route, at Leicester Line Junction, opposite the Burton Locomotive Depot. Beer traffic was also carried in open wagons and in old cattle trucks, the casks of beer travelling in well ventilated wagons to preserve the condition of the beer.

National Railway Museum

Plate 201 Another posed picture at Derby, with a load of what appear to be bridge sections. The track in the foreground is another point for modellers; note the sleepers are well covered with a dirt material, possibly soil or spent casting sand from the works foundry.

National Railway Museum

Plate 202   In the yard at Rugby, this load of timber was en route from Alexandra Dock, Hull to Nuneaton. The timber was badly loaded and not in accordance with the instructions given for loads of this type, and the wagons were detached from the train to await re-loading before continuing the journey to Nuneaton. Instruction booklets were issued to all goods depots on how particular types of merchandise were to be loaded, and the types of wagons which would suit the load. Individual booklets issued covered: paper traffic, linoleum traffic, empty casks and cases of empty bottles, full casks, machinery and similar traffic, e.g. aeroplanes, boilers, castings and rollers etc. round timber and other special traffic. In addition, wagons in which traffic had travelled and which was later found to have been infested with beetle or similar grubs, had to be disinfested thoroughly, in accordance with a further special instruction booklet.

National Railway Museum

Plate 203   The lamps on this platform are of particular interest, but one cannot overlook the rather splendid sight of the 'Coronation Scot' headed by blue and silver streamlined No. 6224 *Queen Alexandra* passing through Brinklow Station in 1939. Another point of interest for the modeller is the station platform – a small block edging with gravel surface, and of course, the ladder conveniently left for lighting-up time!

J. Coltas

Plate 204 The first LMS Compound built to Midland Railway design, No. 1045, alongside Midland Compound No. 1027 at St. Pancras Station one sunny Sunday in 1930. Out of use trolleys stored towards the end of the platform, are of types 200 and 201.

J. Coltas

Plate 205 This locomotive was built to be No. 5642 and after being in traffic for a short period, it was recalled to the works at Crewe, where it exchanged identities with the first of the Class 5XP engines No. 5552. It was then finished in a special livery of black with chromed fittings and named *Silver Jubilee* in honour of the Silver Jubilee, in 1935, of King George V and Queen Mary, and it is seen in this condition at Bletchley later in 1935. This locomotive subsequently travelled to all parts of the LMS system before settling down to work on the Western Division.

A. G. Ellis

Plate 206 No. 6204 *Princess Louise* at Shrewsbury, a locomotive which does not appear to have been well-photographed. A most graceful class of engine.

A. G. Ellis Collection

Plate 207 An express for St. Pancras taking the line out of Nottingham Midland for Melton Mowbray in 1931 on the section which avoided the line through Leicester. The locomotive is No. 5971, the first of the 'Claughton' rebuilds of 1930 which took the earlier 'Claughton' number and name, although the *Croxteth* nameplate is not fitted. This locomotive was renumbered 5500 in 1934, and in 1937 the name was changed to *Patriot*. The large centre bossed wheels of the 'Claughton' were retained on the first and second rebuilds.

V. Forster Collection

Plate 208 (right upper) A Burton-on-Trent to Scarborough excursion passing through York headed by 2-6-0 No. 2767 carrying the Burton ▶ shed code of 17B. Locomotives were often changed at York on the through excursion trains.

Real Photographs

Plate 209 (right lower) The Twentywell Lane Bridge just south of Dore & Totley Station on the Midland line from Sheffield to Derby. ▶ 'Jubilee' Class No. 5615 *Malay States* with one of the ten high-sided tenders and finished with the 1936 sans serif style insignia. An interesting feature in this location is that the two running lines occupy only two-thirds of the bridge width. Dore & Totley Station platforms are visible beyond the bridge, and before alterations to the track layout were carried out, the line to Derby passed through the two platforms and the junction for the Hope Valley line was immediately south of the platforms. The junction was altered and two further platform faces added to the east side of the station necessitating a tighter curve for the Derby line, but this was prior to the LMS period.

A. G. Ellis

Plate 210 (above) The old Sheff[i]
Midland Station with railway cottages
the ground overlooking the station.
LMS built Compound No. 1048 is at
head of a southbound train.

N. E. St

Plate 211 (left) The east end of Tot[ley]
Tunnel with Class 2P 4-4-0 No. [3]
about to enter. This tunnel 6,230 ya[rds]
(or 3 miles 950 yards) long, was [the]
longest tunnel on the LMSR and [was]
reputed to be one of the wettest too!

D. Ibbot[son]

TOTLEY TUNNEL

TOTLEY
TUNNEL
6230 YARDS.

Electrification

With other modes of transport included in this volume, it would be inappropriate to omit some reference to those lines of the Company which were electrified, and a summary is perhaps the most appropriate way of recording them.

	Miles	Chains
Rock Ferry Station to the junction with the Mersey Railway – a section jointly owned by the LMS and GWR and operated by the Mersey Railway		41
Liverpool–Southport–Crossens	24	79
Liverpool–Ormskirk	12	04
Lancaster–Morecambe–Heysham	9	42
Manchester–Bury–Holcombe Brook	13	76
Bow, Barking & Upminster – worked by the Metropolitan District Railway	12	32
Willesden Junction–Earls Court Part of this route was jointly owned with the GWR and running powers over Metropolitan District Railway were also held for a short distance	2	56
Euston–Watford–Rickmansworth and Croxley Green	23	06
Broad Street–Kew Bridge and Broad Street–Richmond LMS trains worked over part of the Southern electrified lines on these routes	15	33
Manchester South Junction & Altrincham line, jointly owned with the LNER (electrified 1931)	9	13
Wirral Railway from Birkenhead Park–West Kirby and New Brighton (electrified 1938)	10	40

LMS trains ran over Mersey Railway to Liverpool Central (Mersey trains worked New Brighton service).

Details of the stock used on these lines is to be found in *LMS Coaches* by David Jenkinson, published by Oxford Railway Publishing Company, and no purpose will be served by repeating such information, save that which accompanies this plate.

One major electrification scheme which has come to fruition under British Rail, that between Euston and Glasgow on the former L&NWR and LMS main line, was first considered by the LMS in the first few months of 1923. Whether the whole trunk route was considered for electrification is not certain, and there has, to date, been little information which has come to hand to throw light on this interesting subject. What is certain is that dynamometer car tests were carried out on Sunday, 24th June 1923, in order to obtain particulars of engine performance at a speed of 60 mph up the bank, with the results forming the basis for calculations in connection with the design of a proposed electric locomotive for hauling heavy expresses over the route between Preston and Carlisle. The train consisted of seventeen L&NWR passenger vehicles and the L&Y dynamometer car, giving a total weight of 497½ tons, and the train was worked by two L&Y 4-6-0 superheated engines, Nos. 1658 and 1511.

What the final deliberations were I do not know, but Mr. George Hughes was the senior LMS man on the train, in his capacity as Chief Mechanical Engineer. The electrification proposals did not materialise, and further electrification by the LMS did not come until some years later with the MSJ & AR, jointly owned with the LNER, in 1931, and the Wirral Railway in 1938.

The MSJ&A stock carried a green livery with lining in the LMS style, but without the waist panelling. Rolling stock had the normal compartment doors, whilst the new stock built for the Wirral services were the first examples outside London to be fitted with air-operated sliding doors. These were normally operated by the guard, but push-buttons were provided for use of passengers at peak periods. Despite electrification of the Wirral in 1938, one steam passenger working continued in each direction on weekdays between New Brighton and West Kirby in order that the through coach between Euston and New Brighton could complete its journey.

Plate 212   One of the three car sets built in 1927 for the third rail London suburban services from Broad Street to Kew and Richmond. No. 8881 is in full livery.

British Railways

Plate 213 An MSJ&A train built in 1931 by Metro-Cammell for this newly electrified jointly owned line.

British Railways

Water Troughs and Softening Plant

The London and North Western Railway were the pioneers of the water trough principal for replenishing the tanks of locomotives travelling at speed, and Mr. John Ramsbottom, the Locomotive Superintendent was the engineer who invented the method. The first troughs were laid down at Mochdre, between Colwyn Bay and Llandudno Junction, in November or December 1860, to enable the Irish Mail express to run through from Holyhead to Stafford without having to stop to take on water. In 1871 this pioneer set of troughs was taken up and re-laid at Aber, between Llanfairfechan and Bangor, possibly because this was on a more open stretch of line and trains were less likely to suffer checks, than they were after passing Llandudno Junction which was a busy traffic point. Sixteen further sets of troughs were laid down by the L&NWR and with the Midland having troughs at five locations, and the Lancashire & Yorkshire a total of ten sets, the LMS became by far and away the largest user of water troughs with a grand total, in 1923, of 32 sets. In addition, one set at Ludlow was used jointly with the Great Western.

The principle of the water trough was simple. The speed of the locomotive provided the force to channel the water up the scoop which had been lowered by the locomotive fireman from beneath the tender and into the trough just below the level of the water. The water tanks were thus replenished without the tedious time-wasting stops to use one of the lineside water columns. Obviously the lower the speed the less water was taken into the tender. The early types of scoops fitted to the underside of tenders were of a simple orifice which was moved through the water. Whilst this was simple and effective it suffered from the disadvantage that when the engine was running at high speeds nearly as much water was thrown clear of the trough as was picked up. Not only was this a complete wastage of water and therefore a financial loss, especially where money had been spent in softening it for locomotive use, but the water splashed out soaked into the track bed which in turn required increased maintenance to the permanent way. The problem was the subject of a number of experiments with various shapes of scoop and although there was some success, loss of water which built up in the areas at the side of the scoop and was consequently spilled over the sides of the trough, remained a problem. A specially modified tender was used in some of the tests, with a compartment constructed in the middle of the tank in which an observer could sit and watch the water entering the mouth of the scoop and also measure the quantity of water picked up on the tank gauge. The loss of water through spillage was ascertained by measuring the water required to return the level in the troughs to normal after the train had passed, and deducting that which was recorded in the tender tank. It was realised that spillages could not be entirely eliminated and to lower the level of water in the troughs would merely mean that less water would be picked up, and the objective therefore frustrated. In 1933 a deflector was designed to be fitted some 16 inches in front of the scoop, consisting of a horizontal plate with two vertical plates projecting down from the edges, the vanes being tapered towards the rear edge of the plate. As the deflector preceded the scoop through the water, it had the effect of streaming the water inwards and to a higher level in the centre of the trough, allowing the scoop to take up a greater volume and wastage was considerably reduced. Savings were envisaged as high as twenty per cent of the water supplied to the troughs. In addition to the 32 sets of troughs in England and Wales, the LMS also laid down three further sets in the Northern Division at Floriston and Strawfrank on the Caledonian section, and New Cumnock on the G&SWR section. The shortest length of trough was at Walkden on the Central Division, 478 yards, whilst the longest set was 642 yards at Hademore, just south of Lichfield on the North Western main line. Most of the others were either just over 500 yards, or to the Midland standard length of 557 yards. The highest set of troughs were those at Garsdale on the Settle & Carlisle main line, 1,169 feet above sea level, and the 560 yards length was heated during the winter period. An interesting feature was the unique set of troughs which were on the level stretch of track in Standedge Tunnel, between Stalybridge and Huddersfield, the only suitable section on the Manchester to Leeds line.

The following is a list of the LMS water trough locations:-

Ex-L&NWR

Main Line

Bushey *	Church Lawford (between Rugby & Coventry)
Castlethorpe*	Christleton)
Newbold*	Flint)
Hademore*	Prestatyn) North Wales route from Crewe
Whitmore*	Aber)
Moore*	
Brock	Halebank (between L'pool & Weaver Junction)
Hest Bank	Eccles (between L'pool & Manchester Exchange)
Dillicar	Standedge

Ex-Midland

Oakley*
Loughborough*
Melton Mowbray*
Garsdale
Tamworth

Ex-L&Y

Lostock Junction	Smithy Bridge
Lea Road	Walkden
Whitley Bridge	Kirkby
Horbury Junction	Burscough
Sowerby Bridge	Rufford

LMS Northern Division

Floriston
Strawfrank
New Cumnock

Water softening plant installed at these locations in 1932/33.

Quite apart from the financial loss resulting from the spillage from water troughs, further financial loss resulted from the use of hard water in locomotive boilers, and the scaling-up process impaired the efficiency of the locomotive to an extent which could not be accurately assessed, although the loss was known to be substantial. The LMS operated in a wide area of the country and the geological structure differed widely. The natural water sources pass through different types of ground and much of the English terrain through which the LMS lines ran were known to be hard water areas, the water permeating the ground and in so doing gathering various impurities which generally caused it to be less suitable for boiler use and liable to cause scale deposits inside the boiler tubes.

It is important to note that the waters found in Scotland did not contain the impurities which caused scaling, and in fact did not require treatment before use in locomotive boilers. Perhaps this is one reason why there is no English whisky! One of the principal impurities is derived from limestone, and water from these sources contains lime compounds which will form scale when the water is boiled to form steam. A greater heat is required to penetrate the scale as its thickness increases and this reduces the efficiency of the locomotive, which is measured in financial terms when more coal is consumed than would otherwise be necessary. The scale is formed into a very hard stone-like layer around the tubes and over the firebox and the normal washing and rodding which takes place periodically is not sufficient to remove the deposits. Temperatures in the firebox ultimately are higher than would normally be expected and this causes erosion to the inside of the firebox, another factor to be measured in financial terms as repairs have to be carried out earlier than normal. In addition to hard-scale, a sludge-like substance is also derived from water in certain areas and this was usually deposited in the lower parts of the boiler and thorough washing disposed of this material.

The LMS estimated, following tests carried out by the chemists on the use of various types of water, that more than 70,000 tons of coal were wasted on the English divisions through using untreated hard water. Water softening plants had been in use for many years, but the early processes were slow and involved a settling period before the water was suitable for use. One of the early softening plants had been installed by the Midland Railway at Derby in the late 1880s, and this was still in use in the 1930s and possibly later. Clearly this was not suitable for railway use where continuous quantities of softened water were required, and in 1932 the LMS embarked on a programme to install twenty-eight softening plants, and in aggregate the largest softening plant on any railway in the world. In addition to the plant installed at water trough locations, others were provided on the Western division, at Watford, Tring, Leighton Buzzard, Bletchley, Northampton, Rugby, Nuneaton, Milford, Kenyon Junction and Preston, and on the Midland division at Kentish Town, Cricklewood, St. Albans, Bedford, Wellingborough, Kettering, Market Harborough and Toton.

All the new installations were of the continuous process type with the largest plant at Bushey capable of processing 50,000 gallons per hour. There were six different types of softener all basically using the same process, comprising a method to proportion and supply the correct amount of chemicals to the water tank, after which the process of precipitation and settling took place before sand filters completed the softening process and the water fed through to storage tanks ready for use.

In installing this plant, the LMS anticipated savings of around £175,000 per annum would be achieved and that the capital cost would be covered within a short time.

The following plates are all taken at water trough locations and again they reflect a personal choice of locomotive types. They will also give the railway modeller detailed information on troughs which may prove of interest and lead to this feature of the railway scene being reproduced in main line layouts.

The following plates are all taken at water trough locations and again they reflect a personal choice of locomotive types. They will also give the railway modeller detailed information on troughs which may prove of interest and lead to this feature of the railway scene being reproduced in main line layouts.

Plate 214   Dillicar troughs in the Westmorland Fells with the 'Coronation Scot' headed by No. 6224 *Princess Alexandra*. There are two types of trough shown here and there is little or no spacing between the sleepers, each of which is chaired. Note the special lamps carried by the locomotive, the lampsides taper back in a wing formation.

Author's Collection

Plate 215   Bushey troughs in 1937 with 'Patriot' No. 5523 before she was named *Bangor* in 1938. Note here the sleeper formations. The locomotive is coasting down to Euston without picking up from the troughs.

Real Photographs

Plate 216   During the first week of May 1936, No. 6202 turbo-locomotive underwent a series of dynamometer car trials between Euston and Glasgow Central on the 'Royal Scot' service, and here she is seen with a sixteen coach load, with the dynamometer car behind the tender, traversing Brock troughs on the stretch between Preston and Lancaster, possibly during one of these tests.

A. G. Ellis

Plate 219 Brock again with 'Jubilee' Class N 5619 *Nigeria* heading a milk train made up of t six wheel tanks and two four wheel tanks betwe them, and a panelled full brake. The tanks are exceedingly grimy and there is very little letter visible. Although the train has only j commenced crossing the troughs there is no in cation water is about to be picked up.

A. G. E

Plate 220 'Royal Scot' Class No. 6151 *The Ro Horse Guardsman* leaving Newbold troughs in J 1948, soon after nationalisation. The tall build immediately over the first carriage is the wa softening plant installed in 1932. Note the trou were on the fast lines only.

J. Co

Plate 217 One of the ex-L & Y R 'Aspinall' 2-4- heading towards Blackpool over Lea Road troug a glorious four track stretch in open country.

A. G. E

Plate 218 Early afternoon as No. 622 *Coronation* with the 'Coronation Scot' takes wate at Brock.

A. G. Ell

Wheel Tapper

△

Plate 222 One of the celebrated railway terms evolved to describe the 'Train Examiner' was, of course, The Wheel Tapper, and here is just one such employee carrying out his duties. The butt of the music hall joker, the description belies the true nature of his job, and the train examiner was not only required to be fully fit to satisfy the Company's doctor, but a comprehensive knowledge of the construction and maintenance of all types of carriage and wagon stock was also a pre-requisite. The characteristic ring as he worked his way along a train was the indication to passengers of his presence, and since the wheel tapper had the responsibility for the soundness of every vehicle examined, his was a most exacting task carried out amidst the general hubbub of a busy station. If a defective tyre was found it was his duty to take whatever steps he considered necessary to ensure the safety of the vehicle, even though delay and annoyance could quickly follow his decision. Not only did he tap the wheel, he also had to ensure that all working parts, such as wheels, axleboxes, springs, buffers and drawgear, brakes and inside fittings, were all in good order. He had other points to look for, in all just everything on every vehicle, and great reliance was placed upon his shoulders by the Company, and in turn his presence could be said to have contributed to the confidence of the traveller in using the railway. On occasions the tapper would be accompanied by a mate, and again a light hearted comment gave rise to the belief that he was just 'the listener'. In fact, the second man was a greaser and oiler, and he worked round a train with the train examiner attending to axleboxes as necessary: fulfilling another important task.

British Railways

Plate 223 As with luggage labels, there was a vast assortment of wagon labels and these examples in regular use. Red and black printing on white or yellow card was usual and special markings, as shown with the diagonal line and cross were in red. The Castle Douglas livestock label reflects the early Scottish style, having 'Glasgow & South Western Section' as a subsidiary title. E R O sequences were applied later.

Author's Collection

Wagon Labels

First Aid

Throughout the length and breadth of the LMS railway, employees were encouraged to undergo First Aid and Ambulance training and many of those who did so were members of the St. John's Ambulance Brigade in their spare time. Teams were formed and their training followed an approved course with one or more local doctors assisting with the training. Knock-out competitions were held each year with a Grand Final staged at locations such as the Midland Grand Hotel at St. Pancras. Individual and team tests were undertaken with the winning contestants taking the usual array of trophies. Such was the success of the LMS ambulance activities that no less than 11,000 employees each year on average were passing the various individual examination classes. Much of the work carried out by the Company's employees was of a heavy nature and whilst accidents and mishaps were bound to happen, the presence of trained ambulance men was an invaluable aid to those in need. Regular local competitions were held in most centres, with departmental teams and others from the other railway companies adding to the interest and inter-company rivalry. At the larger centres the Company provided ambulances, but others were subscribed for by employees and departmental hospital fund raising activities and presented to the Company.

The LMS actively encouraged all its staff to take an interest in First Aid precautions and competitions were held for teams of volunteers to practise their expertise in readiness for any emergencies. Because of the nature of the LMS operations, accidents did occur and first aid treatment was an important matter. First Aid boxes, with a wide range of treatments were provided, and in the accompanying photograph, the bracket to hold a red warning flag can be seen. These boxes were provided at all stations, goods sheds, yards, sheds and other locations wherever LMS staff worked.

Author's Collection

Plate 224 (top) The Company ambulance at Wolverton, which was also available for local use in the town.

National Railway Museum

Plate 225 (bottom) Another Morris Commercial vehicle numbered in the 'S' fleet in May 1945.

National Railway Museum

Publicity and Printed Company Material

Plate 226 A selection of timetables published by the Company.
Bottom left is the early style of cover of the Divisional issues whilst the adjacent one is the mid-thirties pattern, which included all lines serviced and was in contrast a much thicker volume. *Middle of top row* is the standard wartime issue, a much reduced volume concentrating on the services available to the exclusion of much of the additional information provided on hotels, steamer services and maps which characterised pre-war editions. The others are all sectionalised for particular areas. There were many other types of timetable issued and these represent only a token sample. The majority of all timetables were in maroon with black printing. All were for public use and the true cost of production must have far outweighed the 6d or 1/- actually charged to the public.

Author's Collection

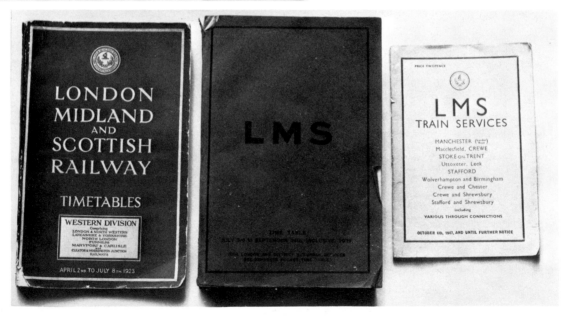

Plate 227 A wide variety of publications was produced by the LMS, most of which were designed to interest the public in the destinations ▶ which the LMS served and to encourage them to travel LMS. This selection includes a Holiday Guide for North Wales; A Summer Season Excursion Booklet with details of all excursions to be run from the London termini and suburban stations for the 1925 season; a very comprehensive brochure 'The Royal Scot' and her forty-nine sister engines which describes the locomotives and the origin of each name bestowed on the locomotives of this class, but preceded by an introduction which characterises the locomotive and other forms of travel generally. The remaining two publications were for internal use of LMS employees. The list of Road Vans for stations in Scotland, a small booklet, details the trains along each route to which the Road Vans or Parcels Vans would be attached and the stations served for which traffic could be carried. The term Road Van is perhaps somewhat misleading, in that it does not refer to Road Motor Vans, but Parcels Vans which were attached to trains for the 'Road' specified. Very strict instructions were laid down for the working of Road Vans and these were intended for small consignments which could be easily handled at the small Scottish stations by the staff available. The second 'internal' publication is the LMS staff magazine produced on a monthly basis and as one would expect, carrying information of interest to the staff on Company operations, new introductions and descriptive articles on particular locations, as well as details of the very many staff activities and societies which existed throughout the system. The staff magazine was also on sale to the public at stations and some bookstalls. During the war years from 1940 onwards, the LMS magazine was replaced by a newspaper type of publication with the appropriately chosen title 'Carry On – LMS Staff Newspaper', produced, no doubt, at a fraction of the cost of the pre-war magazine. There were many other brochures and a vast range of pamphlets to attract the public. The Holiday Guides were published annually and in addition to the descriptive text of places of interest in the area covered by the guide, advertising from hotels and guest houses, and other interested parties, was carried and the revenue raised would defray, if not cover entirely, the cost of production of the booklet. Covers were attractively reproduced from paintings, and in most cases the LMS crest in miniature and in full colour also appeared. Another of the range of brochures with plain white cover was one on the Cathedral Cities of England and Wales.

Author's Collection

Plate 228 The title of this brochure issued in 1923, speaks for itself and many places within easy reach of London for a half or full day were described and illustrated in an attempt to attract short-day excursion traffic.

▽ *Author's Collection*

Plate 229 A typical page – Pinner – is it the same rural area today?

Author's Collection

Pinner (Hatch End Station).

Charming Rural Walks.

PINNER is one of the few places within easy reach of London which has not lost its rural aspect, but in the midst of the suburbanising which is going on all round still remains what it has always been—an old-world village with houses straggling up the sides of the High Street, at the

Pinner—*Continued*.

top of which stands the grand old fourteenth century church. There is a curious edifice in the churchyard which attracts numbers of sightseers, not from any particular beauty of architectural construction, but from the unique legend attaching to it. The lofty cross on the top of the tower of the Church is said to have been placed there by the old-time inhabitants of Pinner to guide people out of the dense forests which surrounded the village on all sides.

Old buildings dating back to 1470 and 1560, are in existence. The Queen's Head Hotel is also very ancient, dating back to 1750.

There are some most picturesque walks to be had in and round Pinner, and round the L M S Station at Hatch End has grown up one of the finest residential localities within twenty miles of London.

Rickmansworth.

Charming Walks, Boating, Fishing, etc.

THERE is no more delightful part of Hertfordshire for country rambles than that within easy reach of Rickmansworth. Less than five minutes' walk from the L M S station brings us to Moor Park (once the beautiful

GOOD FISHING CAN BE HAD AT RICKMANSWORTH.

18   19

SCOTLAND FOR THE HOLIDAYS

LNER   LMS

Plate 230 In Scotland, the LMS combined with the LNER to issue Holiday Guides, presumably because much of the holiday traffic was of tourist rather than holiday-centre based. The 1935 Holidays by LMS Guide for England & Wales covered 493 resorts in 1,000 pages and 270 photogravure illustrations.
Author's Collection

Plate 232 (below) A rather attractiv postcard size print in full colour an printed on the reverse as a postcar enquiry form for the Removal Service When first produced, one of these card was issued with each copy of the LM Magazine.
J. Alsop Collectio

Plate 231 (below) For this Railway Removal pamphlet, the 'British Railways', the four main line companies combined to issue one, rather than individual ones, since a great proportion of Removal traffic would be likely to cross company boundaries, and the most direct routes would be demanded by those using the railway service. Expert removal men to pack and to unload the household accoutrements, fares for every member of the household reduced by one third, and insurance at low premiums, were all part of the package offered, and one side of the pamphlet was printed with an Enquiry Form to obtain estimates.
Author's Collection

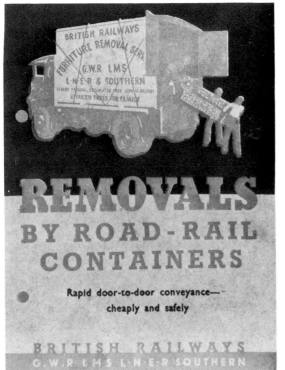

REMOVALS BY ROAD-RAIL CONTAINERS

Rapid door-to-door conveyance— cheaply and safely

BRITISH RAILWAYS
G.W.R LMS L·N·E·R SOUTHERN

Plate 233 (below) The front cover of one of the books of trains, with the contents of des criptive text and photographs, published in late 1937. Another publicity feature was show on the back cover 'And now – the LMS in films', a range of films available to cultivate a interest in travelling LMS. They were popular too, both with outside organisations and LMS employees' clubs, and a programme of films was presented at main centres fo employees when they were first available. A selection of lantern slide sets, of beauty spot served by the LMS was also available without charge.

MODERN LOCOMOTIVES of the L.M.S.

BY D. S. BARRIE

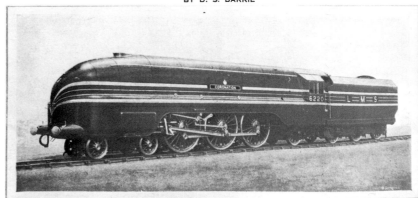

ISSUED WITH THE AUTHORITY OF THE LONDON MIDLAND & SCOTTISH RAILWAY BY THE LOCOMOTIVE PUBLISHING CO. LTD. 3 AMEN CORNER, LONDON, E.C.4

— PRICE —
ONE SHILLING

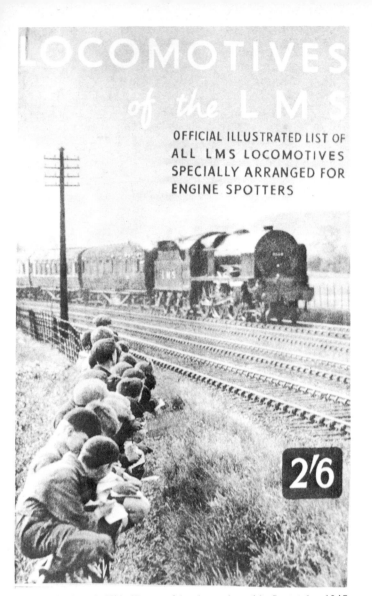

Plate 234 (above) This 'Spotters' book was issued in September 1947.
Author's Collection

Plate 235 (above) There were many small Savings Banks and Friendly Societies in existence prior to World War II, and although many survived the war, amalgamations and mergers retired many to oblivion. It would have been unusual if the LMS, as one of the largest single employers in the 1920s and 1930s had not had its own Savings Bank. Deposit books of the type shown, and conforming in most respects to a normal commercial bank deposit book, were issued to staff who joined to safeguard their savings. Savings business only was transacted — overdrafts and current accounts were not available!

D. P. Rowland Collection

Plate 236 (right) Encouragement was given to railway employees to study for examinations related to their everyday work and a wide variety of courses was available. In addition to commercial subjects, technical courses and lectures in the form of mutual improvement classes were available, and annual examinations were held. This certificate for a 1st Year First Class pass in goods and passenger station clerical work was awarded to Mr. D. Rowland — a name which some of the readers of this book may recognise in connection with the LMS Society's activities. It behoves me, therefore, to add that Mr. D. Rowland is not the LMS Society Chairman, Don Rowland, but in fact Don Rowland's late father.

D. P. Rowland Collection

Plate 237 The mid-twenties saw the publication of a booklet containing 18 of the paintings by members of the Royal Academy which had been specially commissioned by the LMSR. Well known academicians contributed works both for the booklet and to the series of paintings which were the basis for colourful posters advertising the LMS and in an introductory appreciation by Sir Martin Conway, M.P., under the heading 'The Elevation of Poster Art' 'An Appreciation', comments . . . . inter alia . . . . 'Such a series of posters as this now issued will no doubt effect the primary intended purpose, but it will do much more. These posters will carry the appeal of good art to a new strata of society whose appreciation in its turn will react upon artists. They will set a standard for the best form of advertising, which may well be productive in the future of even greater results than we can foresee in the present'. Indeed, such was the appeal of the range of LMS posters that they were sold to the public with no less than 26,500 in the UK and 3,220 in North America being sold between 1925 and 1933. Alas, relatively few have survived the passage of time. This plate is the cover of the booklet.

M. Brooks Collection

Plate 238 This depicts one of the series.

M. Brooks Collection

To Ireland Seven L.M.S. Routes.   Painted for the L.M.&S. Railway by Norman Wilkinson

The Coronation Scot

STREAMLINED
RESTAURANT CAR EXPRESS

LONDON & GLASGOW
IN 6½ HOURS

AVERAGE SPEED THROUGHOUT 61·7 M.P.H

WEEK-DAYS
(SATURDAYS EXCEPTED)

	P.M.		P.M.
LONDON (EUSTON) dep. **1.30**		**GLASGOW** (CENTRAL) dep. **1.30**	
CARLISLE arr. **6.13**		**CARLISLE** dep. **3.17**	
GLASGOW (CENTRAL) arr. **8.0**		**LONDON** (EUSTON) arr. **8.0**	

Calls at Carlisle to set down passengers only. | *Calls at Carlisle to pick up passengers only.*

Will not run on Fridays | Will not run on Friday
July 28th and August 4th, and | and Monday
Monday, August 7th, 1939 | August 4th and 7th, 1939

THE NUMBER OF PASSENGERS IS LIMITED TO THE SEATING CAPACITY OF THE TRAIN AND SPECIAL RESERVATION TICKETS MUST BE HELD.

RESERVATION FEES First or Third Class for Single Journey **2/6**

Seats should be reserved in advance at the following Offices

LONDON *Enquiry Office, Euston Station or any Town Office, Suburban Station or principal Agency in London.*

GLASGOW *Enquiry Office, Central Station or any L M S Agency in Glasgow.*

CARLISLE *Station Master's Office.*

Orders for seats on this train can also be placed at any L M S. Station, Town Office or Auxiliary Agency. In these cases passengers must apply for their Reservation Tickets at Euston or Glasgow Central Enquiry Offices before joining the train.

Plate 239 The 'Coronation Scot' is well known as the LMS Railway's most prestigious service of the late 1930s, and arguably the most prestigious event of the LMS period. It is said to have been the result of some hasty planning and there are many thousands of enthusiasts who would have loved to have seen the train, let alone to have experienced the thrill of the journey. The blue and silver livery was carried through to the posters produced to announce its introduction. In addition to wall posters, a small sheet in blue with white lettering was added inside the front cover of timetables from July 1937, and as can be seen from this photograph gave full information of this reserved-seat-only service. Special reservation tickets, also in blue card, were issued for each seat.

Author's Collection

Plate 240 and *241 (next page)* The 'Coronation Scot' menu card, again with blue face to match the colour of the train. The traveller was well provided for, for after ordering from the menu, there were the facts about the train to be digested. It is worth noting – in addition to what now appears to be a modest charge for so full an offering – that the date of journey is also printed, in this case 13th August 1937. Every traveller by this service also received a booklet on the route of the train, detailing points of interest to be observed and distances travelled.

Author's Collection

SOME FACTS ABOUT THE CORONATION SCOT

THE ENGINE

4-6-2 streamlined Locomotive No. 6220 "Coronation"

Boiler Pressure 250 lbs. sq. in.	Grate Area 50 sq. ft.
Heating Surface 2807 sq. ft.	Cylinders (4) 16½" × 28"
Superheater 856 sq. ft.	Coupled Wheels 6ft. 9ins.
Total Weight, Engine and Tender. 164 tons 12 cwt.	Tractive effort 40,000 lbs.

THE TRAIN

Seating Capacity : 82 First Class ; 150 Third Class

Total Weight 297 tons

The formation is as follows :

Corridor First Class Brake
Corridor First
First Class Vestibule Dining Car
Kitchen Car
Third Class Vestibule Dining Car
Kitchen Car
Third Class Vestibule Dining Car
Third Class Vestibule Dining Car
Corridor Third Class Brake

The Euston Hotel, London, N.W.1., and the Central Hotel, Glasgow, are two of the 29 famous L M S hotels in Great Britain and Ireland

The Coronation Scot

Menu

Luncheon

3/6

Iced Melon

Grilled Halibut   Anchovy Butter

Roast Beef   Horseradish Sauce
Baked & Boiled Potatoes
Green Vegetables
or
Assorted Cold Meats
Salad

Compôte of Fruits Chantilly
Biscuits
or
Vanilla Ice Cream

Cheese, Biscuits, Salad

Coffee, per Cup, 4d.

THIRD CLASS   AFTERNOON TEA, 1/3   13/8/37.

The A.B.C. Railway Guide can be consulted and Writing Paper and Envelopes obtained on application to the Conductor

In the general interest Passengers are requested to refrain from smoking immediately prior to and during the service of meals. Passengers are requested to see that their bills are written out in their presence, and not to pay any money until the bill has been presented.

Wines

CHAMPAGNE	Bot.	½ Bot.
365 Perrier Joüet, Finest Extra Quality	17 6	9 6
318 Lanson, Extra Quality, Extra Dry	18 6	10 0
315 Veuve Clicquot, Dry	19 6	10 6
351 G.H. Mumm, Cordon Rouge, Très Sec	19 6	10 6
345a Geo. Goulet, Ex. Qual., Ex. Dry, 1928	21 0	11 0

OTHER FRENCH SPARKLING WINE

259 Sparkling Muscatel, "Golden Guinea"	15 0	8 0

BORDEAUX RED

30 Bordeaux Superieur	4 0	2 0
31 Medoc	4 6	2 6
32 Margaux	6 0	3 6

BORDEAUX WHITE

52 Graves	4 0	2 0
252 Clos du Gravier, Extra Dry	4 6	2 6
54 Haut Sauternes	5 6	3 0
179 Graves Dry Royal, 1st Growth Podensac	7 0	4 0
185 Château Carbonnieux, Château bottled	10 0	5 6

BURGUNDY RED

56 Macon	5 0	2 6
59 Beaune	7 0	4 0
61 Pommard Superieur, 1923	8 6	4 6

BURGUNDY WHITE

74 Chablis	5 0	3 0

BRITISH EMPIRE WHITE WINES

762 South African Hock Type, Paarl Amber	5 0	3 0
757 Australian Highercombe Amber	6 0	3 6
760 South African Dry Dominion Sp'kling	12 6	7 0

RHINE AND MOSELLE STILL WINES

598 Laubenheim	5 0	3 0
599 Cueser-Berncasteler	5 0	3 0
661 Zeltinger	7 0	4 0
615 Nierstein	7 6	4 0
603 Liebfraumilch	7 6	4 0

SHERRY

4 Amontillado, Pale Dry, per glass, 1/-	
1 Fine Rich	

PORT

15 Ruby per glass, 1/-		
400 Vintage Character	1 6	5 0
401 Finest Old Tawny	1 6	5 0

GORDON "SHAKER-BOTTLE" COCKTAILS

Piccadilly, Martini, Dry Martini, Manhattan Bronx	1 6

WHISKY

138 "Royal Scot" finest procurable	- 10
Other Proprietary Brands	1 0

GIN

Finest Unsweetened	- 10
Booth's Old Matured Dry	1 0
Gin and Bitters	1 0
Gin and Vermouth	1 0
Vermouth, French or Italian	1 0

COGNAC

Fine Old Cognac	1 6
	liqueur glass
134 Cognac Vieux Maison, 40 years old	1 6
207 Hine's Grande Champagne, 25 years old	2 0

LIQUEURS

Drambuie, "Scotland's Own Liqueur"	1 0
Crème de Menthe ; Curaçao ; Cherry Brandy	1 0
Kümmel ; Bénédictine ; Grand Marnier	1 6
Cointreau	1 6

BEER, CIDER, AERATED WATERS, ETC.

Bass' No. 1 Barley Wine	per nip	1 0
Bass' or Worthington's Pale Ale, per bottle		- 11
Guinness' Stout		- 11
Graham's Golden Lager		- 11
"Red Tower" Lager		- 11
Barclay's "London" Lager		- 11
Pilsner Urquell		1 8
Cider		1 0
Bulmer's "Pomagne" per bot. 4/-, per ½ bot.		2 6
Ross's The Belfast Ginger Ale, per bottle		- 8
Schweppes' Sp'kl'g Grape Fruit		- 8
Schweppes' Sparkling Lime		- 8
Schweppes' Aerated Waters		- 5
Schweppes' Soda Water small bottle		- 5
Sparkling Buxton per bot. 8d. split		- 5
Apollinaris per bot. 1/-		- 6
Perrier per bot. 1/-		- 6
Still Malvern per bottle		- 8
Vichy Celestins		1 6

QUARTER BOTTLES

CHAMPAGNE   G. H. Mumm, Cordon Rouge, 5 -

OTHER WINES

Bordeaux Superieur 1/-	Graves 1/-	Sauternes 1/6	Hock 1/6
Moselle 1/6	Macon 1/6	Chablis 1/6	
Sherry No. 1 & 4 2/6		Port No. 400 & 401 2/6	

LIGHT REFRESHMENTS

AVAILABLE WHEN TABLE D'HOTE MEALS ARE NOT BEING SERVED

Tea or Coffee, 2 Boiled Eggs and Bread and Butter, or 2 Poached Eggs on Toast	2 6
Tea or Coffee, Fish or Plate of Cold Meat, Salad, &c.	3 6
Meat Sandwiches each	- 6
Glass of Hot or Cold Milk	- 3

It will be appreciated if patrons will report any unusual service or attention on the part of Dining Car Attendants to Arthur Towle, Controller, L M S Hotel Services, St Pancras Chambers, Euston Road, London, N.W.1. This will enable the management to recognize exceptional efficiency, which they desire to encourage in their services.

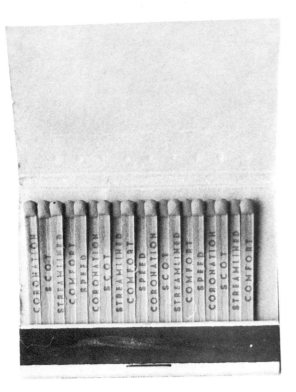

Plate 242 Special book matches were also produced and made available on the train. The LMS went to great lengths to make this a new luxury service and to ensure the 'Coronation Scot' achieved an identity of its own with the travelling public. It is rather unfortunate that the service had a relatively short life before it was withdrawn at the outbreak of World War II.

Author's Collection

Tickets

LMS ticket issues – it would be impossible to include examples of the very many issues of tickets which were available throughout the 25 year life of the Company, but the tickets in these plates are a representative selection which will give added dimension to the task of ticket production which was a very necessary part of the railway organisation.

Early tickets followed the patterns of the pre-group constituent companies, and card colours were very varied. Vertically printed tickets were among the early types issued, and as the issue of specially printed tickets for different categories of passenger had some advertising merit, so the variety of types multiplied.

A study of the types depicted will occupy many, but perhaps the most interesting type is the issue with the Spratt's Ovals advertising card, which slotted neatly into a centre pocket provided for this purpose, and complete with a cut-out for finger grip. These tickets were a patented British design produced by a private company, Insets Limited, and the LMS placed a contract in late 1930 for the supply of 200 million a year of these advertising tickets commencing 1st January 1931. There were very many different advertising insets, some of which were confined to particular types of ticket issue. Petrol from Pratt's, Typhoo Tea, bicycles, vacuum cleaners and pianos, coupons for use with certain purchases which had a discount value, a simple message 'Great Stuff this Bass' and a host of other subjects. Again the LMS did not entirely sell this advertising space, as there were four inserts all with a typical LMS message – 'Transport! Phone the LMS' was one and others referred to Holiday Contract Tickets and 'First Class travel is only ½d a mile more than Third Class' – which was 1d a mile.

The revenue from ticket advertising would go a long way towards covering the cost of the ticket printing, and the LMS was unique in issuing these tickets with inserts. LMS Joint Lines and LMS (NCC) also issued these types. Many experiments were carried out to attract more passengers and amongst these were schemes for the issue of combined travel and theatre tickets from stations selected over a wide area, and including those close to London and further afield, Derby, Leicester, Manchester and others, some on regular availability, whilst others were for shorter trial periods at spaced intervals. This scheme commenced on 1st January 1935, and shortly afterwards the popular 'Summer' classes of ticket became 'Monthly' category.

In April 1935, agreement was reached between the four main line companies to adopt a standard colour scheme to be introduced for all tickets as existing stocks were exhausted. This move was no doubt welcomed by ticket staff, as inter-availability of all the four companies' tickets was in practice, and standardisation would aid identification by ticket collectors and inspectors.

The agreed colour classes were:-

First – White
Third – Green
Day, half-day & evening excursion – First – Yellow, Third – Buff
Workmen's – Grey
Children's tickets – same as adult colour
Bicycles – Terra cotta
Dogs – Red
Perambulators – Pink

Other classes closely linked would take the appropriate colour – e.g., motor cars and motor cycles took the terra cotta ticket appropriate to the bicycle.

Children's tickets were, when separate printed series were not issued, indicated by a child's 'cut piece' being removed, by special nippers, from the normal adult ticket. On Midland style vertical tickets the cut piece was triangular in shape, and on the horizontal LNW and LMS types the cut piece was more rectangular in shape. The piece removed showed the originating station by its number code and the destination by name and an abbreviation for the type of ticket. The class of ticket was indicated by the colour. The cut pieces were retained by the booking clerk and finally forwarded with the account current sheet which was sent to the audit offices for verification, and the number of pieces agreed with the number of child fares recorded.

It is interesting to note that in 1925 not all stations issued platform tickets, but of the 160 listed as issuing them, 7 stations did so through the ticket collectors, free of charge, 93 had automatic issuing machines, 57 stations issued platform tickets at the booking office and there were 3 stations at which they could be obtained both from the booking office and an automatic machine. The free tickets were issued where

the booking office was on the platform and/or there was a subway with exits at both sides of the station, e.g. Stockport. Other than those for which no charge was made – at Crewe, Halifax, Hellifield, Normanton, Rugby, Stockport and Trent – the charge was 1d per hour, except that platform tickets issued at Edinburgh (Princes Street), Glasgow (Central), Glasgow (Buchanan Street) and Glasgow (St. Enoch) were charged at 3d per hour. There were three stations which issued tickets on Sunday only, presumably because fewer staff would be on duty to observe the intentions of platform entrants without travel tickets, and four stations made issues only during the summer period. Mold Station is recorded as issuing platform tickets between 9 am and 6 pm each day.

Examination and the collection of tickets was undertaken in accordance with precise instructions and specially designed nippers were provided. The designs were so different that virtually no two were alike. Some punched a portion of the ticket out, others impressed a coded mark into the ticket, whilst there were those which impressed the surface and also removed a section of ticket alongside. Collected tickets for journeys completed were sorted into strict Issuing Station alphabetical order in classes of ticket, and forwarded to the Audit Section of the Chief Accountants Divisional Office, and were subject to verification checks.

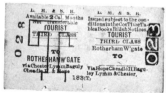 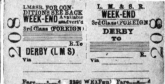 

Plate 243

A selection of LMS tickets

1.	Walking Tour – 273	–	Pink
2.	Walking Tour – 027	–	White with pink stripe
3.	Day excursion – 776	–	White
4.	Cheap return – 067	–	Pale blue
5.	Season day excursion – 8189	–	White with green stripe
6.	Supplemental ticket for reserved compartment – 244 with advertising insert	–	Mauve
7.	Return issued at single fare – 1223	–	Orange
8.	Emigrant ticket – 194	–	Pale green
9.	Police on duty – 862	–	Pale green
10.	Tourist third – 023	–	Pale green
11.	Weekend third class foreign – 208	–	Grey
12.	Single child – 9973	–	Pale green

Note the triangular markings on the vertical tickets to indicate the section to be removed if the ticket was issued for children's travel. On horizontal issues the station code, destination and type of ticket are seen in small print in the centre bottom section, again for removal if issued for children's travel.

(Note: Some of these tickets are pre-standard colours)

Author's Collection

Luggage Labels

Plate 244 Luggage labels — small gummed labels for passengers' luggage. To most people, maybe not worth a second glance, but as with most items associated with railways they were not without interest and there were many patterns, some of which are shown here. The pre-group companies had their own designs and the early LMS labels were repeat patterns, other than the company initials were changed.

1. Liverpool James Street — LNWR pattern, even to the ampersand.

2. Blackburn — Full title, still with MR and the Midland printed form code. Some of the Midland labels also carried a figure for the print run and date, i.e. 10,000 – 3/09.

3. Ballater — Change of pattern close to Caledonian style.

4. Manchester (Victoria) — Initials without ampersand.

5. Gloucester — Similar pattern, but with a changed reference number above the printed form reference. The LMS management were very aware of the vast multiplicity of forms from the constituents and they sought to reduce the number of items and avoid duplication. A Canadian company, Steiner & Murphy Incorporated were engaged in a capacity which today would be termed Management Consultants, to review the stationery in use and eliminate duplication and waste, and a Mr. Murphy and Mr. Joseph O'Neill were invited by Sir Josiah Stamp to undertake this work in 1928. They saved the LMS £1m of its stationery bill in the first year, and Murphy was paid on results, 1% of all savings, and by the time the review was completed he returned across the Atlantic £100,000 better off. This excercise led to a standardised reference index for all items of stationery and publications, and the ERO letters which preceded the figure reference stood for 'Executive Research Office' reference.

6. SE&C Section — The ERO five figure reference was soon followed by an oblique number allocated to the station on the label.

7. Blackpool Central — Lancashire and Yorkshire Railway style label with the L&YR reference M.399 and LMS offset to the right. Reference M.399 also was placed on some examples sitting level with the bottom of the initials.

8. Via Bath — Another type with routing details, possibly used as well as the station destination label.

9 & 10. Scottish labels — Both labels carry their pre-group company form number and originating section.

Larger labels with the station of origin shown on the Caledonian section example, and space for the station name to be written on the Highland one. Most labels were black printing on a white ground but the Caledonian section labels were black on a purple ground.

11. Not an LMS label — but included as an example of another company's issue for use to LMS stations.

12. For Ballymoney — Another larger than normal label issued by the LMS Northern Counties Committee in Northern Ireland. The print run and date are shown, most probably a continuation of the Midland style and influence.

13. Midland & Great Northern Joint issue — included in the LMS ERO series, but with an M&GN reference also.

These examples are typical of the many thousands of labels issued throughout the system and reflect the principal styles used. Evidence of their use came to light only a year or so ago, at an antique auction, when a case with a variety of labels included two labels for Derby LMS.

Author's Collection

The LMS Beyond 1947

Plate 245   Even as late as September 1947, the LMS was planning its future motive power for the main lines, and as is now well known, No. 10000 was built for the Company at Derby in late 1947. Artist's impressions of the new diesel electric locomotives were included in one of the last books published by the LMS *Locomotives Old and New*, a summary of the principal types of locomotive built by the LMS and its constituents, which is dated September 1947, and it is interesting to note the caption accompanying one of these impressions 'New design 1600 HP diesel electric loco which the LMS is to introduce experimentally for suburban and semi-fast passenger trains and for medium work freight services' — two in tandem are described as for main line work. No. 10000 and its B R built sister No. 10001 lasted well into nationalisation and in the late 1940s and early 1950s they spent much of their time on the West Coast Main Line, often paired together on the heavier trains including the 'Royal Scot'.

Author's Collection

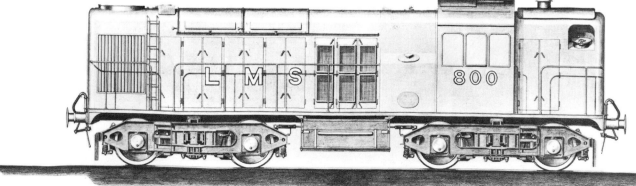

Plate 246   An artist's impression of a Bo-Bo diesel electric for use on the LMS and it is interesting to note that this design is not so different from the BR Bo-Bo's which are seen around the country on freight trains. In fact in 1950 the North British built BR Bo-Bo No. 10800 was very close in reality to this artist's impression.

— the LMS led the way, THE BEST WAY —

Author's Collection